Hitler's
PROPAGANDA
MACHINE

Hitler's
PROPAGANDA
MACHINE

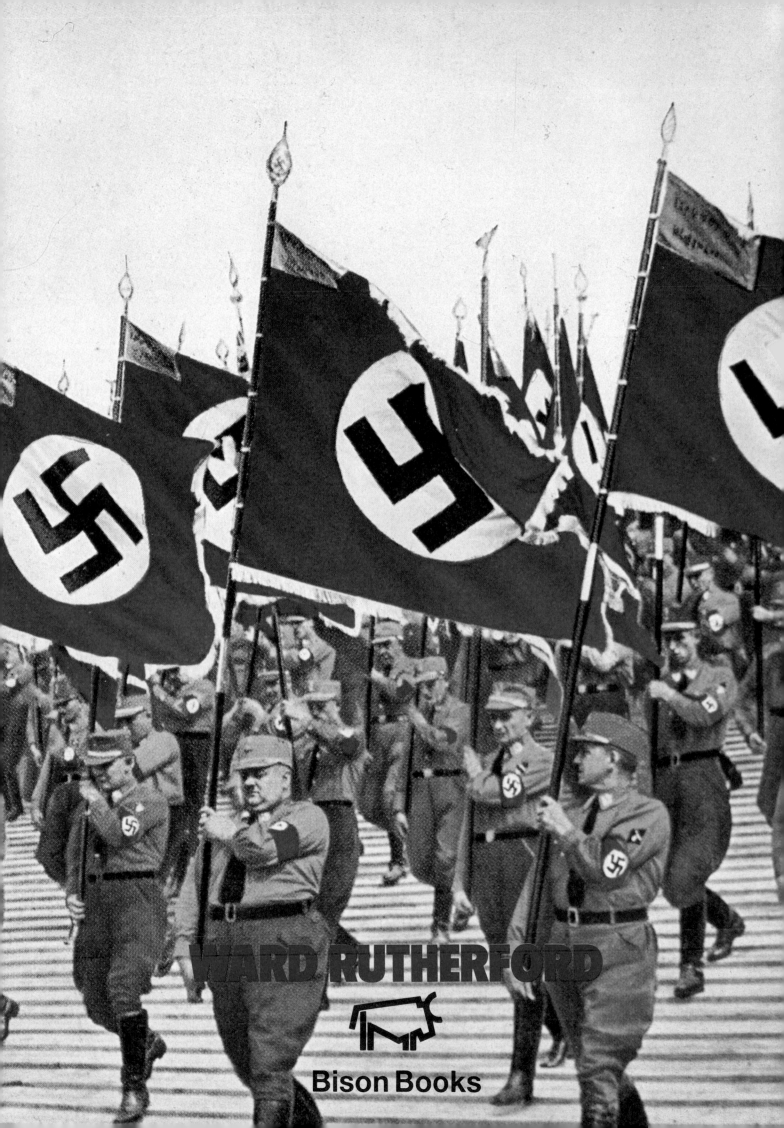

WARD RUTHERFORD

Bison Books

Published by Bison Books Ltd
176 Old Brompton Road
London SW5
England

ISBN 0 86124 255 6

Printed in Hong Kong

Reprinted 1985

CONTENTS

1 The Complex Apparatus of
  Persuasion   6
2 The Writing on the Walls   28
3 In the beginning was the word...   44
4 The Orchestra of the Media   62
5 The Artist Enslaved   92
6 Flickering Images   110
7 Pomp and Circumstance   124
8 Barking of the Dogs of War   154
  Afterword   188
  Bibliography   190
  Index   190

THE COMPLEX APPARATUS OF PERSUASION

From the very beginning Hitler knew what he meant by propaganda and what was to be its place in his scheme for gaining and retaining power. He devoted an entire chapter of *Mein Kampf* to the subject, analyzing it brilliantly. Such was his faith in it that he once remarked that in future wars propaganda 'softening up' would replace the pre-attack artillery barrage. Albert Speer, Hitler's architect, who ultimately became his Minister of War Production, told the Nuremberg War Crimes Tribunal that what had distinguished the Third Reich from all previous dictatorships was its use of all the means of communication to sustain itself and to deprive its subjects of the power of independent thought.

Hitler claimed to have derived his convictions from studying the effects of the British propaganda offensive in World War I which he regarded as having been instrumental in bringing about Germany's defeat. The British operation, led by the highly successful press baron, Lord Northcliffe, from headquarters at Crewe House, London, involved many ingenious minds, among them the novelist H G Wells. Employing such totally new weapons as leaflets dropped from aircraft and trench newspapers, it had successfully driven a wedge between people and government, hinting that once the 'Prussian militarists' responsible for the war had been ousted Germany would be accepted as an equal partner in the comity of European nations.

This gave rise to two great ironies. The first was that the British propaganda promises, which many Germans felt had not been honored after the war, helped to fuel that sense of grievance which brought Hitler to power. The second was that Nazi propaganda was at its least effective when it was used for those very purposes Britain had employed it for in wartime – that of trying to affect the enemy.

In Hitler's propaganda scheme, the target was the 'broad masses.' Recalling the impression made upon him by a march of Viennese workmen, which the Austrian Social Democrats had organized, he saw politics as expressing itself through mass movements. To attract large numbers to policies, they had to be formulated in strong, forthright, uncompromising terms so as to pander to the desire for security of his 'broad masses.' Ideas must be expressed in simple, concrete terms as they were unable to comprehend abstract ideas; issues must be presented in black and white because the subtler distinctions of hue were beyond them.

If it was necessary to lie to gain one's point it was mere 'bourgeois morality' to have scruples. The only proviso was that the lie must be a big one. The big lie carried its own credentials – who would believe another capable of such impudence as to tell a truly monstrous falsehood? What was more, even when discredited it always left traces behind.

There was another factor Hitler thought essential for effective propaganda. It had to appeal to the emotions because the reactions of the masses expressed themselves in crude passions and not through the intellect. Everything had, therefore, to be stated in crudely emotive terms. The very machinery of terror, developed in the party struggles and institutionalized under the National Socialist state, played its part in this. It demonstrated that the enemies of Germany had been identified: terror was no

A ceremonial 'altar' for the SS. Note the photograph of Hitler, ever-present even at intimate family occasions such as weddings and funerals.

Far left: Music box which churned out the Horst Wessel Song, anthem of Nazism.
Left: A paperweight produced at the start of the Nazi era.
Below left: SA men urge the boycott of Jewish merchandise in front of Israel's department store in Berlin in 1933.

Above: The boycott of Jewish shops was the first stage in the 'final solution' in 1933. The placard reads: 'Germans! Beware! Don't buy from the Jews!'

Top left: Hitler greets members of the SA during one of the four elections held in 1932.

Left: Dr. Goebbels visits the makeshift airfield in Königsberg, East Prussia in 1933.

Right: 'Walter's Struggle for Hitler' was a propaganda piece directed at German boys and young men in an effort to have them join the burgeoning Hitler Youth.

Below and above right: Various examples of 'Nazi Kitsch,' which was actually discouraged by the Nazis in their first years and eventually suppressed. The lady's fan and the decals were in this category. The sheet music for *Die Fahne Hoch*, the Horst Wessel song, to be sung barber-shop quartet style, was not.

more than the state, in the name of the people, striking them down. The SA (*Sturm Abteilung* or Storm Troopers) began this process. Originally formed as stewards for party meetings, they were encouraged in the view that the best means of defense was attack. The reputation they soon gained for the brutal handling of hecklers or any who tried to disrupt meetings was meant to stamp them and the party they belonged to 'as a political fighting force and not as a debating society.' Their tradition was worthily continued by the SS (*Schutz Staffeln* or 'Protection Squads') and their various offshoots – such as the Gestapo and the SD (*Sicherheitsdienst* or 'Security Service').

Besides frightening off political rivals, these methods had the advantage of giving the masses an increased sense of mental security in Hitler's view. There was no purpose in bothering their heads about other ideas for, since the bearers of those alternatives were quickly chased from the scene, fate and fortune must be on the side of the victors.

The party did its best to convince the masses that this was indeed the case. It did so, as Hitler intended, by raising politics above the realm of platforms, pledges and policies to that of 'spiritual forces.' The real struggle, he had declared, was not between the competing manifestoes, but between *Weltanschauungen* (life philosophies), a much favored Nazi word. Marxism was one kind of *Weltanschauung* and the reasons its opponents had failed to combat it, even by physical force, was because of their failure to understand its nature. This rendered everything they did defensive. It could be fought only by a political force making its own claims on the human spirit. It is in this notion that the 'mystical' element of National Socialism lies and this was to interpenetrate every aspect of its propaganda. From the political party of men 'who believed themselves the standard-bearers and apostles of a new spiritual doctrine' of which Hitler had spoken, to an actual religion, was a very short step indeed. It was taken by men like Himmler and Rosenberg. The views of both men were, of course, cranky claptrap; Himmler's expressed themselves in his new Jesuits, the austerely clad SS bound by vows to Hitler as their Supreme Pontiff. Rosenberg, however, possessed the gift for expressing himself in something like academic phraseology and so became the party's theologist. His new religion was the religion of the blood, of race. The soul was race seen within and race the external and collective manifestation of the soul. He then proceeded to show the all-transcending racial superiority of the Germans, the ordained bringers of order, logic, discipline to humanity.

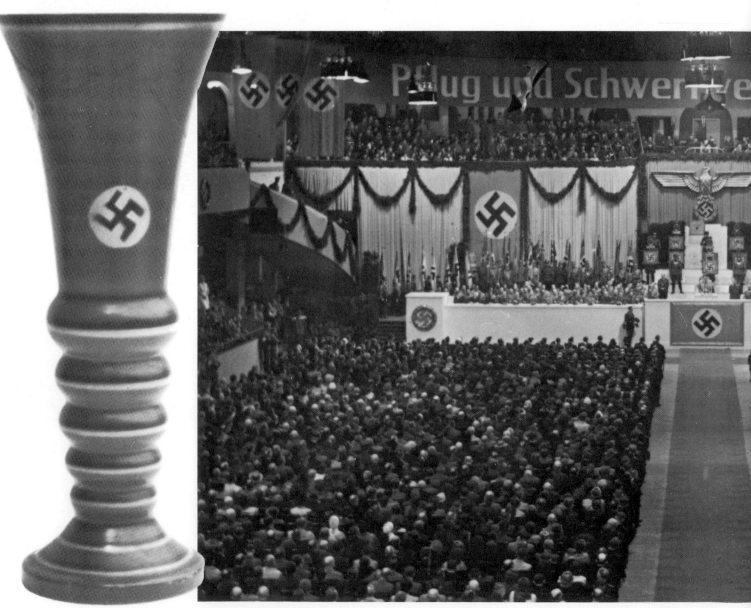

What this really amounted to was, of course, a simple reversion to tribalism, which for Rosenberg meant Germanic tribalism. It was the natural consequence of this that he should hark back to his people's ancestral past, to its sagas, like the *Hildebrand Lied*. Here was reawakened the world of Odin, Freya, Thor and of eternal rewards, as in the *Edda Saga* for those 'who have fallen in the fight, who have borne wounds, who have toiled unto death from the beginning of the world.' In this heroic age of robust, virile, ruthless warriors, there had been no place for moral questioning. Only deeds of daring counted. They had killed, conquered, copulated with healthy abandon until the Christian doctrine came to enfeeble them by elevating the individual soul above the mass and by preaching a love of humanity which ignored race. Now a renewal of that pagan and pantheistic spirit was taking place and under

Far left: A drinking goblet in veritable 'Nazi Kitsch' style.
Left: A wartime rally held in honor of Hermann Goering, who delivered an address that evening.
Above left: Hitler congratulates General Litzmann on his birthday in 1934. The general died soon afterwards. Hitler attempted to ingratiate himself with the military during his first years in power, which convinced the public though not the General Staff.
Above: A bronze plaque in honor of the Nazi seizure of power.

its inspiration there would be a return to the old practices of the true Germanic faith: sun worship, nature and fertility cults, even animal sacrifices. Above all the worship of the warrior.

The new faith had its gospel in *Mein Kampf*; its Messiah in its author; its morality in Rosenberg's 'striving for the freedom and honor of Germany'; its devils in the Jews – the racial polluters; its villains and persecutors in Germany's enemies, historical as well as contemporary, among them Charlemagne who had slain 4500 Saxons. It had its martyrs in Horst Wessel or the murdered Hitler Youth, Herbert Norkus; its seminaries in the Adolf Hitler Schools and the Ordensburgen (Order Castles) where selected youths were trained as future leaders. It had,

Reigen, Freuden Feuer,
HitlerJungens, HitlerMädels.

Flieger S.A., Reiter S.A.,
Arbeitsdienst, Motor S.A.

BraunerRock, S.A.1933,
S.A.1923 + Horst Wessel.

Saalschutz, Wachdienst,
Schwarzer Rock, + Mantel.

Above: Goebbels listens intently to the adventures of a young convert to the *Hitlerjugend*.
Left: A children's book extolling the virtues of the SA and National Socialism.
Right: A page from this book showing everyone in step marching to Hitler's tune.
Below: A Tinker Toy or Lego-style swastika designed to be put together by small children and fixed to a prominent spot in the nursery.

Tra ri tra ra – tra ri tra ra!
Trom pe ter find da.
Tra ra tra ri
trom pe ten fie.
Trom pe ter wer den wir,
im Takt mar fchie ren wir.

Left: Model of an SA man.
Right: Goebbels making an impassioned speech in 1943 which urged the German nation to wage total war on the enemy.

Below: Booklet supporting the German postal service.

Deutsche
Reichspost

Center right: Goebbels addresses a rally at the Kroll Opera House in Berlin on the occasion of the transfer of the Saar territory to the Third Reich.

16

through the party and its affiliates, its rituals and festivals.

At the party's highest levels, many Nazis thought Rosenberg's (and Himmler's) views were so much ludicrous cant. Hitler would have died rather than greet the summer solstice by participating in the hilltop slaughter of a young goat. It is characteristic of their cynicism that the Nazis were prepared to allow these ideas to be preached if they helped to secure their own power or to provide an opium which took people's minds off their oppressions and the abuses of government.

And this the new religion certainly did. Integrated into the National Socialist German Workers' Party, the insignificant and the anonymous found, as so many converts of religions had found before them, identity and status. The party could, and did, claim for its congregation every Aryan German, even those who lived abroad.

During the great ages of faith, the believer had found himself immersed in its outward symbols. There were the churches, basilicas, cathedrals soaring over lesser buildings; there were the wayside crucifixes, grottoes and shrines; there was the constant sight of priests, monks, nuns about the streets. He was expected to take part in the church's festival and required, on pain of mortal sin, to attend mass. He prayed, worshipped, confessed and gave alms. This role of creating a total ambiance was the one now taken over by the Nazi party which would also take over the roles of expurgating heresy and punishing and liquidating heretics.

It can, therefore, be seen that those who had the task of building the party and state's propaganda machine had a gargantuan task.

In 1920, when the party was a mere handful of the dedicated, Hitler himself had been its propaganda chief. His qualifications amounted to more than those ideas he was to express in *Mein Kampf* later for, in 1919, while still an infantry *Gefreite*, his nationalist views and his ability to couch them in incisive terms commended him to his officers. Anxious to stem the advance of left wing and Communist propaganda in the armed forces, he was one of a number of men appointed as 'political officers.' He soon proved his worth and was to prove it again in the party.

He was already clear in his mind when he accepted office in 1920 that instead of the street-corner orators addressing their half dozen or so bored passers-by or speaking to apathetic meetings held in three-quarters empty halls, he wanted mass meetings, part of a mass movement. This, to him, was vital to the 'spiritualization' of politics, since it is among the crowded congregations of filled churches that

Above: Some Nazis and others interested in the subject gaze at a notice board on which the slogan, 'With the storm troopers against the Jews' is written. The board's rubric states that 'The Jews are our misfortune.'
Below: A family portrait in which the grandfather thanks Hitler for giving him the means to live.

the believer sustains his faith and that the convert is won over. One of his earliest efforts – a brilliant advertising campaign – drew nearly two thousand people to the *Festsaal* of the Hofbräuhaus in Munich. There his audience was given an exposition of the twenty-five points of National Socialist policy which ingeniously managed to offer something for everyone. In this relatively modest beginning were the seeds of the vast meetings in the Berlin *Sportpalast* or the Zeppelinwiese at Nuremberg.

By 1925 the burden of organizational work left him too little time for his propaganda duties. In any event, he had no intention of allowing himself to become a backroom boy while others stalked the corridors of power. From this time, Gregor Strasser took over propaganda and it was as his assistant that the young Paul Josef Goebbels first became involved with the party. The name, forever afterwards to be associated with Nazi propaganda, first came to prominence as a result of one of the Führer's more inspired pieces of talent-spotting when, in 1926, he appointed him *Gauleiter* of Berlin. Poet manqué, incurable philanderer and romantic, he was very much a man in need of a cause. He found it in attachment to the person of Hitler.

He was born in the Ruhr town of Rheydt in 1897 where his father was a factory manager. The boy's destiny was to have been the Catholic priesthood, but as he was by nature the reverse of celibate or ascetic, it was obvious that his idealism would need a less restrictive outlet. He was, furthermore, far from unshakable in his faith.

The Nazi leadership, from Hitler down, reveals those who, in the normal course of events, would have been life's losers: those activated principally by grievance and self-pity. One reason for the success of National Socialism must lie in the fact that the world abounds in such people and they would have been even more common in a recently defeated country suffering from economic depression.

For them the party was a sanctuary in which their neuroses could be given free rein. Goebbels, though in many ways intellectually and educationally superior to the general run, was just such a one and the roots of this may have lain in his clubfoot to which have been ascribed various causes, including polio.

He was a studious youngster, and thanks to Catholic charities was able to study at a succession of German universities, among them one of the most renowned, Heidelburg. Here, to the distress of his parents, he lost the last shreds of belief and from this time, although they plainly retained affection for one another, their relationship was frequently stormy, as his diaries show.

At the end of his university studies, during which he had read literature, there was the question of a career. The profession of schoolteacher, such a rich hunting ground for the Nazi party recruiters, seemed the obvious choice, but he disdained it. Instead, like many another deluded young man he decided his future lay in creative writing. Its first fruit was a pretentious novel, *Michael: A German Fate*, whose main character was a latterday Sir Lancelot. As the basis for fame or fortune it was a non-starter. German publishers looked at it, shook their heads over it with pursed lips – and returned it. Later, and with a new character, plainly meant to represent Hitler, added, Goebbels used his position to secure its publication through the party presses. Sadly, even his personal *réclame* was insufficient to persuade German readers to buy it.

Penury drove him into politics, and for all that he was by inclination a romantic socialist (he was to write in his diary later of the tragedy of Communist and Nazi 'class brothers' fighting it out in the streets), he moved towards the nationalist right. In 1925, by now 28, he underwent his conversion to Nazism. He had found his own – and Germany's – redeemer. His diary is choked with entries that read like the gushings of a schoolgirl fallen for a mistress. So he writes of Hitler: 'He spoils me like a child. The kindly friend and master . . . He singles me out to walk alone with him and speaks to me like father to son . . . [He] gives me a bunch of flowers . . . red, red roses.' Such maundering about his encounters with Hitler were to continue, practically to the last. Here, a psychologist might tell us, was latent homosexuality revealed. Perhaps his notorious promiscuity was simply an attempt to conceal the truth from himself – a subterfuge by no means rare.

The principal mark of the man and the party to which he now allied himself was an impassioned loathing of the Jews. There is no evidence that hitherto Goebbels had entertained strong feelings in this direction. He had an affair with a girl who was part Jewish; he read Marx, knowing he was the son of a rabbi; he quoted Heine; two of the professors he most admired at Heidelberg were both

Below: Hitler and Goering (right) are enthusiastically greeted by *Alte Kämpfer,* former combatants in World War I.

Left: A bronze plaque in honor of the Führer.
Below: A group of people in a Franconian village greet the passing motorcade of the Führer.
Bottom: An unusual life-jacket.

ADOLF HITLER

Jews. Now all this, including his love affair which lingered on for a time after he became a Nazi, had to be extirpated. Within a short time he was a convinced anti-Semite. No one was ever able to criticize him for lack of zeal on that score. Even if he could never be accused of direct participation in such enormities as the Final Solution, it was perhaps he more than anybody who paved the way for it to be carried out with public acquiescence. He brought this situation about through the conscientious fulfilment of his role as propagandist. He did it by the constant harping on the themes of Jewish racial pollution, financial dishonesty and cupidity, most of all by promulgating the preposterous stories of Jewish world conspiracies. This made it permissible, when the rest of the world protested against Nazi treatment of the Jews, to hold those in Germany responsible as co-conspirators.

It was because of his efforts that the grain of anti-Semitism in all of us, including not a few Jews, was swelled and ripened. Without them, the anti-Semitic plans of the Nazis might have gone the way of their euthanasia plans, which were stillborn.

By the grace of his new found patron, Goebbels was appointed *Gauleiter* of Berlin; he was alongside Goering and some other party members also elected as a National Socialist deputy to the Reichstag.

By this time, in the way of would-be poets, Goebbels had

already found his true vocation – in journalism. He edited a series of publications which offered him a chance if not to vent his spleen against the denying world, at least to turn upon his political adversaries. These included all those he held responsible for keeping him from his true place: the Jews, the Communists, the 'betrayers of Germany' (and his own birthright) in the Weimar Government.

By 1929 he had succeeded Strasser, who had quarrelled with Hitler over policy, as head of party propaganda and at once demonstrated his genius. As *Reichspropagandaleiter* he also had a seat in the inner council of the party. His rise could aptly be called 'meteoric' and he was now fully occupied on the party's behalf – speaking, writing, organizing publicity. He met, during this time, the attractive divorcee Magda Quant whom he married in September 1931, with Hitler as witness. She already had one child by her first husband, but produced six by her second.

Marriage did nothing to cure his chronically roving eye and it was estimated that he had had some 30 mistresses, some of them with his wife's knowledge. Stories of his peccadilloes, especially about his using his position to lure pretty young actresses into bed provided ample scope for gossipmongers in the party, where he was generally disliked. One reason for this was the scorching attacks he made with his tongue which had the sting of a scorpion. His diaries frequently refer to this or that unfortunate receiving 'a tongue lashing.' He did not endear himself to his party comrades either by his condescending attitude to those he regarded as philistines, a group which must have included the majority of them. They had also heard how he kept the Führer roaring with laughter by his vicious impersonations of the foibles of those he wanted to discredit in his eye.

More serious, however, was the accusation that he was a congenital liar. He had at one time said that his clubfoot was the result of a wound in World War I. Later he claimed to have been a martyr of the French occupation of the Ruhr in 1923. They had imprisoned him, he said, and flogged him daily. When Gregor Strasser and his brother, Otto, made enquiries they found he had never spent a day in prison in his life.

None of this did anything to stay his rise to power and this reached its peak with the Nazi takeover in 1933. He then became Minister of Propaganda and Public Enlightenment. This combination of roles by which he would be able to build up a total environment of Nazism was the fulfilment of a long-nurtured plan.

Perhaps it is hardly surprising that he saw his model in the Catholic Church. He found it particularly impressive that 'every Catholic priest in the whole world read the same prayers on the same day, even at the same hour, in the same Latin language, from the same breviary.' The concept of a single authority which the Church represented, wherein faith and morals were clearly laid down and made obligatory upon all believers also seemed to him something to be envied and emulated. And when he looked deeply into the Church's festivals, its processions and its liturgy, he at once saw their value as a means of building up habits of unquestioning obedience. In their secularized form, they must be adopted by party and state, he believed.

All this was theory, however; practicalities were what mattered now: the actual party policies had to be imple-

Opposite and right: Pages from a girl's booklet urging participation in the *Bund Deutscher Mädchen* (League of German Girls).
Above and below: The seamier side of early Nazism in practice. Guards in front of one of the first concentration camps for political prisoners (above), and a round-up of actual and alleged Communists by the SA in 1933.

mented. These he had to present, interpret, make comprehensible and acceptable. Fundamental to these was, above all else, anti-Semitism and he was a passionate Jew-hater. The Jews were, in themselves, evil and the nation must rid itself of them. It was from them that all other evils flowed: capitalism was a Jewish manifestation; so was Communism; so was enfeebling and pusillanimous democracy which made the masses arbiters of a nation's destiny. And so, too, were other undesirable aspects of society such as Freemasonry, which he thought of as a great and powerful puller of strings. If all these things seem incompatible and it is hard to think of the same minds which produced capitalism producing Communism, one must remember the Nazis were convinced believers in the truth of 'The Protocols of the Elders of Zion.' This forgery, produced by the fanatically anti-Semitic advisers to Tsar Nicholas II of Russia, purported to expose a vast, diabolical plan of world conquest instituted by the leaders of world Jewry. In this capitalism and Communism were alike – merely stages towards the total enslavement of the Aryan races by the Jews.

The unmasking of 'Zionist' intentions had been due to the far-sighted genius of the Führer. Thus, he was to be seen as the saviour of Germany and of the world – if only the world would acknowledge the fact.

Stemming from the menace of Zionism was the need to grasp, with renewed strength, the nature of Germanness, to nourish and hold all that was German. One part of this was maintaining 'racial hygiene,' that is insuring that there was no possibility of miscegenation by which German blood would become polluted by inferior external sources; the other increasing the Aryan population.

It was hardly to be expected that the conspirators of Jewry would accept the challenge to their plans with equanimity. They would strain every sinew to the fight, using in particular their puppets in the capitalist democracies as well, of course, as Bolshevik Russia. It was to be expected, therefore, that there would be strong anti-Nazi agitation in these countries and that this would direct itself towards trying to deny Germany its rightful place. Britain and France would do this by trying to thwart Germany's attempts to consolidate its position in Europe or secure colonies. This is what they had always done. This was what lay behind the punitive Treaty of Versailles to which traitorous Weimar leaders had put their signature. The United States would seek to keep the nation from world markets, while itself exporting its Jewish and Negro culture – this, too, was part of the Zionist plan of pollution. Soviet Russia, on its side, would ceaselessly agitate and try to impose its political system on Germany.

Surrounded by enemies, but determined not to be frustrated in his intention of improving Germany's lot and position in the world, the Führer alone realized it was necessary to build up the strength of the armed forces to the point when they could challenge all comers. For this sacrifices would be necessary on the part of the people.

These were the broad outlines of policy but besides their exposition, the propaganda machine had also the day-to-day task of explaining and gaining support for government acts as they were carried out. These included, for example, the Enabling Act, passed in the Reichstag, which allowed Hitler to rule by decree and hence without refer-

Model soldiers from the Afrika Korps, Wehrmacht, the SA (behind) and, of course, Hitler.

ence to the normal democratic processes; or the 'Nuremberg Laws' of 1935 which defined 'Aryan' citizenship and made Jews into uninvited guests of Germany. There were as well, the thousand small matters of detail. Speer relates how, in 1935, a delegation of women's organizations, visiting Berlin and wishing to give their Führer a bouquet, inquired what his favorite flowers were. No one knew, but since the question was likely to arise quite frequently in the future, it was decided that an answer must be found. In the end one of Hitler's aides, completely on the spur of the moment said it was edelweiss. The only reasons for the choice were that it was rare and came from the Bavarian mountains. From then on the edelweiss was the 'Führer's flower.'

On top of all this were the constant crises mainly of the regime's own provocation – Rhineland, the Saar, the Austrian *Anschluss*, Czechoslovakia. Dynamic, questing and aggressive, National Socialism felt it had to be constantly challenging in order to prove its virility. This, as we know, finally roused the world to ire. When it did, Goebbels was able to say, like a prophet justified that here were the 'Jewish plutocracies' once more conspiring to thwart Aryan Germany's resistance to their machinations.

It looked like further proof of the National Socialist thesis of a Zionist plot when both America and Russia joined the war against Germany. The absurdity in this was, of course, that it was precisely under cover of the war that the Nazis were able to implement their 'Final Solution to the Jewish Problem.'

Goebbels carried out the complex mission entrusted to him, not only with exactitude, but an inspired flair and with a typical, restless, inexhaustible energy. He saw it as a creative activity and expected his subordinates to view it in the same way. The true propagandist was an artist who sensed the 'secret vibrations of the people.' And to him the people were a single unit, they were to be taught to think and react as one, belabored until they succumbed to what was required of them.

Right: Himmler pays a visit to Dachau concentration camp in 1936 and interviews one of the inmates.
Far right: A baptismal scene in which members of Himmler's SS 'christen' the baby.

Above: A pillow lovingly embroidered with the swastika.
Above right: A pewter plate *circa* 1934.

His instrument for the achievement of this end was an organization largely of his own making, whose tentacles embraced every aspect of life in which communication could conceivably be involved. These were subsumed into the twelve departments of his Ministry, whose headquarters was in a converted palace in Berlin's Wilhelmplatz, but which had branches throughout the *Gaus*. Despite the scope of its work he took the view that bureaucracy and paperwork were to be shunned since they impeded contact with the people. Quite late on in the regime's life he was to claim that there were no more than a thousand people under his control, though this is probably an underestimate.

Besides departments with specific interest in a particular field of activity, there were others with more routine functions. Department I, for example, was concerned only

A corpulent SA officer issues hand guns to his men who hold them out for inspection. The importance of the SA as a Nazi private army decreased after the Blood Purge in 1934, when Röhm and his entourage were slaughtered at Bad Wiessee.

with administration. Department II was directly involved in propaganda work, explaining and watching over the decisions of government and party. But it also had other tasks: it was responsible for devising and executing anti-Semitic propaganda. It sought to popularize the government's drive to increase the birthrate. It was concerned with the *Volksdeutsche*, the Germans living abroad, and with seeing that they were kept properly informed about what was happening in the Fatherland and were kept loyal to it. Separate sections within it were concerned with the organization of the great State festivals: the celebrations to mark historic anniversaries, rallies, the naming of ships, even State funerals, which Goebbels regarded as very important occasions. It planned exhibitions whose objectives were mainly political, such as those allegedly exposing the conspiracies of Bolshevism or 'World Jewry.'

It drew up detailed programs for all events in which Hitler was to take part.

In addition to all of this, it was also concerned with sport. For example, it acted as publicist for eminent German sportsmen when they traveled abroad and saw that the State gained the maximum advantage from their prestige, showing, if possible, that their achievements were the result of National Socialism.

There was at one point a section, IIa, whose function was to survey the very limited cultural life permitted to non-Aryans in Germany, but as these dwindled the need for it withered away.

Of the other departments, III was concerned with broadcasting; Department IV with the press, national and foreign, and so on. These, however, will be considered in more detail under the relevant sections of this book.

Besides the State's propaganda there was also, of course, the party *apparat*, under Goebbels' control. Of this the office of the *Reichsparteileiter* (Reich Party Leader) had the responsibility for 'determining the propaganda

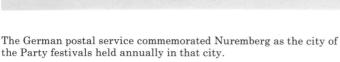

The German postal service commemorated Nuremberg as the city of the Party festivals held annually in that city.

An early photograph of Hitler in the uniform of the SA, the Nazi Party's first private army.

attitude and enlightening the people on the achievements of the Party leadership and State.' It was divided into two broad groupings, and Goebbels controlled one personally, while his chief of staff controlled the other. The first included the Offices of Active Propaganda, of Films, of Broadcasting, of Culture and of Liaison. The Office for Active Propaganda was concerned with publicizing and exploiting every kind of party function. These could be on such a colossal scale that special buildings had to be erected for them, or else so small-scale they concerned only local party branches.

The Chief of Staff's responsibilities included the Management Office, the Reich League for National Socialist Propaganda, the Head Office for Press Propaganda and, with these, the Head Office for Exhibitions and Trade Fairs.

The *Reichsparteileiter*'s office was divided between Berlin and Munich.

An especial mark of Goebbels' endeavors was the high degree of precision with which he sought to fit his propaganda to its intended recipient audience, and in his methods of collating and assessing their reactions, he was a pioneer. It was essential under National Socialism, he would argue, for the state to be informed of the mood of

the people as this was the way in which they could be guided. To obtain the necessary feedback, he employed several techniques. For example, he urged his subordinates to back all evaluations of public reaction to policy measures or to efforts by his own Ministry by statistical data. Information amassed in this way was kept on file to provide guidance in the future. Particular care was given to comparing the divergences between the actual reception a book, film, play or any other piece of propaganda received and his Ministry's earlier predictions about its reception.

Similarly *Gauleiters* and *Kreisleiters* were expected to report back to him not only in general terms, but also in regard to specific campaigns. He claimed that they did this with complete frankness. Other detailed statistics showed the sales of tickets for different types of events, indicating clearly those that were most popular.

Where there was failure among the public to respond to his efforts, he would seek remorselessly for the causes, scrapping his own pet schemes as ruthlessly as he scrapped those of others. He was to claim that he developed such a sensitivity to the nuances of public taste that during actual speeches he could judge how an argument was going down as he propounded it.

25

Es wird künftighin nur noch einen Adel geben: Adel der Arbeit!

Even the degree of supervision to which the media was subjected by his department was decided by a series of scales. These gave ratings to each medium with a separate scale within the medium itself. Although nobody was free from observation, those which rated lowest received the least. So in the press, it was newspapers which stood highest with weeklies and books coming lower down his scale; in the cinema it was the newsreels; in radio news and news commentaries.

Goebbels was, of course, to remain the name most closely associated with propaganda in the Third Reich, and he was certainly master of its main agencies. Assiduously as he tried to gather all the reins into his own hands, however, there were others. This was no accident: Hitler's policy was one of 'divide and rule.' Often he liked to keep some little thorn pricking the flesh of his paladins. It was a source of great annoyance to Goebbels that much wartime propaganda, in particular news of victories, emanated from the Führer himself, announced through the department of the Reich Press Chief, Otto Dietrich, a man he disliked. Dietrich, an early associate and friend of Hitler's, had been given overall control of party newspapers and retained his position after the seizure of power. What was more, Dietrich was responsible to Hess and so virtually outside of Goebbels' control.

Among other potential rivals was Alfred Rosenberg, who had hoped for the office of Minister of Propaganda for himself, and who remained an indefatigable article-writer and pamphleteer. Through him, *Völkischer Beobachter* maintained its own London correspondent. His role was not simply to report Britain back to Germany, but, equally, to interpret his own country to Britain by means of articles and interviews.

Joachim von Ribbentrop, the Foreign Minister, also believed himself to have an interest in propaganda and set up an organization within the Foreign Office to handle it. At one point there were even rival press clubs run by the Foreign Office and Propaganda Ministry to tempt overseas journalists in Berlin. In 1939 Hitler went so far as to increase Ribbentrop's responsibility for propaganda abroad.

Himmler and the SS represented another if less threatening group. The SS, for example, had its own newspaper *Der Schwarze Korps* (The Black Corps) which tended to pursue something of its own policy line. At the same time the mere sight of these grim, crisply uniformed black figures was one more reminder to the man-about-the-streets that he lived in Hitler's Third Reich – which after all is a form of propaganda.

All the same, the SD (*Sicherheitsdienst*) provided Goebbels with copies of its internal memoranda on such subjects as public morale and the way certain measures were being received, so that he could adjust his campaigns accordingly.

With the war, the army had an interest in propaganda, too. Although Goebbels saw to it that he retained overall control, there was a tendency towards 'going it alone' among the soldiers. This became particularly evident after the occupation of Europe. The various Army commands felt they were in a better position to judge on the spot the right emphasis for propaganda than civil servants in Berlin. It was, indeed, through the army's propagandists that people in the occupied countries (of which, by chance, I found myself one) encountered the ideology of the Third Reich.

Each of these bodies represented for Goebbels not just fingers in his own pie, but also potential alternative interpretations of National Socialism. Throughout his career,

Goebbels was concerned about this for two very good reasons. One was that a totalitarian system demanded the 'whole man and his unswerving obedience.' It was therefore urgent that disparate *Weltanschauungen* were synthesized in the interests of state security. The other was the personal threat these interpretations represented. At any moment, Hitler, both capricious and pragmatic, might decide he preferred one rather than another. Despite its urgency for him, Goebbels never solved this problem.

As history has shown it hardly mattered. He maintained his supremacy to the end. Side by side and, to some extent, as a result of his activities, the political system he advocated and used, and his powers of persuasion to advance the German people, brought its untold suffering upon Europe, in the end encompassing the Germans themselves.

*   *   *

One final comment ought to be made so that one can look at National Socialist propaganda in something like a proper perspective. Most writers, German as well as foreign, have tended to look upon Goebbels and his organization as purveyors of nothing more than lies. In doing so they have overlooked the lessons E H Dance teaches in his admirable *History the Betrayer*, a book which should be required reading for every historian. Dance has argued

that the appearance of events depends largely on one's standpoint. Britain sees Wellington as the victor of Waterloo; Germany, Blücher. Neither version is objectively 'truer' than the other.

National Socialists observed events from the viewpoint of extreme nationalism. What they thought they saw was a Germany surrounded by jealous, potential enemies. What was more, hardly any of its leaders had ever set foot in Britain, France or the United States, let alone possessed detailed knowledge of those countries. And in special ways Germany was remoter from the world than either Britain or France. The latter were both imperial powers; Britain was also the world's foremost center of trade; France that of culture. These things brought their peoples into constant touch with other nationalities – including far distant ones – contacts the Germans have never really experienced. Although changing, this sort of provincialism is still a marked German trait.

It certainly did nothing in the 'Twenties and 'Thirties to help the leaders of its government to form balanced judgments.

In any case, almost everything which is now associated exclusively with Nazism antedated their period of power by many years. Anti-Semitism, for example, had a long history in Germany; for all that it took Hitler to carry it to its final excesses. Schoolchildren under the Weimar government were taught about German racial superiority and the legitimacy of the nation's claim to dominate Europe. They were told, too, that Britain, France and Russia had wished World War I on humanity; Kaiser Wilhelm II was the apostle of world peace.

If all this sounds astonishing, one must remember that British and American schoolchildren are similarly misinformed. The defeat of a British Army under General Whitelock by the Argentinians in 1806, for instance, is not even mentioned in most British history books.

Detestable and repellent as the practice of National Socialism was, one must see its propaganda as an attempt to present a viewpoint believed to be right, one different in emphasis, but not in kind from what had gone before. The Nazis simply believed that they were giving paramountcy to those qualities of Germanism which other governments acknowledged, but for such weak reasons as the appeasement of rapacious neighbors, had ignored.

Goebbels, as we know, was a liar by instinct. Hitler suggested how lies should be employed in politics. One has to search diligently to find examples of their employing them. Indeed, there is evidence rather that they eschewed downright lies as too easily detected and so likely to affect their total credibility.

If asked what was the intention behind the total control of communication they exercised, they would have answered, as the Soviets might also answer, that it was to 'prevent misrepresentation.' The most they would acknowledge was that they 'managed' news.

And this, of course, they did with an efficiency never achieved before. It has never been surpassed.

Left: The petit bourgeois character of Nazi Kitsch was as tasteless as plates and cups with a Kennedy motif or an Elvis sweatshirt. Its fascination lies in the grass-roots nature of the movement which the Nazis themselves deplored on an official level, but turned a blind eye to it.

Various German parties campaign for the Reichstag elections in 1932
with their posters. From left to right: Nazis, Nazis, Center Party,
Social Democrats, Communists and National Party.

THE WRITING ON THE WALLS

National Socialist propaganda divides itself naturally into three phases: that which the party itself liked to call its 'time of struggle' before it acquired power; the period after 1933, up to the war; and the war itself.

In each period, the demands made upon the propaganda apparatus were different. In the initial one, the NSDAP was simply another German political party competing for the favors of the electorate against the rest, many of which were better established, more experienced and, at least in the early days before the NSDAP attracted funds from wealthy businessmen, wealthier. During that period, therefore, its persuasive powers were used to try to bring in the uncommitted and to convert the committed. In doing so it was fully aware that its political rivals were similarly employed.

Once the second period had begun propaganda began to take on new functions. The Nazis were aware of themselves as a party enjoying only minority support, and this disagreeable fact was underlined in the elections of March 1933, five weeks after their takeover when their vote was about 1,000,000 below that of the previous election in November 1932. This was despite the means at their disposal – as the government in power during the 1933 election – and their almost open intimidation of opponents.

It followed that after the election they had to set about winning 'the hearts and minds' of the people, and having won them, bind them fast to the Nazi cause. They were optimistic enough, perhaps over-ambitious enough to believe they could achieve a 100 percent success-rate. At the same time, however, they wisely refused to set themselves a target-date and realized they would only be totally accepted as new generations of Germans were born, to be soaked in the atmosphere of National Socialism from cradle to grave, to be absorbed and to merge themselves into its institutions through its schools, the Hitler Youth, the League of German Girls, the Labor Service, the Army, and, naturally, the party proper.

During the third phase, following the outbreak of war, fresh responsibilities devolved upon the state machinery of persuasion. On the one side the German people at large and the armed forces needed their morale sustained and their belief and support for the leadership, political and military, kept intact, even through reverses, which Goebbels, at any rate, recognized must be faced. On the other was the potential enemy audience where every effort must be applied to the lowering of morale and fighting-will.

Since, however, war propaganda in general is a totally different field it will be examined and assessed in detail in a separate, later section of this book.

Naturally, the effort to win over the whole of the German people to Hitler and to National Socialist ideology did not end in 1939. As a matter of fact, the early victories of the Wehrmacht provided a most welcome means of emphasizing their message. Hitler was never so popular or so esteemed as he was after the fall of France, when the whole of continental Europe seemed to lie in the German lap and Britain to be ripe for the gathering. Thus, there is continuity in the prewar political propaganda objectives of winning the whole of the people to the party, which can be followed right up to the time of the regime's collapse.

The immediate objective is to examine the various media through which the Nazis expressed their propagandistic aims and for this the poster offers an obvious and logical starting point. It must have been through seeing some bill, perhaps advertising an impending mass-meeting, that countless Germans made their first acquaintance with National Socialism.

Though the poster was by no means new – the Egyptians were said to have used it as far back as VI Dynasty – its modern development dated from about the middle of the 19th Century with cheap means of color reproduction by lithography. It was developed in Britain, the United States and later in France, where, of course, artists like Toulouse-Lautrec raised it to the level of an art-form.

It had quickly been taken up by political parties, especially during elections, in which the Nazis took part. Hence, a substantial proportion of their advertising was devoted to the type of pre-election posters characteristic of their kind: exhortations to vote for the party or its candidates. In one such, for a Reichstag election, unflattering photographs of opponents, particularly the Jewish ones, were juxtaposed with very flattering ones of the Nazi candidates.

The ballot-box was, nonetheless, viewed with understandable suspicion by the Nazis: a party which derided the democratic system could hardly be expected to enter wholeheartedly into its processes. There is, accordingly, a certain tepidity in their efforts in fighting elections, particularly when compared with the other and more important objectives of their propaganda. Even one of the most effective of the posters of the time, a gray line drawing showing dejected, unemployed men with the caption 'Our last Hope – Hitler' is comparatively mild. Only the words 'last Hope' betray the Nazi hand behind it. It was typical for them to present issues in such terms: 'Germany awake!' with the implication that if it failed to do so some appalling fate would strike. This was the 'language of imperatives' they so loved and which gave the spectator, willy-nilly, the feeling he ought to be doing something, no matter what, when affairs were at such a pass.

Goebbels specialized in playing on such vague feelings of discomfiture: 'THE BOURGEOIS STATE STAGGERS TO ITS END!' proclaimed great red posters in February 1927. Building the new Germany readers were told, was the task 'of you, worker of brain and of fist!' The nation's fate was in their hands. They must act. Then it told them how they could act: by attending a meeting to be addressed by Dr Goebbels in the Pharus-Saal, in the heart of working class Berlin.

This was where the National Socialist poster came truly into its own – as an adjunct to the main method of conversion – exposure to the ritual of public meetings with their showmanship, hypnotic oratory, paramilitary organization and sheer brute force which often overspilt into violence. To draw audiences to meetings almost anything was permissible. 'KAISER OF AMERICA – SPEAKS – IN BERLIN' was the startling wording of one of their bills. The passer-by had to go very close to read the rest. Then it became clear that the 'Kaiser' was the American millionaire Henry Kaiser and that Goebbels would be speaking at a meeting in Berlin devoted to the evils of this and other dollar-capitalists, who were holding Germany in pawn.

Left: Placard for the 1936 'election' which, traces the course of the Nazi party.
Above: A poster for the 1933 election, urging voters to support Hindenburg and Hitler. 'Fight with us for peace and equality.'

All this, of course, was merely following the ground plan of propaganda as already laid down by Hitler, which encompassed the poster as part of a total visual effort. Every message was, on this view, to be confined to the barest necessities, expressed in stereotyped formulas, so frequently repeated that their underlying idea was imprinted on the memory. For such a purpose, posters were an almost ideal medium. For one thing they were difficult to escape if only there were enough of them. Wherever a man moved he would find himself confronted by one. The aim was to give these constant encounters sufficient impact and it was here that Goebbels' skill lay.

Aggressive, almost physically violent in the impression on the beholder, it could be said that their visual ground base was in the ubiquitous swastika flag. It had been Hitler himself who had chosen this symbol and, after much thought, had chosen also the red, white and black in which, henceforward, it was always represented.

Every detail was the product of premeditation. There was, for example the thought given to the proportion and relationship of each color: the dominant areas of red, the white carefully picked to accent both the red and the black. There was the thickness of the arms of the swastika itself and the angle at which it was displayed. If the arms were too thin the image conveyed was one of timidity; if too thick, of dumpy inertia. Equally, it was placed aslant instead of on strictly horizontal and vertical planes, thus imparting to it a sense of relentless forward motion. This technique of placing the images at an angle to give dynamism was one the Nazis continued to use in their posters, which were also dominated by black, white and – especially – red, the color of revolution, a choice intended to pre-empt their Communist rivals.

There was, in addition, the actual choice of tone: the red of the brilliance of new-spilt blood, the white of a semi-fluorescent purity, the black, dense, without highlights. There were stories of whole batches of posters being rejected when they came off the press because the colors were thought to be too weak.

Of course, all this was partly the result of evolution, of trial and error, but the final result was a triad of colors which, to those who like myself have been exposed to it, can never fail to reawaken memories of the flags, bunting, vistas of banners and standards. Their impact was extraordinary.

There was extreme care, too, in making sure it was shown off against the blandest backgrounds: on the brown-uniformed arms of Storm Troopers; on the walls of gray, downtown areas; in drab meeting halls; on flags borne high through squalid streets. In all these places it stood out like poppies in a cornfield.

If visual symbols can be violent these, assuredly, were violent visual symbols. But this was consistent with Hitler's stated opinions. He once asked a friend: 'Haven't you ever seen a crowd collecting to watch a street brawl?' Brutality and physical strength he believed to be the two things the 'broad masses' respected. Propaganda consisted in attracting these very people, not, he declared, in educating those already educated. For him, therefore, the battlefront was not among the seats of government, but in the streets; its warriors, not the politicians, but the politically ignorant. And to appeal to them there was only one course: unacquainted and unable to digest abstract

Cover of an in-house SS magazine, atypical of the graphic art generally employed by the Party.

ideas, their reactions lay in the realm of feelings – the gut, as one might say today – it was at this level they must be appealed to. And such an appeal was the primary purpose of poster advertising.

Hitler had himself shown his skill in using posters, shortly after his appointment as head of party propaganda. He managed to attract 2000 people to a meeting in the *Festsaal* of the Munich Hofbräuhaus, an achievement unparalleled in the party's history. And it was here that he laid down his famous 'twenty-five theses' in imitation of Martin Luther, a clever amalgam of ideology and manifesto which managed to offer everything to everybody.

Goebbels, too, when he became party propaganda chief in 1926 saw the winning of the streets as a first objective, and when, in addition, he was made *Gauleiter* of Berlin gave this practical application. His opponents in the struggle for the allegiance of working people were the Communists and he decided to take the fight right into their heartland, using the very terminology of the left.

'Lenin or Hitler' was the choice offered by posters plastered all over Düsseldorf – a choice not, perhaps, totally apposite since in 1925, when it was used, Lenin had been dead for a year!

A particularly virulent anti-Semitic poster claiming that the Jews are devouring the peoples of the earth.

Right: 'Only Hitler' is the slogan for the 1932 Presidential election in which this famous poster appeared. Hitler narrowly lost to Hindenburg, the incumbent.

Party poster urging voters to opt for 'Greater Germany' April 1933.

'Every ten-year old to Us' is the appeal of this poster to join the BDM.

Expressing themselves, as the Nazis usually did in terms of struggle and warfare, the message emblazoned on the walls was always uncompromising: 'Perish Judah,' 'March with Us,' 'Fight with Us,' 'Join our Struggle,' 'For Germany and Freedom,' 'Onward – to Berlin,' 'Forward, over the Graves.' It was the vocabulary from the language which talked of 'the infamy of Versailles,' 'the Virus of Jewry,' 'the evil of Bolshevism,' 'the honor of the race,' and later 'the call of duty,' 'the nobility of a soldier's death,' and simple as it was, it was hard to ignore.

At the same time, in their design the posters were models of the art, using techniques well in advance of their times – which is why they always stood out from others. They were never overloaded with text; their drawings simple, straightforward and bold.

When Germany's reparations payments to its ex-enemies were being blamed for the nation's economic distress with the National Socialists in the forefront of the attack, posters were tellingly used. In one a clenched fist is shown menacing a baby, which raises its tiny arms in pathetic self-protection. By the child's side is a German worker, worn out toiling to provide the money handed over by his feeble government to rapacious foreigners. Only a Brownshirt, heroic and virile, offers resistance, shouting into the father's ear: 'Father! Rescue your child. Join the NSDAP.'

Left: Poster rallying farmers to a rally in Goslar in 1937.

It was in this field of presenting a fighting Germany, a Germany refusing, for example, to truckle under to foreign thrall, that the Nazi posters artists specialized. Their creations have a fierce power. Typical of them was the famous 'Three Storm Troopers' poster. It shows a trio of heads, marching, bodies canted forward like infantry advancing under fire. The three are of different ages: one is young, injured but not knocked out of the struggle for he wears a bandage heroically round his forehead; the second is middle aged; the third an older man with the face of a worker. The poster is captioned: 'National Socialism – the Organized Will of the Nation.' In a similar one, using techniques reminiscent of the woodcut, with its high contrasts, the three advancing Storm Troopers are dubbed: 'The Iron Cohorts of the German Revolution.'

The creator of both, 'Mjölnir,' was later to make a second reputation as cartoonist in Goebbels' paper *Der Angriff.* The pen name, which concealed the identity of Hans Schweitzer (later 'Dr' Hans Schweitzer), had been chosen as a Nordic form for 'hammer.' His speciality was the German hero with cleft chin, larger than life, hard of fist and rather low of forehead, all conjuring up pictures of strength, challenge and will. It was said of him by one Nazi leader that he did far more than lengthy speeches could do by 'the glowing fanaticism of his powerful art.' Beyond pure technique, it is hard to admire his work, for it seems to epitomize and idealize the street-corner thug and the bully-boy who, throughout the previous history

Film poster of 'The Eternal Jew.'

'The word: Freedom! We reach it only through Order.'

of civilized nations ancient and modern, had been regarded with detestation and contempt.

To this extent he was the most Nazi of all their poster artists and was duly honored for his services. He was made head of a special department of the Reich Fine Arts' Chamber, with the rank of commissioner, where he was responsible for designing all the symbols of the National Socialist state from stamps to statuary.

Not all the poster art of the Nazis was of this type. Other artists would try to evoke the nation's artistic past. In one case the great Albrecht Dürer provided the artist's inspiration. A knight on horseback holds in his hand a species of etiolated swastika, which is drawn in the manner of a Dürer woodcut. Yet another artistic style is demonstrated in the work of Ludwig Hohlwein, who has preserved an international reputation and is still cited as one of the pioneers of poster art in Germany. Looked at today, his work reminds one of nothing so much as those advertisements for seaside resorts which used to enliven British railway stations in the 'Thirties. Invariably, they would show a smiling girl in a bathing costume beckoning to the traveler to join her on a sunlit, silvery strand. In Hohlwein's case, the girl was replaced by a young Nazi, male or female, also smiling that same cupid-lipped, slightly rectangular smile, often advancing with outstretched hand in greeting. As for the beach backcloth, this has been replaced by a swirling swastika flag or some other symbol

of the party. Perhaps not surprisingly his work was particularly in demand for the Hitler Youth, and the League of German Girls and their various functions.

With the seizure of power, the scope widened immeasurably for the poster and its creators. To the ordinary man of today, used to seeing posters, including political posters, as part of his everyday environment, they may seem innocent enough, propaganda easily dismissed. This overlooks the fact that he sees them in competition with one another. It is not only the Republicans in America or the Conservatives in Britain who claim to have the only answer to the nation's troubles. Side by side, the Democrats or the Labour Party will be making similar claims. In a one-party state the process by which one largely cancels out the other ceases to function. The poster is no longer a stimulus to skepticism, it is the way the state reinforces the beliefs it wants its citizens to hold. There is no refutation. And backing these persuasive forces is the fact that life in a totalitarian society is tolerable only insofar as the individual accepts society's tenets and makes them his. If he fails to make this adjustment, not only is he a potentially dangerous subversive, he is suffering constant aggravation and, since he has no way of knowing the real truth, frustration is added to his

Right: 'Youth serves the Führer. Every ten-year old into the Hitler Youth.'

36

Jugend dient dem Führer

ALLE ZEHNJÄHRIGEN IN DIE HJ.

EINSATZ
DER DEUTSCHEN KRIEGSMARINE

aggravation. Questioning becomes less and less desirable, less and less possible, less and less necessary.

Typical of this was the campaign to convince Germans that Hitler was the nation's sole saviour. It is not always realized how repugnant the excesses of the Hitler cult were to most Germans. To evade the necessity of greeting each other with the mandatory 'Heil Hitler,' they bowdlerized it to '*Ein liter*,' two words which if said quickly enough had approximately the same sound. A whispered story ran: '*Heil Erd zu essen*; *Heil Tee zu trinken*; *Heil Hitler zu kotzen!*' '*Heil Erd*' and '*Heil Tee*' were respectively a health food and a health drink. Thus, the translation might run: '*Heil Erd* to eat; *Heil Tee* to drink; Heil Hitler to make you vomit!' Nonetheless, confronted by the leader's image at each street corner, there must have been many who asked themselves the question: 'Perhaps, after all, this man is the answer to all our problems.' And from this 'perhaps' they were on the way to being utterly converted to the cult.

In one poster typical of its kind, the anonymous knight of the Düreresque drawing has been replaced by the Führer himself, in white armor, with the red, white and black swastika streaming behind him. In another, mercifully uncaptioned, he is shown with left fist clenched, right hand holding aloft a swastika banner, lips grimly set, wind blowing hair, backed by a lowering gray sky and a

Opposite: A poster appealing for support for the German Navy.
Left: 'We are for Adolf Hitler,' an electoral appeal indicating that the millions of unemployed in Germany in 1932 supported the Nazis, which was only half true. The rest backed the Communists.
Below: Nazi propaganda van during the Prussian regional elections of 1932.

Unterstützt das hilfswerk
Mutter und kind

Above: 'You must save five marks a week if you want to drive your own car,' a slogan for the 'Strength Through Joy Car' later called 'The Peoples' Car,' or Volkswagen. Few were able to gain the benefit of this program, since the money was diverted to the war effort along with the factories which made them.

Above and below right: Two appeals for family life by the Party, urging motherhood (above) and large families (below).

sea of SA-men. Behind him, like the Holy Spirit descending, is a German eagle in the epicenter of a sunburst.

Before his death in 1934, the popular and prestigious figure of Marshal Paul von Hindenburg was frequently placed side by side with that of Hitler over the title *Der Marschall und der Gefreite* – the Marshal and the Corporal. (In fact, Hindenburg, a kindly if not outstandingly intelligent old gentleman, hated Hitler whom he invariably spoke of as 'the Bohemian corporal.')

In yet another, much beloved of both Goebbels and the Führer himself, Hitler is shown in what is virtually a colored photograph, enlarged to its maximum, wearing the brown Nazi jacket, eyes fixed on a distant horizon, penetrating, sad, thoughtful. One hand, fist clenched, is on his hip; the other rests on the back of a chair. The caption – to become the refrain of the regime – was *Ein Volk, Ein Reich, Ein Führer.*

The psychology of sowing seeds of doubt, which could be nurtured, applies to other forms of poster propaganda: that directed at rousing anti-Semitic feelings, for instance. A specialist in this was 'Seppla' (Josef Plank). In his work

Left: Poster supporting the Hitler Youth, which eventually incorporated every German boy of school age.

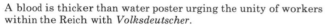
A blood is thicker than water poster urging the unity of workers within the Reich with *Volksdeutscher*.

'The Eternal Jew' exhibition was held in the German Museum in Munich.

every critic of National Socialism was given either a Jewish appearance or, where this was impossible, shown as a puppet of a frock-coated, top-hatted Jewish capitalist.

The most repellent example of anti-Semitic posters was that of an unnamed artist for an exhibition under the title of *Der Ewige Jude* (The Eternal Jew). The figure of an archetypal Jew dominated the picture, represented in hues of yellow and green, hook-nosed, caftanned, skull-capped. In his right hand he shows off his shekels, connecting him with money-grubbing; under his left arm is a relief map of the USSR and a whip.

Besides the reiteration of the main themes of National Socialism – anti-Semitism, the people's oneness with the leader, the need to breed ever more young Aryans – posters were of course used for many other purposes. For example, posters were used for recruitment for the various party organizations: the Hitler Youth, the League of German Girls, the SA, the SS and the Waffen-SS. They were used for exhibitions, and other party occasions. There were the activities of the 'Strength Through Joy' organization with its festivals and entertainments. All had to be shown in colorful posters. From time to time, too, there were the special campaigns. For example, Goebbels, who saw the radio as the principal means of reaching the people *en masse*, was concerned to see that as many as possible of the German people possessed receivers. For this purpose a cheap, so-called *Volksempfänger* (People's Receiver)

was produced, only capable of course, of receiving home transmissions. A poster campaign was used to publicize it across the country.

Naturally, posters were employed for purely commercial purposes at the same time – for selling lager or toothpaste or the German beauty-spots which could be reached by means of the State railways. There were also things like films and where these were produced with an ostensibly propagandistic purpose, posters were expected to do more than just draw in audiences. They were supposed to contribute to an overall propaganda offensive. So the posters for the violently anti-Semitic *Jud Süss* restated the image of the venomous Jew of Nazi stereotypes.

So until the crack of doom over the regime's head, posters went on playing their part in sustaining it. Advancing troops of the Allied Armies found them, flapping off crumbled walls – *Kampf bis zum Sieg* (Fight on to Victory), *Der Sieg wird Unser Sein!* (Victory will be ours!), *Adolf Hitler ist Der Sieg!* (Adolf Hitler is Victory!). For them, the message was merely funny. But Nazi propaganda had been no laughing matter, as the ruins about them showed. In the Germany, so like Orwell's *1984* where Hitler had been Big Brother, posters had helped materially in providing the total environment by which friends and foes of the Nazis alike felt themselves to be immersed.

Right: A poster celebrates the rally for peace on Party Day in 1939.

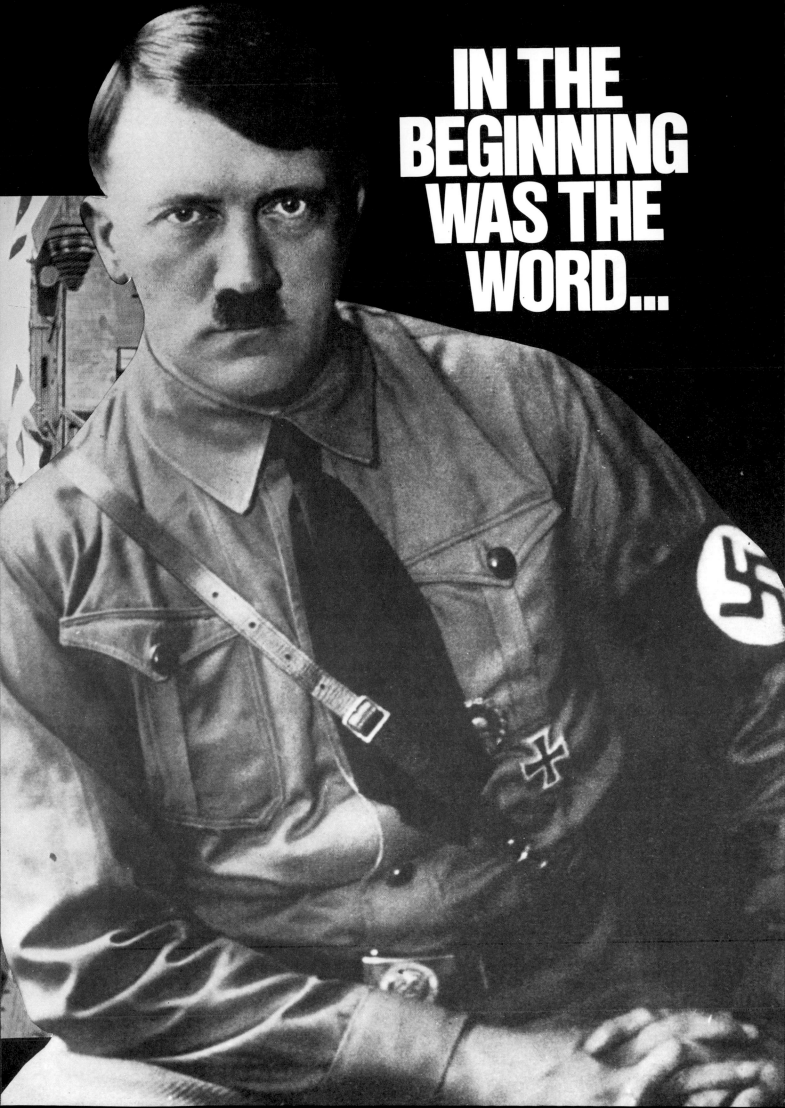

IN THE
BEGINNING
WAS THE
WORD...

'The force which ever set in motion the great historical avalanches of religious and political movements is the magic power of the spoken word. The broad masses of the populations are more amenable to the appeal of rhetoric than any other force.' So said Hitler in *Mein Kampf* and these words, having come from on high, it followed that the party's efforts were principally directed towards seeing that as many people as possible were exposed to this magic power.

In its pursuit, the grandmasters, Hitler and Goebbels – who thoroughly agreed with his master's view – as well as other leading Nazis, fulfilled a killingly arduous program of public speaking engagements. During one election campaign, Goebbels achieved a record of addressing 6000 meetings. In addition, all long-standing and high-ranking party members were expected to be capable of speaking to an audience. To ensure that they possessed at least minimal competence, they went through the Reich Speakers' School in which they were exposed to lectures in the Hitlerian techniques of oratory, given ideological training and, in test sessions, expected to hold their classmates enraptured. There was a Party Speakers' Certificate, resplendent with eagle and swastika seal, for those who did best.

Election meeting in Upper Bavaria in 1932. The banner urges votes to give Hitler power by supporting the National Socialists.

It was obvious, however, since party and then government placed such importance on the spoken word, that the unaided efforts of this select band alone would be inadequate. For one thing such luminaries of the movement tended to restrict themselves to the great issues of national and international affairs, though with occasional excursions into the byways of culture or racialism. There remained the more local issues, often as important or, to those involved, more important than remote questions of high policy. It was, in any event, regarded as of paramount importance to the Nazis that their ideas percolated from top to bottom. The good Aryan German was expected to hate the Jews not simply in broad principle, he was expected to carry this hatred actively to his Jewish neighbors.

From the outset the party was anxious to prove its local involvement: an attitude which distinguished the NSDAP from other parties of the extreme right. The Spanish *Falange*, for example, showed a total and arrogant disregard for the lowest strata of society. Goebbels and many others in the party were in Ernest Bramsted's words 'restless radicals,' and placed the emphasis unhesitatingly on the 'Socialist' rather than the 'National.' Goebbels had declared himself an enemy of the bourgeoisie – its profits and its peace and order. They would get a shock, he said in opposition, when they saw the radicalism of the party's demands. The nearest he came to a break with Hitler was over what he thought to be the leader's willingness to reach a composition with capitalists. In any case, the party's proclaimed intention of drawing upon the innate power of the masses could only come about if those masses felt the party to be concerned in their everyday affairs. Insofar as the Nazis won the 'Battle of the Streets' before 1933, they did it not merely by brute force, but by convincing the denizens of those working-class areas which were the battlefields that they were on their side in a far more direct way than the party's Communist rivals. It was regarded as essential to the continuing success that this state of affairs should persist.

There was, of course, never any question of involving others in government. It was a simple matter of elucidation, but of elucidation carried out in such a way that at the end government decisions received only enthusiastic endorsement. And this attitude was extended downward to local matters.

To meet the demand for party apologists, virtually an army of speakers was required and this is what the propaganda apparatus, both before and after the seizure of the power, strove to provide. They all came under the *Hauptstelle Rednerwesen* (Head Office for Speakers' Affairs), one of the two main sections of the office of the *Reichsparteileiter*. The resources of talent available ranged through the entire gamut, carefully categorized and graded. Some were part-time speakers, some fully employed by the party and in some cases extremely well-rewarded. A *Gauredner* (roughly, a constituency speaker) or a *Kreisredner* (district speaker) who specialized only in the affairs of the area and was expected to keep himself informed about them, functioned only part time. He might earn his daily bread by working for the party in another capacity. Next came the regional speakers whose domain could cover an entire province. There were besides

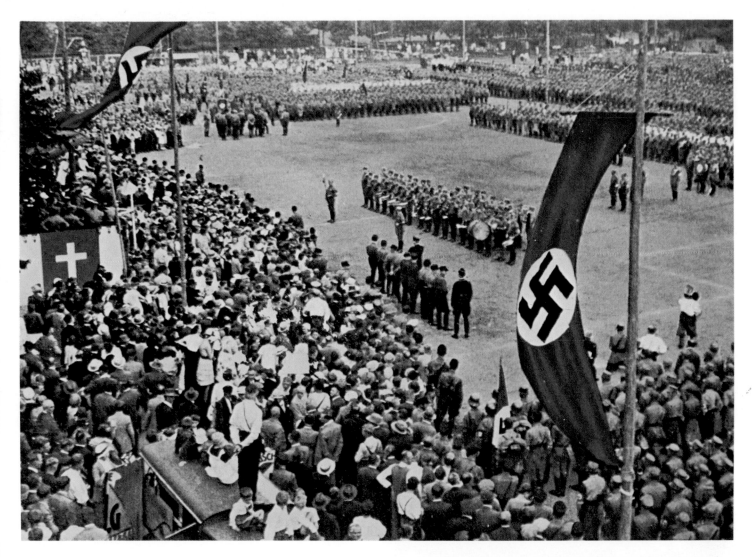

Above: Electoral meeting in Dresden in 1932.
Right: Hitler on the campaign trail in Brunswick in 1931. The repetition of monster rallies with shouting of slogans combined with street violence by the SA put an increasing pressure on the electorate to submit to Hitler's demands to gain power.

specialist speakers who limited themselves to particular themes: foreign relations, the economy, the so-called 'Jewish problem,' Bolshevism, even the British 'plutocracy.' There were Shock Troop Speakers and Shock Troop Speaker Cadets, used for short, intensive campaigns on one topic or another. At the pinnacle, were the *Reichsredner* (Reichs speakers), well paid and as heavily publicized as pop stars, who were used only on major occasions. There were in parallel with all these, other organizations like the Labor Front, the Strength Through Joy movement and even the Hitler Youth or the League of German Girls, which had their own speakers. All came, however, under the general umbrella of the *Reichsparteileiter*, and all had to fulfil exhausting programs, since supply never equaled demand.

Besides the Speakers' School the *Hauptstelle Rednerwesen* maintained a subsection for speakers' training, which among other things offered refesher courses. There was also a Speakers' Information section providing background notes on current and general issues, and handing down directives.

Comprehensive as this organization might seem, it remained overtopped by the real giants of Nazi oratory.

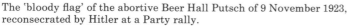
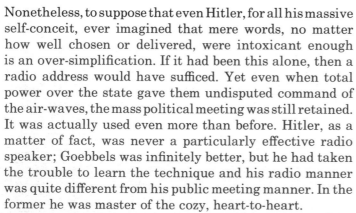

The 'bloody flag' of the abortive Beer Hall Putsch of 9 November 1923, reconsecrated by Hitler at a Party rally.

Hitler Youth salute their Führer at a rally in Berlin's Lustgarten on 1 May 1933.

Nonetheless, to suppose that even Hitler, for all his massive self-conceit, ever imagined that mere words, no matter how well chosen or delivered, were intoxicant enough is an over-simplification. If it had been this alone, then a radio address would have sufficed. Yet even when total power over the state gave them undisputed command of the air-waves, the mass political meeting was still retained. It was actually used even more than before. Hitler, as a matter of fact, was never a particularly effective radio speaker; Goebbels was infinitely better, but he had taken the trouble to learn the technique and his radio manner was quite different from his public meeting manner. In the former he was master of the cozy, heart-to-heart.

The truth is that words – that is to say pure ideas and argument, the engagement of reason and dialectic – were never foremost in the armory of National Socialist speakers. The party ideology could scarcely bear that kind of analysis. The relation between speaker and audience was, in Hitler's thesis, purely demagogic, since what marks the demagogue is that he tells his audience what it wants to hear. At his lowest, he appeals to sub-conscious instincts of sadism, prejudice and hatred. He could be said to go before his audience scarcely knowing what he intends to say, but relying on his instinctive feeling for the baser of human motives and his gifts for divining the mood of his listeners. This view is borne out in the

cases of Hitler and Goebbels. The first used to treat the preparation of his great speeches with a casualness which alarmed his staff; the second, to ask jokingly, 'Well, what shall we give 'em today?'

Speer, too, speaks of both of them, apparently molding the opinions of audiences but actually being molded by them. And this is the paradox of dictators, that they are actually more at the mercy of the mob than democratic leaders. On the one hand, there is the dictator's insatiable megalomania with its demand for ever greater acclaim and adulation, and on the other is his nightmare that those from whom power flows may turn upon him. So it was, as Speer says, that though Hitler and Goebbels both had the pornographers' instinct for the base, 'in a deeper sense they derived their whole existence from the reactions of their audiences.' There is little doubt that Hitler thrived on the roars of applause, even if he never left us any record of his gratification. Goebbels, on the other hand, is un-sparing in self-admiration: 'I soon have them spell-bound' (1925), 'They rave, they shout' (1926), 'breathless tension' (1926), 'a frenzy of enthusiasm' (1928) and so it continues.

All the same, a National Socialist party meeting was more than an exhibition of rabble-rousing oratory. The meeting was placed in its ideal psychological setting, produced, presented, stage-managed with no trick of theater missed, so that it became an emotional experience.

Above: At least 100,000 gathered at Potsdam on 21 March 1933 to honor their past and future warrior heroes.

The ordinary individual, drawn perhaps by a poster, wandering into his first meeting might find, as it was intended he should, that it was all rather intimidating: the premeeting street parade; the hall draped in its swastika banners; the uniformed SA stewards; the unison choruses of 'Heils'; the singing of marching songs with their aggressive tempos. During the meeting itself there might well be one of those incidents of violence when a persistent heckler was manhandled with the brutality the stewards specialized in. Intimidating, as a Black Mass, but also in some terrible, dark way, exhilarating.

Yet it was still the words of the speakers which set the tone of the whole thing. For the listener, what they offered was the subtlest form of incitement: there standing before him was this authoritative public figure, putting into words, making not merely permissible but actually laudable, that which hitherto had lain in the realm of the half-shameful, unconfessed fantasy. And here, about him, fantasy was being acted out.

'For a few short hours,' says Speer, 'the personal unhappiness caused by the breakdown of the economy, was replaced by a frenzy that demanded victims. And Hitler

Right: Hitler and Vice-Chancellor von Papen on the way to the Garrison Church in Potsdam for the ceremonies. Hitler deliberately played down his NCO rank by dressing formally while the heroes of World War I dressed in full military regalia.

49

Above: Eager Nazi students prepare to burn 'forbidden' books and leaflets on the Unter den Linden shortly after Hitler took power. *Left:* Hitler at the start of a speech made in March 1936 on the occasion of his bid for 're-election.' By this time all other opposition parties had been banned.

and Goebbels threw them the victims. By lashing out at their opponents and vilifying the Jews, they gave expression and direction to fierce, primal passions.'

The half-skeptical individual who had wandered through the doors, paid his few pfennigs entrance, shuffled to his seat, sat looking apprehensively about him, like one strayed into the place of worship of some alien faith, could well find himself experiencing catharsis.

No wonder audiences became utterly intoxicated. Not long after he became a Nazi, Speer watched a crowd leaving a meeting at the *Sportpalast*. They took over the entire broad street, he relates, moving down it like 'a marching throng' so that cars and trams had to stop for them. For a moment, they, the deprived, had been given a sense of mastery and of being in control. Could they not be excused if they imagined that by putting a National Socialist party in power this would become their permanent condition?

And this was just the state of mind which was being striven for. Perhaps the most terrifying aspect of all was how the architects of Nazism were able to calculate the way in which such effects were achieved, in the case of Goebbels to a nicety, before they even faced their hearers. Of all the Nazi leaders who made such an impression in

their times, three in particular – Goering, Goebbels and Hitler – could have been said to owe it primarily to their speaking talent. Each, however, had his individual style. Goering was the bluff, straight-speaking soldier. Perhaps it was logical that it was he who uttered the direct threats. At the time of the Czech crisis, he challenged the democracies, in a speech to Labor Front delegates 'to come out and fight' if they did not like what Germany was doing, boasting of her strength and warning the world that 'this nation of workers and peasants stands firm; threats have no effect on us.' He was cheered to the echo for minutes on end.

Elsewhere he used the same blustering tone to warn Britain to establish peace in 'that little Jewish state of hers' – meaning Palestine. His apparent candor, his outward cordiality and his rotundity, so often equated with

Above: Hitler at Brunswick in 1931 prior to a speaking engagement.
Right: Explaining a point. Hitler usually began a speech calmly and slowly built up to a crescendo.

Above: Burning of the books on the Opernplatz in Berlin, 11 May 1933. An early example of Nazi repression.
Right: Hitler tells Hindenburg and the throng gathered in the Garrison Church in Potsdam, 'We want to give the people peace.'
Below: Two old people in Hesse listening to a Hitler speech.

Left: Burial service held by the Nazis in honor of those who died in the street-fighting against the Communists on 30 January 1933, the day Hitler seized power.

honest good-nature, assisted his pose and won him popularity and the trust of the German people, who christened him 'Papa' Goering. It was a pose, nevertheless, for when it came to the crisis he was as devious as the rest. When it came to the more ruthless kinds of Jew-baiting he was ahead of them. After Crystal Night it was he who suggested that the Jewish population should be collectively fined to pay for the damage done to their own property by the rioters. In this way, the German insurance companies were relieved of an embarrassment. The memorandum which set in motion the Final Solution carries his signature.

And when it came to lies, his were the most bare-faced. It was Goering, for instance, who invented the myth of a Reich 'surrounded by a ring of steel,' through which no enemy bomber could penetrate. As a flyer himself – he had commanded the famous 'Richthofen Flying Circus' in 1918 after the death of its founder – he must have known this was nonsense. If he did not, there were his air ministry advisers to tell him so. He was also responsible for the declaration that the Luftwaffe was the 'world's most modern, most technically advanced and most numerous' air force. True to Hitler's prediction that 'the big lie' left traces behind, this is still accepted (among other reasons, because it was gratifying for the British Royal Air Force

of 1940 to believe it had vanquished such a giant). The real truth is that the French Air Force was larger and it is at least arguable that its aircraft were more modern and more advanced.

In almost direct contrast to Goering was Goebbels. He was the voice of reason or so he wished to appear. His first appearance as an orator was in his days at *Gymnasium* when he was invited to give the graduation speech on behalf of his class. Afterwards, in one of those joyous little ironies of history, his headmaster congratulated him on it: 'The content was excellent – but you'll never make a good orator.' As the need to develop his talent came, he set about self-training with characteristic penetration and thoroughness, buying a three-sided mirror before which he could posture for hours, trying out and improving gestures. The result was a formidable skill for swaying audiences, for whipping men to emotional frenzies which even Hitler found impressive. He was, Hitler declared, the only speaker he could listen to without falling asleep.

For Goebbels everything was premeditated and calculated. It was an exercise in sheer histrionics executed with the skill of the actor who knows how to render his audience silent at one moment so that not a single cough is heard and at another to rock them with laughter. As proof that he succeeded in giving the impression of 'the man of reason,' there are still Germans who will tell you they preferred Goebbels to Hitler as a speaker, leaving the inference to be drawn that their taste was somehow more discerning. Certainly his speeches bear re-reading, carry

53

An electoral meeting in Frankfurt am Main during one of the 1932 campaigns.

through a sustained and often ingeniously worked out argument in a way Hitler's rarely do; his tarnished invective now only evokes boredom.

An example of Goebbels' skill is a speech called 'Communism with the Mask Off' delivered in 1935. It was intended to be an answer to a leader in the London *Times*, headed 'Two Dictatorships,' and likening the Soviets to the Nazis. He painstakingly took the argument to pieces. Bolshevism was a terror imposed on a reluctant people. Foreign observers had only to speak to Germans to see what loyalty Hitler commanded. Bolshevism aimed at world conquest; National Socialism was concerned only with Germany and its problems, and wished to live in peace with the world. He listed the examples of Soviet terror; labor camps, mass executions, starvation of the *kulaks* as part of a drive to farm collectivization. Gradually he brought this register of atrocities nearer home – Bela Kun's short-lived 'Red Terror' in Hungary, not missing the point that Kun was a Jew. In Germany itself, some 300 NSDAP members had fallen victim to the Communists.

If, therefore, Germany seemed to be taking stern measures, it was doing so only to deal with the threat posed by the Communist International. Other Europeans, instead of criticizing Germany, should be emulating her example since they too were likely victims of the conspiracy.

As a piece of advocacy it was typically brilliant, tricked out with half-truths, deliberate misinterpretations and statistics without foundation or quoted source. But because the tone remained so reasonable throughout, the listener does not suspect or question the bases.

His repertoire of tricks included a flair for inventing terminology. He used words like 'penetrant' or 'schizophrenic.' Where no word was available he coined: *Kritikaster* – a small-time critic; *moralinsauer* – made sour by constant moralizing. Antagonistic newspapers were staffed by the *Journaille* (a combination of 'journalist' and *canaille* – rabble). He could turn out memorable phrases: 'We pursue aims by no means hypocritical,' he said in a wartime address. 'After the war we shall gladly live up to the principle: Live and let live. But during the war, the maxim is: Fight and let fight.' Or, on another occasion: 'We know what we want, but what is still more important, we want what we know.'

But perhaps most significant of all was his gift for subtlety and gradually changing the very meaning of words. A typical example is the word 'freedom.' Most people know what they mean by this – they mean the freedom of the ordinary citizen to act as he wishes within the law, which includes the freedom to criticize the government. Although this had totally disappeared in Nazi Germany, the word 'freedom' was used as much as ever. What it meant then however was the freedom of Germany as a nation to do exactly what she pleased without reference to others as, apparently, the Nazis thought other nations behaved.

President Hindenburg and his new Chancellor on 1 May 1933. Hindenburg thought he would be able to control Hitler but in fact Hitler was able to use the President as a puppet.

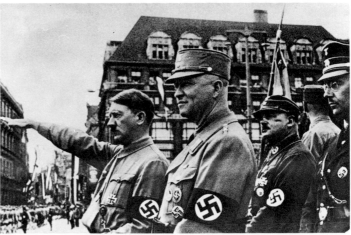

An SA rally in Leipzig in 1933. From left to right: Hitler, Mutschmann, the Party leader of Saxony, Ernst Röhm, Chief of Staff of the SA, and Heinrich Himmler, leader of the SS.

For all the rationality, the wit and the language more likely to please the educated than the uneducated in his audience, emotionalism, the emotionalism of the demagogue was still the main driving force. Often he would achieve his effects by a modulation of his fine speaking voice. Speer, observing him in a demonstration at the *Sportpalast* only weeks after his own first encounter with Hitler, speaks of Goebbels rousing his audience to greater and greater frenzies of enthusiasm and hatred. It was, he said, 'a witches' cauldron of excitement such as I had hitherto witnessed only at six-day bike races.'

Among many remarkable performances it is difficult to single one out. There was his speech 'Lenin or Hitler' in 1925 in which he carefully built up arguments to show National Socialism as more radical than Communism and hence providing the true spiritual home of the proletariat,

particularly since Communism was itself in pawn to the Jews, themselves in league with the stock exchange capitalists.

Still more striking, however, was his address at the *Sportpalast* in February 1943. This was not long after Stalingrad when doubt about the war's outcome was beginning to chill the hearts of the German people, bringing in its train a disillusionment with Hitler's promises. Before a carefully picked audience of loyal party members, Goebbels, without compromising his belief in final victory, frankly admitted the seriousness of the crisis in the east. To meet the needs of the moment he put forward three theses: that the German armed forces were the bastion against the engulfment of Europe by a Bolshevik tide; that alone of the nations, it had the will and the power to fulfil its mission; that in the prevailing crisis this could

The SA marches in triumph through the Brandenburg Gate on the night of Hitler's takeover.

Hitler meets with SA members in the Casino of Brown House, Nazi Party headquarters in Munich.

only be done by prompt and drastic action. Then, using a technique of question and answer which he had seen employed by Mussolini, he asked if Germany should do what must be done to bring the war to a successful conclusion without consideration of the cost – in other words wage 'total war.' The 'Jawohls' were shouted from thousands of throats to echo through the living rooms of millions of homes as the occasion was broadcast live. He was later to flatter himself that this effort served to stay the tide of pessimism and defeatism and gave the nation the will to struggle on.

By this time, of course, Hitler had very largely withdrawn from the public arena. There is no doubt, however, it had been he who had set down the outlines of a pattern in oratory all others followed. Speer recalls his speaking, pre-1933, to students and lecturers from the University of Berlin and from the Institute of Technology which Speer himself attended.

Dressed in a restrained suit, where Speer had seen him only on posters, formidable in party uniform, Hitler began in low key, quiet, almost diffidently 'as if he were candidly presenting his anxieties about the future.' Gradually, the appearance of shyness gave way to tones of urgency which swept his audience, the young Speer included, along with it. Now an almost tangible wave of enthusiasm was born among the hearers. In such an atmosphere,

Left: A meeting at the House of Culture in Nuremberg on the Fourth Party Day in 1929. The Nazis used these occasions to identify themselves with the traditional values they actually sought to undermine. *Below:* A Hitler Youth rally on 1 May 1933. The traditional Labor Day demonstrations were banned once Hitler was in power.

1933 · Sieg!

Above: 'Victory-1933' – the torchlight parade through the Brandenburg Gate in Berlin the night Hitler took power, 30 January 1933.
Below right: A child reaches up to grasp the hand of the Führer.
Bottom right: An old lady fervently thanks the Führer in the Saar after its return to the Reich by League of Nations plebiscite in 1935.

skepticism died, an opponent would have sounded like a temperance campaigner appealing for sobriety at a Bacchanalian orgy.

As the speech moved towards its climax, speaker and audience became so completely at one, the first appeared to be no more than the articulation of the mind of the other. And this, as the writer points out, was an audience by training critical, claiming to exalt reason over emotion. He goes on, 'It was as if it were the most natural thing in the world to lead students and part of the faculty of the two greatest academies in Germany submissively by a leash.' In these circumstances, it is not hard to imagine the effect it must have had on lesser, uncritical mortals.

What was here exemplified was no more than principles long enunciated and laid out in *Mein Kampf*. It was the application of the idea of releasing an uncompromising assault upon adversaries, disdaining to offer any qualification and presenting all issues in sharp contrasts, as one might say, in the strident hues of the Nazi flag. The least modification implied uncertainty on the speaker's part as to the total justice of his cause. It was, observably, an essay in rousing passion and fanaticism which alone, in Hitler's view, attracted the great masses to a cause. 'For those masses always respond to the compelling force which emanates from an absolute faith in ideas put for-

ward, combined with the indomitable will to fight for and defend them.'

The catch with this particular audience was in the term 'masses.' Speer's fellows were convinced that intellectually they stood, head and shoulders, above the 'broad masses.' They thought of themselves, therefore, as immune to the devices by which these inferiors were ensnared.

The skill which Hitler unfailingly displayed was, no doubt, in a very large measure innate, that born 'gift of the gab' which he certainly possessed. But it had also been trained and refined in a very hard school, as a street-corner speaker, where confronted by, at best, ridicule and at worst, and more commonly, indifference, he learnt how to rivet attention, how to gain sympathy from his hearers. He also developed to the finest pitch that unbelievable, mind reader's flair which could seek out and probe into sensitivities, and cajole, flatter, then reinforce prejudice. As Schacht was to remark 'he could play like a virtuoso on middle-class hearts.'

Compared with Goebbels, Hitler's style was more personal, more reminiscent. He would recall 'the days of struggle,' the malice of enemies and, by contrast, the comradeship within the party in ways calculated to stir and warm his listeners' hearts. He also preferred the oracular to the reasoned statement. He prophesied, but seldom analyzed. His speeches are laden with abuse and menace, sometimes incorporated into the fabric of his address in such a way as to give them an almost conversational air as a man might confide his feeling to a friend. Sometimes they would be shrieked with hammering or brandished fists. At others, he could make a comparatively innocent remark like 'my patience is exhausted' sound like a terrible malediction by raising his harsh voice to raucous shrillness. There was the heavy sprinkling of words like 'hatred,' 'ruthlessness,' 'smash,' 'force' – all presented as justifiable, even commendable attitudes. Goebbels, who used such terms too, would represent them as attitudes made necessary by the moment to give way to more conciliatory ones when circumstances allowed.

Hitler's plane flies over Nuremburg, on Party Day, 1934, in a scene later depicted in Leni Riefenstahl's classic, *The Triumph of the Will.*

All this was built by Hitler into a crescendo in which he worked himself up to a pitch of near-hysteria, screaming and spitting out resentment, knowing it was not merely his own emotion, but also that of his audience. Continued for minutes on end, men would groan, women sob to release the tension, until they reached some final point at

Hitler visits a wounded victim of street fighting in hospital. Compassionate scenes of this type were commonplace and were effective propaganda vehicles.

Hitler decorates a grave at Tannenberg in East Prussia in 1931, commemorating the famous victory won by Hindenburg over the Russians in August 1914.

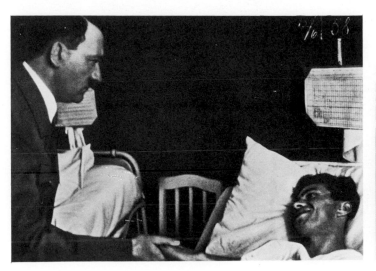

59

which they broke out into the exaltant, relieved cheering of 'Heils.'

In July 1932 Speer drove Hitler to a mass meeting in the Brandenburg Stadium in Berlin, but was prevented by various duties from going into the meeting. As he waited outside in his car he could hear the great storms of applause interrupting the speaker for minutes at a time.

In their printed form, Hitler's addresses often abound in underlinings and double underlinings. So in a speech, 'One Year of National Socialism in Germany,' delivered to the Reichstag on 30 January 1934, he speaks of his own role in events: 'I have never for a moment regarded the task that became mine as other than a

<u>commission entrusted me by the whole of the</u>

<u>German people'</u>

In the same address, he issued a general warning: 'I can only once again repeat to the world at this moment that no threat and no force will ever move the German people to give up rights which cannot be denied sovereign nations.

<u>Germany demands equality of rights.'</u>

Of course translation removes much of the feeling of the original. This is made worse in the case of German by the fact that it lacks the Latin-based vocabulary of English, usually drawn on for formal addresses such as those delivered by heads of state. To fill the lacuna Germans have to make up combinations of words and cumbersome

as these can be, the language is often the more graphic for them. Thus, for example, 'patriotism' in German becomes *Vaterlandliebe* or, literally, 'Fatherland-love.'

The problems of translation apart, the written form of his words always fails because the true demagogue is dependent on a live audience. Some pale simulacra of his intentions may come over in broadcasts or, occasionally, even on film. Written, they defy the efforts of the typographer to capture their hypnotism.

In the light of history one question remains: what purpose did this unprecedented deluge of words serve? The question is as inevitable as its answer is obvious. Given a system of ideas so utterly disconnected one from another and so devoid of a rational, intellectually justifiable basis, there was a need for constant justification and, most importantly, blocking the dams of doubt or criticism by sweeping them away on flights of emotion. It was only in that direct, live contact, in which one man was able to exert his personality upon others, that this was possible and that people could be sent away believing that they had been given satisfactory answers. Or, at least, that they had got something better than answers.

Below left: The Führer at a party congress in Nuremburg, 1929.
Below right: Greeting the Führer upon his arrival in Hamburg harbor for a review of the growing German fleet in 1935.
Bottom right: Hitler returns the congratulations of the throng gathered beneath his balcony in Berlin on the occasion of the return of the Saarland to the Reich in the same year.
Right: Hitler at Nuremberg with the 'bloody flag' of the Beer Hall Putsch of 1923 carried triumphantly by an SS guard.

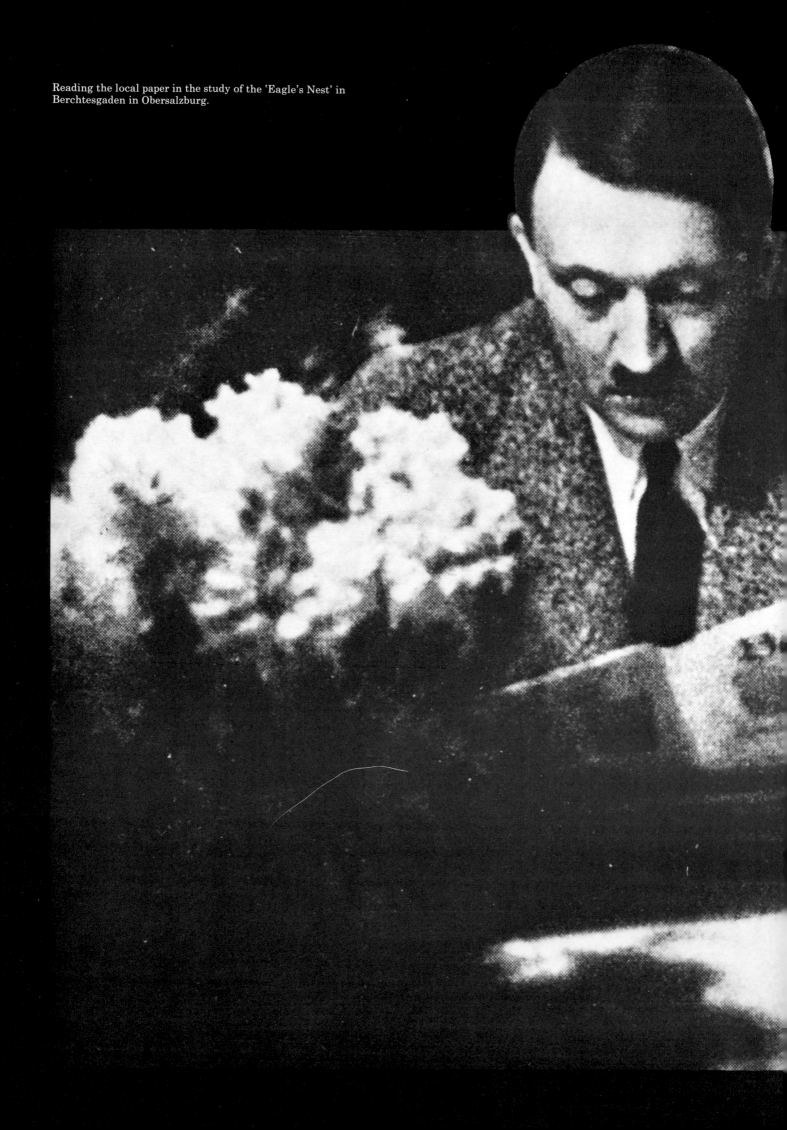

Reading the local paper in the study of the 'Eagle's Nest' in
Berchtesgaden in Obersalzburg.

THE ORCHESTRA
OF THE MEDIA

As with the poster and the public meeting, until the seizure of power, the National Socialist press was simply a political alternative, another tool in the manipulation of the people's minds. Indeed its political journalism suffered from an inherent disadvantage. Once a site had been found for it a poster would always be seen. Equally, the message of party meetings could always be guaranteed to reach ears beyond its immediate audience. On the other hand, no one could be compelled to buy, let alone to read, a journal he did not want. It followed that their publications were usually reaching only the converted, in search of sustenance for their belief, rather than carrying out a task of evangelization.

This, naturally, meant that readership was comparatively small, though there was some growth with the increases in party membership. Nonetheless, even after 1933, the strictly party organs made only a small dent on the reading public. Although the entire press was composed of party hirelings the average German still preferred to stick to his old favorites, provided these had not actually been banned, as if they were still to be relied upon.

In these circumstances, it is somewhat surprising to find how early in its existence the party already had a flourishing and, given the rigid limits of ideology, varied press: *The National Socialist Newsletter, Völkischer Beobachter, Der Stürmer, Der Angriff, Illustrierter Beobachter, Der Brennessel*, and later *Das Reich*. Each had its own character and appealed to its own readership. The *Völkischer Beobachter*, for example, was something of a popular daily, in broadsheet format, with a marked bias towards the 'blood and soil,' ersatz religious brand of National Social-

ism. *Der Angriff*, Goebbels' own paper, presented the news from a less restricted point of view. The *Illustrierter Beobachter*, Hitler's own particular favorite, was the popular tabloid par excellence, its front page covered in pictures. *Der Brennessel* was a so-called satirical sheet. Its contents, which can have raised a laugh only among the most dedicated and purblind of Nazis, oscillated between heavy jokes and nauseating cruelty. Even Hitler was led to comment on its total lack of humor. *Das Reich*, finest of all the Nazi newspapers and also the brain-child of Goebbels, sought to appeal to a cultured and intellectual readership and carried a particularly good arts' commentary.

Apart from these papers, the various party organizations – the SS, the Hitler Youth, the League of German Girls and so on – also had their own journals, all, of course, suited to the needs and tastes of their readers, but also incorporating the mandatory heavy dose of indoctrination.

The *Völkischer Beobachter* was the eldest of this witches' brood, having come under the Nazi banner as early as December 1920. Ernst Röhm, head of the SA and former army captain, managed to obtain the money for the purchase of what was then called the *Münchener Beobachter* (Munich Observer) from his former commanding officer, Major General Ritter von Epp, one-time *Freikorps* leader

Below: 'National Socialist Press – Today the press of the Nazis; Tomorrow the press of the Nation' reads the slogan at this press conference which prophesied the collapse of a free press in Germany after Hitler took power.
Right: Front page of the *Völkischer Beobachter,* the official Nazi Party journal, the morning after Hitler took over as Reichs Chancellor.

Norddeutsche Ausgabe / Ausgabe A
31. Ausg. ★ 46. Jahrg. ★ Einzelpreis 20 Pf.

Freiheit und Brot

Ausgabe A / Norddeutsche Ausgabe
Berlin, Dienstag, 31. Januar 1933

VÖLKISCHER BEOBACHTER

Herausgeber Adolf Hitler

Verlag: Frz. Eher Nachf., G.m.b.H., München 2 NO, Zweigniederlassung Berlin SW 68

Kampfblatt der national-sozialistischen Bewegung Großdeutschlands

Ein historischer Tag:

Erste Maßnahmen der Reichsregierung Hitler

Interview des „Völkischen Beobachters" mit dem Reichsinnenminister Frick — Tagung des neuen Kabinetts

Der Reichspräsident von Hindenburg hat Adolf Hitler zum Reichskanzler ernannt. Der neuen Regierung werden neben Adolf Hitler als Reichskanzler der frühere Minister Pg. Frick als Reichsinnenminister und der Reichstagspräsident Pg. Goering als Reichsminister ohne Geschäftsbereich und Reichskommissar für den Luftverkehr angehören. Pg. Goering wird gleichzeitig mit der Wahrnehmung der Geschäfte des Preußischen Innenministeriums betraut.

ADOLF HITLER

Reichsinnenminister Dr. Frick   **Reichsminister Goering**

Berlin, 30. Januar.

Die im Anschluß an die Ernennung Adolf Hitlers herausgegebene amtliche Mitteilung hat folgenden Wortlaut:

„Der Reichspräsident hat Herrn Adolf Hitler zum Reichskanzler ernannt und auf dessen Vorschlag die Reichsregierung wie folgt gebildet:

Reichskanzler a. D. von Papen zum Stellvertreter des Kanzlers und Reichskommissar für das Land Preußen;

Freiherrn von Neurath zum Reichsminister des Auswärtigen;

Staatsminister a. D. M.d.R. Dr. Frick zum Reichsminister des Innern;

Generalleutnant Freiherrn von Blomberg zum Reichswehrminister;

Graf von Schwerin-Krosigk zum Reichsminister der Finanzen;

Geheimen Finanzrat M.d.R. Hugenberg zum Reichsminister der Wirtschaft und zum Reichsminister für Ernährung und Landwirtschaft;

Franz Seldte zum Reichsarbeitsminister;

Freiherrn von Eltz-Rübenach zum Reichspostminister und zum Reichsverkehrsminister;

Reichstagspräsidenten Goering zum Reichsminister ohne Geschäftsbereich und gleichzeitig zum Reichskommissar für den Luftverkehr.

Reichsminister Goering wurde mit der Wahrnehmung der Geschäfte des Preußischen Innenministeriums betraut.

Reichskommissar für Arbeitsbeschaffung Gereke wird in seinem Amt bestätigt.

Die Besetzung des Reichsjustizministeriums bleibt vorbehalten. Der Reichskanzler wird noch heute Verhandlungen zur Aufnahme der Bayerischen Volkspartei aufnehmen. Heute nachmittag 17 Uhr findet die erste Kabinettssitzung statt."

Das Ziel der neuen Regierung:

Die geistige und willensmäßige Erneuerung des deutschen Volkes

Erklärt Reichsinnenminister Dr. Frick in einer Unterredung mit dem „Völkischen Beobachter"

Während der Platz vor dem „Kaiserhof" sich immer mehr mit den Menschen füllt, die in freudiger Erregung auf den Augenblick warten, wo der neuernannte Reichskanzler Adolf Hitler mit seinen nächsten Vertrauten das Hotel verläßt, während Zeitungsreporter mit Photoapparate aufzubauen, Schupozüge die Regelung des notwendigen Verkehrs übernimmt, ist oben in den Räumen des Führers ein geschäftiges Kommen und Gehen.

Hitler befindet sich in eifrigem Gespräch mit seinem neuen Reichsminister des Innern Pg. Dr. Frick, um die zunächst zu ergreifenden Maßnahmen zu besprechen. Das Vorzimmer füllt sich inzwischen mit den Berlin anwesenden Fachreferenten der Partei, die aus kommen sind, um die Glückwünsche zu übermitteln. Die Tür geht auf — der Führer erscheint, zur Seite ihn mit Dr. Frick, und führt ihn ins Zimmer. Nach einem kurzen Gespräch mit einigen Herren seiner Umgebung erhebt sich unser Mitglied der Schriftleitung und hat dabei Gelegenheit, von dem neuernannten Minister einiges über die nächsten Ziele und Absichten der neuernannten Regierung zu erfahren.

„Die geistige und willensmäßige Erneuerung des gesamten deutschen Volkes ist die Voraussetzung für jede andere nationale Erneuerung und Erhebung und wird somit im Mittelpunkt unserer gesamten Politik stehen",

erklärte Minister Frick mit scharfer, bestimmter Stimme.

„Denken Sie, Herr Minister, dabei noch an besondere Maßnahmen gegen die KPD.?"

„Ich werde vorerst in dieser Richtung keine einzelnen Kommunisten in den letzten Woche Flugblätter verteilt wurden, in denen zum Generalstreik aufgefordert wurde."

Sollte sich dies die Kommunistische Partei so anders überlegen, so werden wir mit den schärfsten Maßnahmen gegen einen derartigen Generalstreik vorgehen."

Die Richtung unserer Politik deckt sich mit unserer bisherigen nationalsozialistischen Stellungnahme zu dieser Frage.

„Es wurde mir mitgeteilt, Herr Minister, daß in gewissen Gegenden Berlins schon die gepackten Koffer bereitstehen und gewisse Fern-D.-Züge heute nicht stark belegt sein sollen. Glauben Sie, hier etwas unternehmen zu müssen?"

Der Reichsminister winkt ab. „Ich glaube kaum. Wenn die Leute rausgehen, kann es uns nur erwünscht sein. Von mir aus hat es dazu keinen Anlaß."

„Die Reichstagseinberufung ist bekanntgegeben und auf die morgigen Tag festgelegt, in den nächsten Stunden wird der Aeltestenrat zum Zusammentritt des Reichstags noch Stellung nehmen. Sind hier entscheidende Schritte der Regierung zu erwarten?"

„Die Einzelparteien werden wohl tagen wollen, wer den Aeltestenrat tagen beschließt, kann ich noch nicht sagen. Jedenfalls aber," und hier erhebt sich die

Der Reichsminister äußerte sich sodann mit einigen Worten über das Verhältnis zwischen der Reichsregierung und Preußen:

„An dem bestehenden Zustand wird vorerst nichts geändert. Wir haben die Einrichtungen der Reichskommissare übernommen, neben denen die marxistische Regierung als zurzeit noch im Amte ist. Dagegen wurde der bisherige Reichstagspräsident Goering als Minister ohne Portefeuille und Reichskommissar für die Luftfahrt auch zum kommissarischen preußischen Innenminister ernannt. Für Minister Gürtner wurde als neuer Nachfolger bestimmt. Es bleibt also die zur endgültigen Regelung zunächst geschlossene Verhältnis der Länder zum Reich in diesem Zeitpunkt nicht akut.

Stimme des Innenministers etwas, „kann mit den wenigen Vollmachten nicht mehr regiert werden. Wir werden dem Reichstag ein Ermächtigungsgesetz vorlegen, das dieser entsprechend den Bestimmungen der Verfassung der Reichsregierung ausstellen soll. Wir brauchen diese Vollmachten, auf das große Werk, das wir mit Einsetzung aller Kräfte durchzuführen gewillt sind, nämlich die geistige und nationale Erneuerung unseres Volkes, endlich zur Tat werden zu lassen."

Der Grundstein zum Dritten Reich

Der 30. Januar 1933 wird einmal eingehen in die Geschichtsschreibung als ein Tag, der einen historischen Umschwung in der deutschen Entwicklung darstellt. Nach 14 Jahren unerhörter Opfer und Arbeit steht Adolf Hitler heute an jener Stelle, die ihm seit langem gebührte. Ein Gefühl unbändigen Stolzes geht durch alle Millionen jener, deren Sehnsucht, Kampf und Hingabe diese Jahre über im Zeichen des Willens stand, die Schande von der 9. November 1918 zu sühnen. Sie wußten, daß Deutschland in dieser Schande nicht untergehen, daß die Geschichte der Deutschen damit nicht zu Ende sein konnte. Adolf Hitler nahm aus dieser seelischen und materiellen Not erwuchs der Nation ihr großes Schicksal. Sie setzte aus jener selbsterlebten Nöten der deutschen Arbeitermassen hinführte zum Schicksalskampf von 1914, und aus diesem Frontsoldatentum, nach dem Dolchstoß der Novemberbrecher, zum politischen Kampf um die Erneuerung seines Volkes. Adolf Hitler als der Charakterkreuzung, die deutsche Nation in letzter Stunde vor dem Verfall vornahm. Gleichnis des deutschen Selbstbehauptungswillens, einer großen Zukunftshoffnung.

Denn das Entscheidende war, bleibt die Erkenntnis, daß diese große nationalsozialistische Volksbewegung niemals das Zeichen der Verzweiflung trug, sondern stets ein Zeichen eines großen Glaubens gestanden hat. Sie fühlte in ihr Ströme deutscher Sehnsüchte zusammenfließen, weit aus vergangenen Jahrhunderten: aus den Bauernkriegen, aus dem friderizianischen Preußen, aus den gewaltigen Quellen der Arbeiterbewegung des 19. Jahrhunderts. Der Glaube an die geschichtliche Sendung, war jene Kraft, die den Führer und die Bewegung nimmer müde werden ließ, über alle Widerwärtigkeiten und Anfeindungen triumphierte. Dieser Glaube wurde immer stärker gefestigt, wenn wir immer neue Gegner am Werke sahen, deutsches Wesen aus untergraben, in immer mehr überzeugten, wie innersinnlich berechtigt und lebensnotwendig der Kampf für die nationalsozialistische Bewegung war. Wenn das

Stürmische Huldigungen

Berlin, 30. Januar.

Der Ernennung Adolf Hitlers zum Reichskanzler ging ein kurzer Besuch beim Reichspräsidenten voraus. An diesem Besuch nahmen teil: Adolf Hitler, Frick, Goering, Papen, Hugenberg, Schmidt-Hannover und General von Blomberg. Unmittelbar nach dem Besuch beim Reichspräsidenten wurde die Betrauung Adolf Hitlers mit der Kanzlerschaft bekanntgegeben. Die Mitglieder der neuen Regierung wurden sofort vereidigt.

Im Regierungsviertel hatte sich die Nachricht von der Betrauung Adolf Hitlers mit Windeseile herumgesprochen. Beim Verlassen der Räume des Reichspräsidenten brachten große Menschenmengen in der Wilhelmstraße und hinter der von Adolf Hitler und Goering stürmische Kundgebungen dar.

Nationalsozialistische Staatssekretäre in Preußen

Berlin, 30. Januar.

Wie wir erfahren, bleibt die Neuernennung des Kabinetts auch für Preußen ohne Folgen. Es ist damit zu rechnen, daß Reichslandbundführer Pg. Willikens zum Staatssekretär für Landwirtschaft in Preußen ernannt wird. Pg. Gauleiter Studienrat Kube, Hannover, dürfte das Staatssekretariat des Preußischen Kultusministeriums übertragen bekommen.

An Stelle des Herrn Planck wird aller Voraussicht nach Ministerialrat Pg. Lammers zum Staatssekretär der Reichskanzlei ernannt werden.

Flaggen heraus!

München, 16. Juli 1941
46. Jahrgang / Nummer 29

30 Pfenn

SIMPLICISSIMUS

VERLAG KNORR & HIRTH KOMMANDITGESELLSCHAFT, MÜNCHEN

Huldigung der Demokratie S. M. des Königs von England

(Karl Arnold)

Ein Ölbild englischer Heiligenmaler für Stalins Hauskapelle im Kreml

Omaggio della democrazia di S. M. il Re d' Inghilterra . . . un quadro ad olio di pittori di Santi inglesi per la cappella privata di Stalin nel Cremlino

and ultimately a Nazi deputy in the Reichstag. The agreed price was 60,000RM and since it is unlikely that von Epp had so large a sum at hand it is possible as Bullock suggests, that the secret funds of the Army were also used.

Its name was promptly changed to *Völkischer Beobachter* widening it from a local to a national publication. The name itself is not easily translated, but it could be rendered approximately as 'National Observer.' The version 'Racial Observer' sometimes offered is stretching the meaning a little too far, notwithstanding the fact the '*Volk*' came to imply under National Socialism '*deutsche Volk*' or, exclusively, 'German people' as distinct from the allegedly non-German people such as the Jews.

Among its earliest editors was Alfred Rosenberg. He was one of those men whose intellectual pretension was greater than either his intelligence or his education. Goebbels, who used to delight Hitler with his crushing description of other leading Nazis, commented that 'Rosenberg almost managed to become a scholar, a journalist, a politician – but only almost.' He was a 'Baltic German,' that is to say he came from the German communities established in the Baltic lands, which in his boyhood, as now, were under Russian hegemony. German influence in them was considerable. Enough to infuriate the Slavic Russians on the one hand who regarded the 'Baltic Germans' as exercising far too much influence via the Tsar's court and the top echelons of the army and the civil service, and metropolitan Germans, on the other. This was because they tended to regard themselves as in some way purer than other Germans.

It was this, no doubt, which led Rosenberg into a nationalist movement. At the same time, while living under Russian influence he had come into contact with anti-Semitism and, in particular, that fevered invention 'The Protocols of the Elders of Zion,' originally printed on the Imperial Russian presses. Like so many people to this day – when their falsehood has been exposed beyond doubt – he believed its story of Hebrew plots.

If his motives for joining the Nazis were emotional, he certainly did his limited best to give them an intellectual gloss and so far succeeded that in Britain and France he was spoken of as 'the philosopher of Nazism,' a title, which if he knew of it, must have given him deep gratification. Its basis was his book, *Mythus des zwanzigsten Jahr-*

hunderts (The Myth of the Twentieth Century), a hodge-podge of crypto-paganism, of 'blood and soil' crankiness, and blatant anti-Semitism all offered as support for the notion of German master-race.

His claim to consideration resides in the fact he was in many ways the rival of Goebbels as the overseer of the German thought-process and, indeed, felt deeply aggrieved that he was not entrusted by his Führer with the portfolio of 'Propaganda and Public Enlightenment.' One reason why he was passed over was the very way in which he had handled the editorship of *Völkischer Beobachter.* Its attempt to restate the tortuous arguments of his *Mythus* was predestined to fail. Hitler believed that the refusal of the reading public to listen to the case he believed so serious and urgent had embittered him. During one of his lunchtime monologues, the Führer said that Rosenberg's 'contempt for mankind was only increased when he found the more he lowered the intellectual level of the journal the more sales increased.'

In fact they increased considerably and by the time that Rosenberg relinquished the editorship and another took his place, it was selling something over 1½ million copies a week, making it the most widely distributed newspaper in Germany. Only Goebbels' *Das Reich,* when it appeared, provided any sort of competition. Nevertheless, Hitler once remarked that for laughs he preferred the *Völkischer Beobachter* to *Der Brennessel* any day.

Second in seniority was *The National Socialist News-*

letter which began in 1925 and appeared twice a month. Its editor was Goebbels, who at once set the seal of his style – lively, provocative and vituperative – on it. Compared with other party publications it had a markedly left radical bias, though in his rejection of capitalism its editor tended to equate this with Jewishness. Among other surprising policies it advocated was one of *detente* between Germany and Soviet Russia (purged of course of those Jewish influences which had perverted the 1917 revolution). Looked at today, the reader can only be amazed that a publication so obviously counter to the views Hitler canvassed and later stood for, should have been possible.

The claims of the *Völkischer Beobachter* or the *Newsletter* to propound some kind of rationale were totally missing from *Der Stürmer*. Its editor, Julius Streicher, so despised intellectuals that he would have disdained doing so. His physique was unprepossessing: a droopy paunchiness his tailor was unable to disguise in making his party uniforms; diminutive stature; head shaved bald; glinting eyes; he was the epitome of the street-corner thug ever promoting fresh causes for violence. The pages of *Der Stürmer* make plain that he judged his audience was drawn from the lowest and bitterest dregs of German society whose monosyllabic speech was varied only by their frequent insertion of the grosser expletives.

To these people he was able to offer reassurance by making it clear that there was one social rank still lower than their own: it was occupied by the Jews. It described

Right: A spread from the *Hamburger Illustrierte* claiming Danzig as a German city.

in the closest detail the alleged sexual assaults of Jews on Gentile girls – always blond and blue-eyed. Its cartoons featured thick-nosed, blubber-lipped Jews often in lavatory situations and it carried on its front page the rubric: *'Die Jüden sind unser Unglück'* (The Jews are our Misfortune). Yet it was not this which made the paper so disgusting. For its editor, the Jews were lower even than the animals. They were excreta. They were the *Scheissjuden* or the *Juden-Scheisser* – the shit-Jews and the Jewshit. Even allowing for the more common currency of the German word than its English equivalent, this terminology still repels. Even the most dedicated Nazis found *Der Stürmer* an embarrassment and many sought to have it, if not banned, at least tamed. One was Rosenberg who, in 1941, proposed that his Institute for the Investigation of the Jewish Question should take it over. Despite the fact that Streicher had fallen from grace the previous year, this was not done. One reason was because Hitler was said to be an avid reader.

Sharing this favor was the *Illustrierter Beobachter* which, according to Speer, he read from cover to cover. As its name indicates, it was an illustrated weekly aimed down market at the masses newspapers everywhere were beginning to court. While less virulent than Streicher's *Der Stürmer*, it did not try to emulate the *Völkischer Beo-*

This cover from a Cologne weekly celebrated Germany's swimming champions during the 1936 Olympics.

Die Woche, a wartime weekly, blamed the connivance of the British aristocracy and the Jews for bringing about the war.

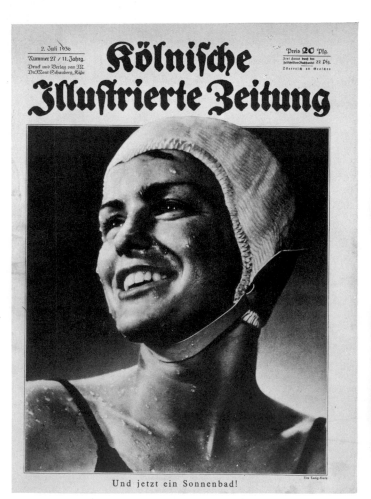

UNSER DANZIG!

Vier Wahrzeichen Danzigs: Sternwarte, Rathausturm, St. Marien und Krantor. Jeder Stein in dieser Stadt spricht von der deutschen Geschichte ihrer Bewohner, die 1920 durch das Diktat von Versailles von ihrem Vaterland losgerissen wurden. Von 20 Danzigern sind 19 Deutsche — glaubt wirklich irgendein auch nur halbwegs vernünftiger Mensch in der Welt, gegen diese elementare Tatsache handeln zu können?

Aufnahme: Volk und Reich (Hege)

Was würde Tommy gesagt haben, wenn man ihm Ähnliches angetan hätte wie 1920 dem deutschen Michel? "Das? Undenkbar!" So würde er geantwortet haben. Die in der ganzen Welt als maßvoll anerkannte Forderung des Führers aber war nicht etwa Wiederherstellung der alten Grenzen, sondern nur formelle Rückkehr des ohnehin deutschen Danzig zum Reich und Abtretung eines Verbindungsweges nach Ostpreußen. Dagegen sollte die in Versailles festgesetzte deutsch-polnische Grenze ausdrücklich von uns anerkannt werden. Fairer konnte kein Staatsmann der Welt handeln! (Zeichnungen von O. Garvens aus "Reparationsfibel")

Eine neutrale Statistik aus dem Jahre 1937 stellt fest, daß die Bevölkerung des Freistaats Danzig 93 % Deutsche, 3,6 % Polen und Kaschuben, 2,2 % Juden und 1,2 % sonstige umfaßt. Diese Tatsache wird auch Polen beachten müssen!

Parifer "Witzbolde" am Werk

Sie zeigen den Führer bei der Beschäftigung, Danzig einen deutschen Anstrich zu geben. Zu spät, meine Herren, denn Danzig ist, solange es besteht, eine deutsche Stadt gewesen. Auch gelegentliche Änderungen der formellen Zugehörigkeit zum Reich durch "demokratische" Zwangseingriffe haben daran nichts ändern können

bachter and argue. It simply stated, but it did so only after stimulating the maximum emotional response from its readers by photographs, if not by the written word. Its front page was always given the appearance of a poster. Typical ones contained a picture showing Russian children being taught about firearms by a uniformed Red Army man. It bore the caption: 'Russia arms – and Germany . . . ?' Another showed a pair of Storm Troopers, bandaged after being injured in a brawl, with the caption: 'They fight and bleed for Germany's freedom.'

Newspapers were by no means restricted to the mere recording of events, even though this was done with a pro-party slant. They were the actual instigators of them. German editors, like their counterparts elsewhere, could claim and went on claiming under the Nazis, that they had special access to public opinion. In the name of the people, therefore, they would call for some special action by the government, such as more stringent measures against the Jews, having been apprised beforehand that this action was already in hand. Hence, the government was made to appear as if responding to public demand. This technique reached its apogee in a leader in *Der Angriff*, in November 1938, after the murder in Paris of a German diplomat. The killer was identified as a young Jew, unheard of before the incident, which itself bore the hallmark of a Gestapo conspiracy. The murdered man was under their surveillance; his killer accepted arrest and his return to Germany with an equanimity which astounded the French. Murders carried out by the Germans themselves and then attributed to supposed enemies were a common device used as the excuse for launching attacks, as happened notably in Poland. The murder of a minor official in a foreign country by an unknown assassin can hardly have inspired the wrath which followed. Nonetheless, Goebbels wrote of mass indignation and predicted that it would turn on Jews in Germany. What followed was a series of riots in which hundreds of thousands of marks' worth of Jewish property was destroyed. It marked the beginning of organized anti-Semitism in Germany, and Goebbels later acknowledged his agency in it.

No doubt this was consistent with the view of a man who believed that effective political propaganda entailed 'making a noise.' It was through 'the making of noise' that the public was impressed, encouraged and intoxicated, while conversely opponents were intimidated. As one of the means of doing this, *Der Angriff* owed its inception to a ban placed on the National Socialists by the Berlin police in May 1927. Such had been the behavior of certain elements in the SA that even the right wing was impelled to condemn it as criminal.

But with the Berlin party interdicted, some means of maintaining contact became essential and there was, at the same time, a reluctance on the part of the Nazis to abandon the attack on 'the system' even for a short period. Goebbels' thoughts turned towards a newspaper. Funds, mostly small amounts, were subscribed, including 2000RM from Goebbels himself, and a printer, who belonged to the party, offered him credit.

Its launch was typical of its founder. The word *Angriff* means attack and full use was made of this. Over the days preceding publication of the first issue a series of posters began to adorn the walls of Berlin. 'The Attacks?' asked the first, while the second ran, 'The attack takes place on 4 July.' The last explained the mystery: 'The Attack' was to be a German Monday newspaper, standing for the only program which could save Germany. It would be the paper every German would want to read and subscribe to.

This last supposition was so wildly over-optimistic it can only have been the freest advertisers' license: its entire first print was only 2000 copies and most of these were sold to party members. One disappointment for its publishers had been the refusal of all but one wholesaler to handle distribution.

Beside *Der Stürmer* it looks like a paragon of moderation, but its tone is strident enough for all that. Its language was aggressively demotic, its content such that any other government but that of Weimar would have regarded it as sheer sedition. It constantly assailed the 'November traitors' of this government and particularly its police officials, especially one who happened also to be Jewish. Only when the ire of the reader had been thoroughly roused did it make its dark threats of a revenge to come.

Its technique was very much that of modern journalism. Its articles were short and always began with an arresting sentence. Its leading article Goebbels treated as a sort of 'written poster' or 'street-corner oration.' It made itself attractive as a whole by this very vigor. Even the title had a certain vivid quality. In the first issue its editor justified it. National Socialism, out to create the worker-state, was on the attack against international finance, which like Bolshevism was the tool of Jewry, the spawn of whose union was three million German unemployed.

The newspaper brought a new eminence to its cartoonist, Mjölnir, already known for his poster work. Through his black and white drawings the handsome, heroic Nazis struggled for power with the forces of evil, portrayed as well-known Weimar politicians, recognizable Jews or, where possible, both.

Vicious, destructive and seditious as the Nazi press was from its beginnings, it was still capable of affecting and infecting only a small section of the population as long as the German press as a whole was unfettered and the majority of the reading public preferred its offerings. With the seizure of power this situation changed dramatically, for now, suddenly, Josef Goebbels found himself with every publication in Germany, down to the most specialized technical journals, prospectively within his reach. He was not the man to let such an opportunity go by default. On the contrary, seeing the nation's press as another means of immersing the population in National Socialist ideology and practice, the party had been longing to get its hands on it. As early as January 1932, a year before they took office, Goebbels had talked over with Hitler plans for an all-embracing ministry under whose control it would fall.

The party's own publishing activity had been under the control of Max Amann, Hitler's former sergeant major, through its main publishing house, Franz Eher Nachfolger GmbH of Munich, responsible, *inter alia*, for the *Völkischer*

Right: Der Grosse König, publicized in this wartime weekly, was a heroic cinematic history of the life of Frederick the Great, the Prussian king who defended Berlin against allied armies in the 18th century. By the late 1930s the entire press was mobilized in support of the Führer's aims.

NEUE

IZ

ILLUSTRIERTE ZEITUNG

erlin, den 29. April 1941

17 XVII. Jahrgang Preis 20 Pf.

en 2 Lire, Jugoslawien 4 Dinar, Frankreich 4 Francs,
weiz 40 Rappen, Schweden 48 Öre, Niederlande
Cent, Bulgarien 5 Lewa

-20

NEUE ARTIKELREIHE:

DER GROSSE KÖNIG

FREI NACH DEM GLEICHNAMIGEN FILM

In der Titelrolle: Otto Gebü
Aufnahme: Tobis-Klagema

NEUE IZ

ILLUSTRIERTE ZEITUNG

Berlin, den 20. April 1939
Nr. 16 XV. Jahrgang Preis 20 Pf.
Schweiz 40 Rappen, Italien 2 Lire, Frankreich 2.50fr.
Jugoslawien 4.50 Dinar

Sie bewundern das Werk
des Führers

Junge Japanerinnen, die, wie viele
tausende Fremde alljährlich, das
Deutsche Frauenwerk und seine Einrichtungen besichtigt haben, tragen
sich in das Gästebuch der Reichs-
frauenführung ein   Aufnahme: Bitt

Aufnahme im Flugzeug des Führers von P. J. Hoffmann

Am 20. April begeht Adolf Hitler, der Schöpfer und Führer Großdeutschlands, seinen fünfzigsten Geburtstag

Links: Die Karte zeigt das Deutschland des Versailler Schandvertrages, wie es der Nationalsozialismus bei der Machtübernahme vorfand

Rechts: Das Deutschland von heute

Adolf Hitler führte das Saargebiet, die Ostmark, Sudetendeutschland und das Memelland wieder heim zum Reich und nahm das tschechische Volk und die Slowakei in die Obhut Deutschlands

Previous page, left: Japanese visitors at the Women's group in 1939 underline the importance of the Anti-Comintern Pact to which the two countries adhered. Four months later Germany signed a non-aggression pact with the Soviet Union.

Previous page, right: In a page from the same journal Hitler notes the incorporation of Bohemia and Moravia into the Reich and the establishment of the protectorate over Slovakia after Czechoslovakia collapsed in mid-March 1939.

74

Beobachter. Within weeks of the Nazi takeover of the state, a Reich Press Chamber was established under his presidency. Its ostensible aim was 'to put the membership of [the] professional groups [working in the press] in a position to create a press answering to the needs of the political leadership.'

Newspaper publishing was made subject to a government issued license and as one of the chamber's declared functions was that of controlling competition, Amann was able to use this as a pretext for denying licenses to the publishers of periodicals which had opposed the Nazis (and, incidentally, to any which he felt threatened the purely commercial interests of his own companies). In November 1933, with the assistance of the so-called 'First Decree,' Amann stopped nearly 1500 publishers in this way. The Chamber could lay down or vary at will the terms and conditions of licensing and so could readily silence an opposing voice. No claim for compensation was entertained.

Its ostensible aim the Chamber advanced by measures which brought every single worker in the industry within its jurisdiction. This was done by drawing all the various representative organizations – those of editors, journalists, printers, distributors and so on – into it.

One of these was the Association of German Newspaper Publishers. In theory, every member firm was entitled to use its facilities, without which their work was almost impossible. In practice, the publishers of those periodicals which were looked upon with disfavor were denied them and had their appeals airily dismissed.

Another body, the Association of the German Press, acted as a Labor Exchange for journalists and editors and kept a complete register of all workers in these spheres. Under the new regime, its aim, as expressed by the editor of *Völkischer Beobachter* was to breed National Socialist journalists. These were to be a race quite different from journalists of the past, disregarding professional ethics and, in particular, the pretence of objectivity. Instead they would be propagandists, combining journalism with party oratory and probably membership of the SA. Thus engaged they must have had little time for that other activity the party regarded as paramount: that of the breeding of Aryan German children.

The publishers of periodicals were bound together through the Reich Association of German Publishers of Periodicals. Organized with commendable thoroughness, it had no fewer than 30 sections and these were subsumed into six major groups covering specialist periodicals, illustrated and entertainment journals, political and related journals, those for the applied sciences, the young, the export trade, as well as, somewhat oddly, periodicals carrying insurance for their subscribers.

There was a special organization covering religious papers, divided as between Catholic and Protestant ones. The aim here was to see that the churches restricted themselves in their publications to what the party regarded as their legitimate functions and did not trespass into the discussion of even local social issues.

Every section operated its own bureaucracy, reading,

censoring, reproving or, if necessary, banning publications.

Yet another division was involved in supervizing every aspect of selling newspapers and periodicals down to the smallest street-corner newsstand or the local lending library. The right to sell, or merely to transport, newspapers was also subject to licenses and among those to whom these licenses were unavailable were, inevitably, the Jews.

Although the government's control of the presses gave them the potential capability to oversee and censor every piece of printed matter down to a wedding invitation or a visiting card, naturally, this power was most thoroughly exercised towards the major daily newspapers. They had their reporting staffs covering events, but, at the same time, the Propaganda Ministry released news of political events, national and international and, especially, the government's attitude to them. These were issued at two daily conferences held at the Ministry and they were often attended by representatives of whatever ministry had been involved in the event itself. Here, however, any resemblance between Government briefing of journalists in free countries and in Nazi Germany ended. These conferences were not an opportunity for reporters to question government ministers. They were simply occasions for them to be told how the news was to be treated.

There were, in fact, three well-defined and well-understood categories into which all information fell. The first was news for immediate publication, to be released in full;

The editors of *Der Angriff*, who 'exposed' this ersatz scandal.

Left: An anti-Semitic spread from a journal edited by Goebbels showing the lascivious activities of Isidor Weiss, formerly assistant to Berlin's Chief of Police.

Streifzug durch die deutschen Westbefestigungen

Bollwerk aus Beton und Eisen

Bildbericht von einem ersten Besuch der Hauptkampflinie — Hunderttausende schaffen am Wall der Grenzmark

Das Wort des Führers.

Der Führer verkündete in seiner Rede auf dem Schluß=
kongreß des Reichsparteitages Großdeutschland 1938 die
folgenden Maßnahmen:

„Ich befahl den sofortigen Ausbau unserer Festungs=
anlagen im Westen. Ich darf Ihnen die Versicherung geben,
daß seit dem 28. Mai dort das gigantischste Befestigungs=
werk aller Zeiten im Ausbau begriffen ist.

Ich möchte Ihnen nur wenige Zahlen nennen: An der
deutschen Westbefestigung, die seit zwei Jahren an sich
bereits im Bau begriffen war, arbeiten nunmehr: In der
Organisation Todt zusammengerechnet 278 000 Arbeiter,
darüber hinaus 84 000 Arbeiter, darüber hinaus 100 000
Mann Reichsarbeitsdienst und zahlreiche Pionier-Bataillone
und Infanterie-Divisionen. Ungesehen des Materials, was
durch andere Transportmittel angeliefert wird, schaffte
allein die Deutsche Reichsbahn täglich rund 8000 Eisen=
bahnwaggons. Der Gesamtverbrauch an Kies beträgt täg=
lich über 100 000 Tonnen. Die deutsche Westbefestigung
wird noch vor Einbruch des Winters vollkommen fertig
sein. Ihre Abwehrkraft ist schon jetzt im vollen Ausmaß
gesichert. Nach ihrer Vollendung umfaßt sie insgesamt über
17 000 Panzer= und Betonwerke. Hinter dieser Front aus
Stahl und Beton, die zum Teil in drei Linien und an
einzelnen Stellen in vier Linien eine Gesamttiefe bis zu
50 Kilometer erreicht, steht das deutsche Volk in Waffen.
Ich habe diese gewaltigste Anstrengung aller Zeiten gemacht,
um dem Frieden zu nützen."

Ueber Berg und Tal
ziehen sich diese höckerigen Hindernisse. Sie sperren jeder angreifenden Panzerwaffe den Weg.

Fast fertig
ist dieser Bunker, den gerade MG-Schützen nach einer ersten Uebung verlassen.

Glück auf!
Einfahrt in eines der unterirdischen Werke.

Erdbewegung
beim Bau eines Sperrgrabens und einer Talsperre zur Ueberflutung des Befestigungsgürtels.

Zielübung

Die Besatzung eines Bunkers richtet ihr MG ein.

Schützender Graben

Gewaltige Bagger ziehen im Gelände tiefe Furchen, die kein Panzerwagen überwinden kann.

Das Höckerhindernis

Zur sicheren Verankerung sind die ungleichmäßig hohen Höcker untereinander durch Betonsäulen verbunden.

Wachtstube

Alle Räume im Kampfwerk sind auf das zweckmäßigste eingerichtet.

Bunkereingang

Die fertigen Bunker sind durch Strauch- und Baumwuchs getarnt.

Wie in der Kaserne

Vorzüglich eingerichtete Waschgelegenheit für die Mannschaft eines größeren Verteidigungswerkes.

Beim Exerzieren

TAK wird vor dem gutgetarnten Bunker in Stellung gebracht.

Aufnahmen: Wolkenstörfer (8) und Schröter (3)

Previous page: A double-page spread from *Das Illustrierte Blatt* showing construction work along the West-Wall, or Siegfried Line opposite the French frontier.

the second was information originating from the Ministry but to be used without attribution; the third was *Vertrauliche Information* (Confidential Information) which was an order on the treatment of a particular story. This last category was highly classified. On no account were editors to give any indication that they had received such instructions. If they were given it in writing, it was to be destroyed immediately. Any failure to do so was met by heavy fines and imprisonment and many journalists were sent to concentration camps for allowing it to be known, even inadvertently, that they were less than free agents.

By 1937 the two daily conferences had been further extended with pre-conference meetings for a circle of select journalists. This was concerned solely with interpretation and comment and it was here that special instructions would be passed on. Editors would be told of the necessity of winning the people's support for this or that new government measure or to quietly drop some other issue which had been kept in the public eye previously. For example, in 1937, newspapers were told to give less attention to colonial questions as it was obvious that Germany would now acquire no colonies and it was pointless to keep up vain expectations.

The Ministry's control might seem all-embracing, but to the press itself it seemed suffocating. Yet there was a second source of surveillance: this was the party itself. The head of its press department was Otto Dietrich, a serious-minded ex-Army officer, who although also a journalist by profession was a very different one from the mercurially brilliant Paul Josef Goebbels. In February 1938 he was installed in the Ministry over Goebbels' head and much to his annoyance. He made repeated efforts to get him dismissed, but always failed since Dietrich's appointment had been made by Hitler personally.

From the point of view of the newspapers, this involvement of the party meant that news had to be considered and treated not merely from the point of view of political expediency – frustrating enough for the independent-minded journalist – but also with possible ideological considerations kept in mind as well.

With controls so far-reaching and with sanctions which reached down to the man who carried a wad of proscribed literature from printer to newsstand, making it possible to deny him his livelihood or consign him to a concentration camp, it is easy to understand why the Press Chamber's, the party's or the Ministry's merest wish could be converted into an urgent, panic-inspiring command in the ears of those to whom it was expressed. Goebbels intended this should be so. What must also be realized, however, is that through it the ordinary German citizen and later those of the occupied countries, too, lost a right taken for granted in free societies. This is the right, when all else fails, to take his grievance to the newspapers in the hope they may back his fight for justice through publicity. With the press muzzled, government or party at any level could act without having to consider this possibility.

Yet, not everything was as Dr Goebbels would have liked it. For one thing a subservient press was also an atrociously dull one: a fact of which he frequently complained, though without realizing the reason for it was that all creative initiative had been taken from journalists. He was also in a ticklish position when it came to newspapers with an international reputation of which a leading example was the *Frankfurter Zeitung*. Simply to have closed it down would have been to announce to the world the nature of National Socialist totalitarianism and he was very conscious of world opinion.

The editors of the *Zeitung* had not failed to realize his dilemma and, viewing it as a trump card, felt confident enough to sit down at the bridge-table with the Minister. They believed that by winning a few hands at one moment and not losing too heavily at another they might continue the game their own way indefinitely. What they failed to take account of was the power and deviousness of their opponent. Although piqued by the *Zeitung*'s impudent show of independence, Goebbels soon saw the advantages that might accrue from retaining one newspaper, at least, which gave an impression of editorial freedom. In fact, the paper had bargained this away quite early on so that while its comments might make it appear that press and government were unanimous, this was a pure fiction. The only small measure of freedom it had was a certain lack of interference in the day-to-day work of its writers. The remote control which operated over it was quite as insidious and far-reaching as the closer form. Nor was it permitted to go on playing any longer than its Nazi master chose. Although during the war the *Zeitung*'s high reputation and appearance of independence made it an ideal place for publishing 'black propaganda' stories, in 1943 Hitler, who had long hated it, demanded its closure.

Another source of concern was the foreign press and its reporters in Germany. There was some harassment of correspondents whose work did not please the regime and among those who were asked to leave the country was Dorothy Thompson, wife of the Nobel Prize Winner, Sinclair Lewis. The result of such actions as these was, naturally, to make a bad press still worse and Goebbels was deeply alarmed, particularly, about the effect this could have on American opinion. As a result he employed a US woman public relations expert on a $33,000 a year retainer to advise him. He began to make a habit of exerting his charm on foreign reporters and, in particular, provided splendid facilities. At the 1933 rally for instance, 200 foreign journalists were invited to attend all functions and a press headquarters with sufficient sound-proof telephone booths for one per reporter was set up. Even more spectacular arrangements were made during the 1936 Olympic games in Berlin and resulted in a special telegram thanking Goebbels and his department for their efforts and praising the magnificent organizational efforts.

The success of all these efforts was, of course, only partial and the many hostile stories reaching the world's press continued to cause him chagrin. Some attempt to redress this was made by establishing propaganda attachés in all the German embassies and something over £20 million a year was spent on propaganda abroad. Glossy,

Right: Foreign Minister Joachim von Ribbentrop initials the adherence of Bulgaria to the Tripartite Pact which linked Germany, Italy and Japan.

NEUE
JZ
ILLUSTRIERTE ZEITUNG
Berlin, den 18. März 1941
Nr. 11 XVII. Jahrgang Preis 20 Pf.
Italien 2 Lire, Jugoslawien 4 Dinar, Frankreich 4 Francs,
Schweiz 40 Rappen, Niederl. 20 Cent, Bulgarien 5 Lewa

-20-

Eine Unterschrift von weltpolitischer Bedeutung

Reichsaußenminister von Ribbentrop unterzeichnet Bulgariens
Beitritt zum Dreimächte-Pakt, der zum Hinauswurf Groß-
britanniens vom Balkan führte. Die Befriedungspolitik des
Führers hat abermals einen unblutigen Sieg errungen

NEUE IZ

ILLUSTRIERTE ZEITUNG

Berlin, den 23. Juli 1940
Nr. 30 XVI. Jahrgang Preis 20 Pf.

Schweiz 40 Rapp., Italien 2 Lire, Jugoslawien 4.50 Dinar

Französischer Kolonialsoldat beim Fr
Anders kann man diesen Vorgang nicht bezei
Mit den Zähnen reißt er Stücke des
Fleisches vom blutigen Knochen, ein Bild,
uns die Erinnerung an die Besatzungsze
Rheinlandes wachruft

beautifully produced publications on the New Germany – on the rallies, or its art, or the youth movements of the party – began circulating all over Europe. They presented an image of something new, vigorous and exciting, but most of all clean and orderly, in contrast to the squalor and disorder which, in the western public mind, was thought of as marking the Soviet revolution. All sorts of people, from Oxford undergraduates to successful businessmen, were invited on visits to Germany, all expenses paid by their hosts. At the same time, all Germans visiting other countries were expected to be emissaries of National Socialism, patiently explaining that Germany could have taken no other road, and that it wanted nothing but peace and friendly relations with other countries to carry through its revolution. Later, this role was taken over by the young soldiers of the German occupation armies, friendly, open-faced, intense and deeply shocked – at least in the first years of the war – that there were still those who believed in and hoped for the defeat of Hitler and his system.

Control of the press was, of course, one of the fruits of power. Another benefit of power was the increased opportunity for the Nazis to extend their own publishing efforts, if they wished to do so. In fact, they did not until May 1940 when the first issue of *Das Reich* appeared. It had for its model the British Sunday newspaper, *The Observer*, whose most typical characteristic was its open-minded liberalism. *Das Reich* slavishly copied it in layout and manner. The word 'Reich' means 'Empire' and this very much represented the new publication's objective: it was the voice and spiritual mentor of the new German Empire. Every effort was made to give it a style of its own and a quality not hitherto noticeable among party-sponsored publications. This went to the extreme of appointing staff on literary and journalistic rather than on ideological credentials or on years of service to the party. It had its own correspondents in all the major cities and its contributors included such names as Theodor Heuss, later to be president of the Federal Republic, while another, Friedrich Luft, is still regarded as doyen of German theatrical critics.

As much subject to censorship as any other publication and as suspect as to its news content, it was none the less technically a deservedly successful paper, rapidly acquiring a circulation of 1½ million (Goebbels claimed it could have been more but for newsprint rationing). It was widely read outside Germany and even by the nation's enemies.

The editorial was written by Goebbels himself and over the course of the war years reflected with special poignancy the changing fortunes in German arms. From the celebration of success – always done with a measure of sober dignity – it became gradually more and more a medium for explaining failure, or of exhortation to steadfastness.

The only other publication of note to come out of the years of power was the wartime picture magazine *Signal*. Broadly copied from the British magazine *Picture Post* and the American *Life* it was printed in some twenty

languages for distribution particularly among the peoples of the occupied countries, extolling the joys of life in the Third Reich and giving evidence of its military might. Its long articles, purporting to prove how Britain must lose the war in one way or another, were scarcely taken seriously by the readers, but its photographic coverage of the war was hard not to admire, and the complete series of *Signals* represents, in the words of S L Mayer, 'the finest collection of photographs of the Second World War in Europe.' It is the greatest of ironies that these were produced by the hamstrung journalists and photographers of a dictatorship. Often in color, their efforts have a directness and vigor rarely seen elsewhere.

The term 'media' as a portmanteau word into which all the news disseminating organizations could be placed had not come into currency in the 'Thirties, perhaps because since television was yet to arrive it was easier to talk of 'the press and radio.' Goebbels certainly looked forward to television's advent, seeing it, above all, as the super-medium of indoctrination.

His other and more immediate concern was, however, radio and perhaps this was to be expected in view of the Nazi preoccupations with the spoken word. For Goebbels control of broadcasting went beyond mere points of principle (in any case, radio broadcasting was quite different from public-speaking to large audiences). He believed and stated that radio would be to the 20th Century what newspapers had been to the 19th: revolutionizing national life by bringing people and state together. Oddly enough, at an earlier period in his life he had been against radio, declaring in 1925 that it would lead to the 'bourgeoisification' of the nation and make the German forget work and Fatherland, views diametrically opposed, in fact, to those he now held.

Before the seizure of power, there had of course, been no way in which the party could broadcast its message, though Goebbels reported in September 1932 that he had a functioning radio organization. This was given its first real task after January 1933. In the elections held in March, 48 percent of voters had declared themselves against the new government. Goebbels saw the radio stations as the means of remedying this, although his party had kept their rivals off the air throughout the run-up campaign and used it wholly for themselves. Addressing station managers after the election he told them that it was for them 'to make public opinion.' If they did their job successfully the recalcitrant 48 percent of voters would be won over. 'Once we have them,' he continued, 'radio must hold . . . defend them, must indoctrinate them so thoroughly that no one can break away any more.'

To bring this about, he aimed to make radio programs more entertaining and amusing, and to drop much of the heavy, serious matter which formed an important part of the stations' current output. Broadcasting had to keep up with the times, be modern, help to 'lighten the daily round.'

Among his first actions on taking office was to create a Radio Department within his ministry and then to unite the radio services, hitherto organized on a basis of the German *Lände*, through the *Reichs Rundfunk Gesellschaft*, a concept borrowed from Fascist Italy's corporate radio system. At the same time, as with the press, a Radio Chamber was brought into being with everyone working

Left: This cover shows French colonial soldiers from North Africa eating raw meat after their capture during the campaign in June 1940.

in the industry united within it. This included not only performers, producers and engineers employed in individual stations of the RRG, but also the manufacturers and retailers of receivers – plus, potentially, the audiences throughout the Reich.

Goebbels also saw radio as a means of exporting the National Socialist message. The external broadcasting services which he established continued to grow through the years of the regime until they reached a total of 27 languages. These included Gaelic, Hungarian, Swedish, Turkish, Belorussian, Italian and, of course, English. It was in the English service, during the war, that the British traitor, William Joyce, nicknamed by the British *Daily Express* 'Lord Haw-Haw' on account of his plummy voice, broadcast. Short-wave transmitters carried German transmissions to the United States, the Far East, the Arab world, Latin America, Africa and the British Colonies and Dominions.

On taking over the German radio services, Goebbels found himself confronted by an immediate technical obstacle to his intention to reach every home in the country. Radio was still comparatively in its infancy and only the better-off owned receivers. As a matter of personal inclination, he would have liked to have instituted a system like that of the Soviet Union where wired services provided uniform programs across the country without listeners having the means of listening to the voices of other nations. The Soviets had had the advantage of being in at the birth of radio where the Nazis were not, so that while efforts were made to organize community-listening through the party, a long term solution had to lie elsewhere. This was through the production of a cheap receiver, the *Volksempfänger* (People's Receiver), costing 75RM or US $24 in the money of the time.

It was already beginning to appear within less than a year of the Nazi takeover. By the outbreak of the war, there were twelve and a half million radio listeners in Germany, practically a four-fold increase on the figure for May 1932. Just before the war, Germany began production of the world's cheapest receiver, the *Deutscher Kleinempfänger* (German Small Receiver), costing under US $12. All its propagandistic objectives apart, the government could feel able to reach the entire population at any moment. And, as an indicator of the importance he attached to radio, Goebbels had his own office equipped with a switch which enabled him to cut into broadcasts all over Germany and address the nation, if need arose.

He also placed the greatest emphasis on the careful analysis of listeners' tastes and instituted a system of surveys carried out through a nationwide body of part-time radio-wardens who were supposed to gather criticism and report back on it. They were also to encourage people to listen to any program the Ministry regarded as being of special significance and, generally, to popularize radio listening. All this information was collated first through the regions and then nationally and it was in the light of it that program policies were changed or modified. It was, for instance, as a result of these studies that from about 1943 the whole tenor of broadcasting was changed. It became more flippant with the emphasis on comedy and escapist programs, because it was seen that listeners wanted their minds diverted from the disasters at the front.

Over the years of the regime, radio policies underwent ceaseless change. One manifestation of this was the gradual dissolution of the Radio Chamber itself. The entire

Below: Model of the new radio broadcasting center in Berlin, which was never built.
Right: 'All Germany hears their Führer with the people's receiver.'

Ganz Deutschland hört den Führer mit dem Volksempfänger

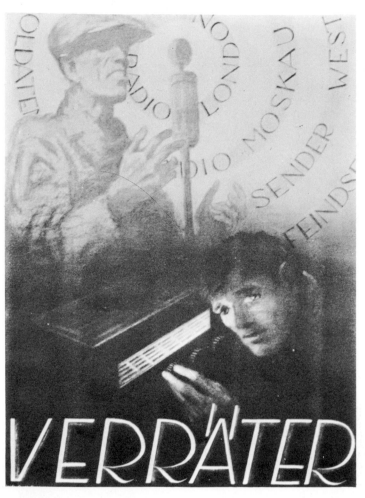

VERRÄTER

concept had been so all-embracing that it soon proved unworkable and various groups were removed from its control. The first was that of the manufacturers and retailers, who, in March 1934, came under the Ministry of Economics, not without protest from Goebbels. Then the Ministry of Justice objected to the Chamber's power to draft legislation affecting the industry and this right was taken from it.

This left only program production under its wing and since this was controlled through the RRG, itself controlled by the government, the Chamber had lost its *raison d'être* and, after lingering for a time, was abolished in October 1939.

With both newspapers and radio under its direction, the ministry had the means for comprehensive news management and this became total after the outbreak of war when listening to enemy broadcasts was made a serious offence. Even in the regime's early days, however, it rapidly and efficiently acquired the means of exhibiting its own activities in the most favorable light and of presenting only those aspects of foreign reaction – negative or positive – as suited its case, with little to fear from contending voices. This became most important in times of crisis or, as was constantly the case in so restless a

Left: 'Traitor' says this poster depicting those who listened to foreign broadcasts.
Below: Hitler addresses a rally and several radio stations in a broadcast sent by short-wave around the world.
Right: Special number of the *Berliner Illustrierte* celebrating the Olympics held in Germany during the summer of 1936.

Berliner Illustrirte Zeitung

BERICHT
in Wort und Bild

Die 16 olympischen Tage"

Germany won the Olympics in 1936 and publicized their triumph with a series of stamps.

society, when new moves were being planned. Then media and government worked completely hand in hand.

An example of this occurred in 1936. At French insistence, the Versailles Treaty had created a buffer-zone along her borders with Germany in the Rhineland. It had always been Hitler's intention to re-occupy this, but it was a question of timing. The moment came when, in 1936, France signed a treaty with Soviet Russia. During the days of negotiations leading up to the announcement of its signature, a carefully orchestrated campaign of denunciation was carried out. With this went veiled hints that if it was signed, Germany would be forced to re-assess her own position since she would feel herself threatened by potential enemies on both her western and eastern frontiers. German newspaper correspondents and radio speakers gave detailed, apparently independent analyses of how the whole balance of power in Europe would be drastically altered if the pact were completed. Finally, its accomplishment was reported in tones of pained surprise

as when one, who has been treated as a friend, assaults one's wife.

In March 1936, certain it had justified itself before the nation and the world, the Nazis did what they had always meant to do and marched their troops into the Rhineland, explaining that this restoration of the buffer zone of Reich sovereignty was in 'the interest of the elementary right of a people to secure its frontiers and preserve its chances of defense.'

Yet another example of this 'orchestration of the press' is in the coverage of the Olympic Games in 1936. Berlin had originally been offered as the venue by the Weimar government, but when he took over Hitler had set his heart on seeing they took place. For a time this was in doubt as Germany's anti-Jewish policies were regarded as running counter to Olympic ideals. In consequence, anti-Semitic activity was at once played down. As foreign guests began to arrive Streicher's *Der Stürmer* was taken

Right: The German team makes its entry into the Olympic stadium in Berlin, 1936. The occasion afforded excellent opportunities for propaganda.

Previous page: Hitler in the company of Field Marshal von Mackensen (left) and Reichs Minister Frick and SS-Führer Julius Schaub (right) enjoy the opening ceremonies of the Berlin Olympics.

off the newsstands and all references to Jews ceased. There was even one half-Jew in the German hockey team. Sports editors were instructed that for the time being race was irrelevant. At a special conference editors were told to exploit to the utmost the opportunities for propaganda the occasion afforded and were given extra paper to enlarge their issues.

Special arrangements were made not merely to welcome foreign correspondents with lavish hospitality, but also to provide them with facilities on a scale previously unknown. Attention was given to radio reporting and arrangements were made for direct transmissions from Berlin to 32 countries – an astonishing achievement for the time.

On top of the actual Games' events, there were others organized by the party, the government and army, including cavalry displays and demonstrations by machine gun and tank units, at which Hitler and Goering took the salute.

A gigantic open-air party thrown by Goebbels on an island in the Havel included among guests ambassadors, generals, admirals, as well as writers and artists. Entertainment was provided by a ballet company, while pretty young actresses mixed freely, sometimes too freely, with the guests. There were several bands for dancing, brilliant illuminations among the trees, lavish supplies of food and gallons of champagne. It was little wonder that the ultimate result was a success for the three-year-old Nazi government which continued to echo for months.

The world was to grow accustomed to the process of news management of this sort. In those days it was new, and for those who could penetrate below its often glossy surface, it was a portent of something shocking. There were, alas, too few who could see beneath the glossy surface in 1936.

Above: The torch bearer races to the podium to light the Olympic flame during the Opening Day ceremonies.
Below: 'Deutschland Uber Alles' is played in honor of the German winner of the shot put. Another German placed third, while the winner of the silver medal was from Finland. He is the one on the right, not saluting.
Right: A diver beneath the massed flags of the nations participating.

The shadow of Erwin Piscator, a pacifist who staged political theater in Berlin until he left in 1933. He spent the war in Moscow and returned to Germany after the collapse of the Third Reich.

THE ARTIST ENSLAVED

In January 1932 Goebbels was writing excitedly of plans for the Ministry to which he, as *Reichspropagandaleiter* for the party, would succeed when they had won power. It was to be an 'immense project,' 'the kind of which the world has never seen before.' Its function was to educate the people and it would bring within its scope art and culture. 'I have already started drawing up the basic plan for such a Ministry,' he added. Thus the intention was conceived by which the entire creative endeavor of a highly creative people was to be made subservient to the causes of party and ideology. And this at a time when it was experiencing a resurgence in the arts.

In the theater there were figures like Bertholt Brecht and Max Reinhardt; players like Emil Jannings, Marlene Dietrich, Elisabeth Bergner: film-directors like Fritz Lang; composers like Richard Strauss, Arnold Schönberg, Paul Hindemith and Kurt Weill; painters like Ernst Nolde, Georg Grosz; architects like Bruno Paul and Mies van der Rohe. In the *Bauhaus* was one of the most original and exciting groups of applied artists to appear in Europe since William Morris in late 19th Century Britain. It numbered the painters Paul Klee and Wassily Kandinsky among its members, but also included brilliant architects, interior and furniture designers. Its director was the architect Walter Gropius. All were to achieve immortality – though for many, in exile. *Bauhaus* designed wallpapers, fabrics, furniture are still being made and sold to the discerning because of their refreshing combination of modernism and intrinsic beauty. Yet, in their own country,

in only a few short years, it was to be as if it had never existed.

And here lies the ultimate measure of the damage National Socialism inflicted on Germany. It left it an artistic backwater.

This was actually far from Goebbels' intention. He was, in artistic matters, if no other, something of a liberal, putting the creator in a special category, beyond ordinary conventions. Even latterly, he constantly defended artists, in some cases including those of Jewish origin, if he felt their work merited it.

Pressure upon him came from elsewhere, however, from Rosenberg and Hitler, and, in the interests of his own survival could not be ignored. We can now perhaps understand that for all Goebbels' efforts the fate that overwhelmed Germany's artistic life was inevitable. It is a fact of political life, as Helmuth Lehmann-Haupt points out, that while an affluent democracy may tolerate art and artists, seeing both as no more than a superadded luxury to be taken or left, dictators have entirely different attitudes. Recognizing that art is fundamental to the fabric of human societies they pay it the left-handed compliment of taking it very seriously indeed. This is demonstrated by the way they seek to bring it within the

Right: Hitler on the tribune of the Luitpold Arena in Nuremburg at a party rally.
Below: Goebbels and Hitler visit an auto show in 1937 in which a number of technical breakthroughs were exhibited. These auto shows promised a car in every German's garage.

accepted that all these artistic movements were yet another part of the Jewish plot to subvert the world. The glories of Nordic man were to be commemorated, therefore, in a sterile, stylized, imitative neo-classicism.

But with power in their hands the Nazis soon found that it was not only the glories of man they wished to commemorate. They also wanted to see that the National Socialist state and all it stood for was given permanent delineation. Hitler, in one of those great cultural speeches at the Nuremberg Rallies, always preceded by a movement from a Bruckner symphony to set the tone, made these ideas clear. If the object was to make a people proud, then they must be given something to be proud of. 'History,' he declared, finds no nation really worthwhile except when it builds its own monuments.'

There was, therefore, a double reason for seeing the the arts were brought into total subjection.

The means for achieving this was in the main two-fold. First of all, there was control of artists through a network of Reich Chambers, each dedicated to a specific activity. Collectively, they absorbed the entire artistic life of the nation, since it was laid down that 'anyone who takes part in the production, the reproduction, the artistic or tech-

Left: Himmler (center) and Hess (right) inspect the macabre bas-relief at the entrance to Dachau in 1936.
Below: Alexander Moissi, a famous German actor in 1930, who was subsequently purged and died shortly thereafter in 1935.

postulates of their ideologies. Where it fails to fit, it must be suppressed. This was precisely the case with the Nazis.

During the period of struggle, their theories of art had first to be squared with their racial conception, extending as they did from the notion of a German herrenvolk at one extreme to the 'subhuman' Jews, Slavs and Negroes at the other. Ingenious racialist theoreticians like Hans Günther, the author of *Rassenkunde* (Race Knowledge), had shown themselves able to adduce interesting proofs that the Hellenic image of beauty was in essence Nordic and hence Aryan. In opposition to this was the 'degenerate' spirit introduced by lesser races, sullying the stream of classicism. For the Nazis, however, the teaser lay, not so much in defining what was degenerate, especially in contemporary art, but in making sure the results tallied with the strong and highly-subjective opinions on art which Hitler – a failed artist – was known to hold. Needless to say, as was invariably the case in National Socialist Germany, a way out of this dialectical impasse was found. As was also the invariable case, it consisted in first discovering what Hitler liked and disliked and then proving by irrefutable argument that the one represented all that was good in human culture and the other all that was evil.

Hitler, on whom Günther had exerted a strong influence, was known to detest such modern manifestations as Dadaism, Cubism, Expressionism and Futurism, whose executants were 'fools or cheats.' Within a very short time from the Nazi accession to power loyal Germans

96

Claire Waldoff was one of Germany's greatest character actresses and comediennes well into the war period.

Trude Hesterberg in 1937. She was a well-known dancer and actress during the Third Reich.

nical elaboration, the publication, the presentation, the wholesale or retail selling of cultural goods must be a member of the chamber relevant to his activities.' So if you were an author or a publisher, you were a member of the Chamber of Literature. If you were an actor or a producer or a scene-shifter or just the girl in the box-office, you belonged to the Theater Chamber; if you were a composer, a musician, a repairer of violins to the Music Chamber; if you were a painter or sculptor or the owner of an artists' supplies shop you were a member of the Fine Arts Chamber. Nor was this enough, you had also to be quite certain you dealt only with accredited Chamber members. As an artists' supplier you sold your goods only to those who were entitled to purchase by virtue of their membership. Jews, naturally, were not eligible so that a Jewish artist was effectively cut off from acquiring the very materials of his profession, unless, as was mercifully often the case, a shopkeeper was prepared to take the risk of supplying him clandestinely.

The second principal means of subjection was through the 'guidance' of artists exercised by the Ministry itself, which had its own departments corresponding to the Reich Chambers. Department VI was for the theater, Department VIII for literature, Department X for music and so on.

Some idea of the thoroughness with which the chambers and the ministry supervised the arts can be seen by a brief glance at the situation of the fine arts, which came under Department IX. Not only did this comprehend painting, sculpture and allied activities, it also maintained a watching brief on arts and crafts and the shops which retailed their products. Even Heydrich's Security Service was brought in on this and once produced a report criticizing the quality of glassware, furniture, picture-framing and postcards. In 1937 a committee of the Fine Arts Chamber was established to see that standards even of individual potters and weavers were maintained – which meant that they, too, were brought under state control. Nor was this all for there were also sections covering the activities of the interior decorator and landscape gardener, while ideology was introduced into such small details of life as typography and handwriting.

But, as if control through Ministry and Chamber were not enough, there was besides the surveillance exercised by other bodies. The Labor Front had its *Schönheit der Arbeit* (Beauty of Work) Division with the aim of creating an esthetically desirable working environment. Robert Ley's *Kraft durch Freude* (Strength through Joy) Movement promoted a range of activities from artistic appreciation classes for workers to orchestral concerts and variety shows. Alfred Rosenberg's office whose snappy title described it as 'concerned with the Custodianship of the

Typical example of 1930s cum Third Reich architecture at the
Potsdamer Platz in Berlin, taken in 1937.

Entire Intellectual and Spiritual Training of the Party
and All Co-ordinated Associations' had an obvious interest
in the arts and even produced its own magazine *Kunst in
Dritte Reich* (Art in the Third Reich). If it lacked the power
physically to harass artists, it could make life harder for
them through criticism that their work lacked the desirable National Socialist spirit. Even a composer of the
stature of Paul Hindemith was not exempt and had his
work *Mathis the Painter* declared 'unacceptable from the
standpoint of cultural policy' in 1934.

In addition there was the party itself maintaining a
watching brief and, at times, acting as patron of the arts.
One of the young Albert Speer's first commissions was to
redesign the decor of the Munich Brown House, party
headquarters in the city which cradled Nazism. On other
occasions artists and sculptors were commissioned to
provide suitably grandiose works to decorate entrance
halls – though needless to say, only in the approved styles.

As a result of this, an artist, if he happened to be a Nazi-
supporter and prepared to produce what was needed,
might feel that the state offered him rare opportunities
and it is a fact that some did well from it. On the other hand,
he might feel that never before had he had to tolerate such
interference in his work.

Having once organized the creators, National Socialism embarked on its tasks of discrediting 'degenerate art'
and seeking to establish one properly exemplifying the
ideological spirit of the hour. The first, it must be said,
was more easily and more completely accomplished than
the second.

This success was due largely to the fierce, destructive
energy invested in the assault. Hitler pulled no more
punches in cultural than in political matters. The language in which he condemned the 'mutually . . . sustaining
cliques of chatterers, dilettantes and art forgers,' ranged
from the jeering mockery of the entrenched philistine to
overt intimidation, sometimes coupled together. Thus:
'These fellows claim that they see nature that way. We
should examine their eyesight. If they are really afflicted
with defective vision, we can only feel sorry for these poor
creatures. We must make sure that they do not pass their
defect on to their children . . .' Or, in 1937, where he warns
'those pre-historic stone-age culture bearers and art
stutterers' that they will be picked up 'and liquidated.'

To make sure that no German was corrupted by being
forced to gaze on such works, no art show could be held
without official permission which was granted only after
the nature of the exhibits had been described and the
racial and political credentials of the exhibitors established. Similar permission was necessary before an art
school could open its doors.

At the same time, under party auspices, exhibitions of
degenerate art were held, the exhibits being so presented

Above: Foyer of the German Opera House in the Charlottenburg section of Berlin, as reconstructed under the Führer's orders in archetypal Third Reich style.
Right: Hitler at the Bavarian State Library inspects some rare books. He liked to be portrayed as a patron of the arts and antiquity.

as to show them in the most unflattering light. Among those so honored were such world-renowned figures as Jacob Epstein and Georg Grosz.

Most of the works involved came, of course, from the modern departments of German art galleries and museums so that, by ridiculing the artists, scorn was also being poured on the taste of those who had originally acquired their work at public expense. It followed from this that there had to be a campaign to purge the art galleries as well. In many cases, the entire modern sections were forced to close and if their curators refused to co-operate they were dismissed. This, naturally, left the government in possession of a large number of works of art, including paintings by Chagall (who was Jewish), Braque, Derain, van Gogh, Modigliani, Matisse, Archipenko, Gauguin and Munch. The manner of their disposal was typical of the system. The paintings were sent to Switzerland and sold there, netting some £10,000 for the Exchequer. In many cases, too, with stunning hypocrisy, they were even offered for private sale to Germans themselves. Goering built up the foundations of the art collection of which he was so proud from cheap purchases of this kind. The director of the Lübeck museum was offered back almost all the works

'Soldier in Poland' by Franz Eichhorst, was displayed prominently in the House of German Art's exhibition in 1940.

from his gallery. He bought what he could afford and persuaded friends to purchase the remainder. When at last no further purchasers came forward, the remaining works were handed over to the Berlin Fire Brigade, who burnt them.

If this act of vandalism cannot leave one unmoved, greater compassion still is aroused by the wretched plight of the proscribed artists. Some, the more fortunate, escaped to Britain, France and the United States. Others were hounded into the concentration camps. A few survived, usually by a quirk of bureaucracy or the mediation of a high-placed acquaintance. Nonetheless, they were usually cut off from friends and other artists, living a life of constant fear. Occasionally, they would find those brave enough to risk acquiring their work and occasionally a shopkeeper who would supply them with paints and brushes.

Writers and dramatists suffered a similar fate. As early as May 1933, less than three months after the National Socialist seizure of power, the books of some two dozen 'undesirable and pernicious writers' were consigned to a great pyre in Berlin's Franz-Josef Platz. This destructive orgy was led by Alfred Bäumler, Professor of Political Pedagogy in the University of Berlin, who encouraged students to break into private libraries to seize works. Writers so treated included Freud, Marx, Heinrich Mann (brother of Thomas), and Stephan Zweig. One author, Erich Kastner, writer of the much-loved children's classic, *Emil and the Detectives*, actually witnessed the destruction of his own books. At the height of these revolting proceedings. Goebbels addressed the nation by radio, commending the student-vandals on their 'strong, great and symbolic act.' In future, he told his listeners, writers would subserve the state, which alone could define what was 'wholesome' and 'unwholesome' in literature. 'Now, like sword and plow, the pen will serve the nation,' he declared.

To this Ernst Krieck, rector of Frankfurt University, added his own amen: 'In future, we recognize no intelligence, no culture and no education which does not serve the self-fulfilment of the German people and derive from that its significance.'

This plain declaration of the regime's nature was not lost on the world. In 1936, Carl von Ossietzky, a pacifist writer, who was immured in a concentration camp, was awarded the Nobel Prize for Literature and to appease international opinion, a furious Goebbels was compelled to arrange his release. He got his revenge by declaring that from now on Germans were forbidden to accept Nobel Prizes, and the government inaugurated its own National Prizes.

Yet, for all his support of the book-burners, Goebbels remained deeply concerned about the barrenness of literary life in the Third Reich and tried desperately to find means to persuade those writers who had fled the country to return to it, with promises of government support. Among these was the most illustrious of his generation, Thomas Mann, who had left the moment the Nazis came to power. In his wooing of Mann, the propaganda minister was by no means actuated solely by his desperate anxiety to show the world that some, at least, of the old vitality of German artistic life had survived, he also had a deep personal admiration for the author of *Buddenbrooks* and *The Magic Mountain*. As we know, Thomas Mann opted for exile until after the war.

Not even music was spared from the government's purges. The Music Chamber at first had as its president the eminent figure of Richard Strauss, who shortly afterwards retired on the pretext of old age.

As with painting and sculpture, the party ideologues quickly discerned a 'degeneracy' in music. Into this category fell Jewish composers from Mendelssohn to Mahler, but the weight of the proscription fell hardest on those who were both Jewish and originators, like Arnold Schönberg. His 'twelve-tone' system was denounced, his music banned and other German composers were prohibited from emulation. A Nazi reference work listed and described Jews and Jewishness in music. Equally detested was jazz, as having derived from the sub-human Negroes, though in fact it became very difficult to efface its influence from German music, particularly popular music and Goebbels was forced to accept it and 'explain' why it was being tolerated.

In the case of drama, the application of a ban on works whose theme was politically undesirable or which were written by Jews deprived the German theater of its greatest springs of creativity. It was compelled to fall back on classical works or those by foreign authors which could be presented so as to convey a National Socialist message. Thus, Marlowe's *Jew of Malta* or Shakespeare's *Merchant of Venice* were used to underscore the policy of anti-Semitism. Strangely, one contemporary British writer who remained acceptable to the Nazis was George Bernard Shaw, perhaps because they believed there was a similarity between his ideas and theirs. Indeed, his 85th birthday in 1941 was marked by a celebratory production of *Candida* in Berlin.

The control of artistic output was made even more complete by a ban on criticism introduced by a decree of 29 November 1936. The reasons for it are not clear. It could perhaps have been that a critic, by suggesting that a particular work contained elements of propaganda, would put audiences off seeing it. There must also have been a connection, however, with Hitler's pathological hatred of critics whom he regarded as having vilified every great man, himself included. Certainly in his explanations of the reasons for the ban, Goebbels emphasized the incompetence of many critics and, obviously to curry favor with the artistic community, pointed out how unfair this was to their endeavors. If there were performers who welcomed the measure they must soon have realized their mistake. Criticism, even when harsh or unjust, is a necessary part of the creative process, for the critic is always in some measure the mouthpiece of the public. If he is silenced, then it too is reduced to passive muteness. One of the essential interactions between artist and spectator – the reasons for the former's existence – has ceased.

After the introduction of the ban all that was permitted was a factual description of an artistic event. How total the ban was is shown by an incident which involved the *Frankfurter Zeitung*. Chafing under it, the paper sent its music critic to cover the première of Alban Berg's *Lulu* in Zurich. His review appeared under the headline, 'A Great Day for Zurich.' At the Propaganda Ministry press conference the following day editor and critic were unmercifully castigated for their 'quite unheard of behavior.'

The wife of Prof Troost, Hitler's artistic and architectural expert, at the Munich Art Museum.

Controls and prohibitions were, of course, part of the negative side and National Socialism was supposed to have its positive side as well. Indeed, Goebbels was aching with anxiety to demonstrate this to the world. Precisely how it was to be done remained nebulous, however, beyond a few hints that the ideology of art was to be grounded in a largely apocryphal German folk-culture.

Prof Gall, Hitler and his chief architect, Albert Speer, inspect the construction site of the House of German Art in Munich.

Composers were urged to turn their attention to folk-song, probably in emulation of the Russian and Spanish 'nationalist' schools of musical composition. Perhaps the sole worthwhile work to emerge from these directives was Carl Orff's *Carmina Burana*, a cantata based on secular Latin poems of the Middle Ages, many of them highly erotic in character. While there can be little doubt that this work was within the bounds of what was regarded as desirable National Socialist music, listening to it today it seems refreshingly free from the influence of the regime under which it was born.

In the fine arts, equally, much was made of what were regarded as the truly Germanic art-forms such as wood-carving. With their caricature-like proportions, these seem completely at variance with that other pillar on which the new art was supposed to stand – 'Nordic' Hellenism.

In drama, the sole original National Socialist contribution was the 'Thing-Theater,' derived by some circuitous route from an early form of German folk drama. It was something akin to a pageant, allied to speaking choruses and stylized movement. Typical of most Nazi projects it was intended for mass audiences and some 25 auditoria, including one capable of holding 20,000 people, were specially built for 'Thing-plays.' Hopes that this new art form, which Goebbels called 'National Socialism turned to stone,' would become popular proved vain, however, and in the end even the most ideologically committed ceased to patronize the 'Thing-Theater.'

This drama form was one of the ways in which propaganda was introduced into the lives of children. In addition there was, of course, the doctoring of school-books so that from the earliest age, with their reading primers, children were being taught love of the Führer – because like God, he first loved them. The process reached right down to the teaching of handwriting. Germanness was inculcated into this by encouraging the use of the Gothic script in preference to Copperplate or Italic hands, notwithstanding the fact it was painfully slow to write and difficult to read. In print, too, the Gothic 'Fraktur' type was used by loyally National Socialist publishers and urged upon others. *Der Stürmer* and *Der Angriff* both purveyed their respective venoms in a type based on that in which the Gutenberg bible had been printed. Books in Roman type, in san-serif faces or in those designed by the detested Bauhaus were gradually reprinted.

Ironically enough, in one of those *volte-faces* at which totalitarian systems are so skilled, the whole machinery for teaching and printing Gothic script was suddenly put into reverse in 1941. It was then discovered that the Gothic script had actually been polluted from Jewish sources, that is to say, Hebraic writing. From now on everything was to be in Roman and a fresh reprinting of books was embarked upon. The truth was that Gothic type was so unreadable, especially among those for whom German was not a first language, that Goebbels was afraid it might discourage foreigners from struggling to read his finer outpourings!

Although the power of the state over art might be said to be complete, what was being produced under the new system can scarcely have been to the taste of the party leadership, especially that of Goebbels and Goering, who

could claim to some discrimination in artistic matters. The sterility of neo-classicism led only to the portrayal of the human figure, naked but sexless, in rigid motions of sport or combat. Artists whose reputations had been established before 1933 and who tried to co-operate with the new government and its absurd requirements, found the sources of their inspiration drying up under the effort. A typical instance was that of Arno Breker, a sculptor who had demonstrated his fine and subtle sensitivity in the freer Weimar days, and had established an international reputation. Treated by Hitler and the Nazis virtually as a court sculptor, his work rapidly deteriorated into a barren, aggressive harshness.

For painters, there was of course the soft option of a well-trodden path: unexceptionable landscapes or representations of peasant life at home or in the fields. A second possibility was 'combat art.' The image of a sweaty, battle-begrimed soldier leaning on his Mauser in the doorway of a smashed, burning house, is hardly one that most people would care to have staring down from over the mantelpiece, but in a society so uncompromisingly militarist it was the accepted alternative to mallards in flight or rubicund monks sipping port round the refectory table. As a genre it reached its zenith in the early stages of the war when both government and Wehrmacht were anxious to immortalize their triumphs. So seriously was it taken that a full range of tanks, guns, anti-tank weapons, horses and their accouterments were kept at Potsdam Army School so that they could be set up to provide artists with the facilities for the accurate reproduction of 'battle' scenes.

Apart from these limited and formalistic styles, so startlingly similar to Soviet 'social realism,' the only direction in which Nazi art could turn was towards technical

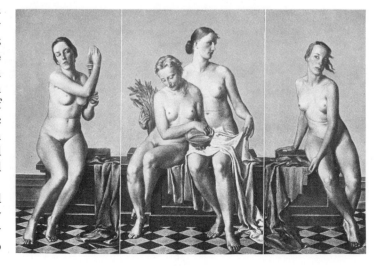

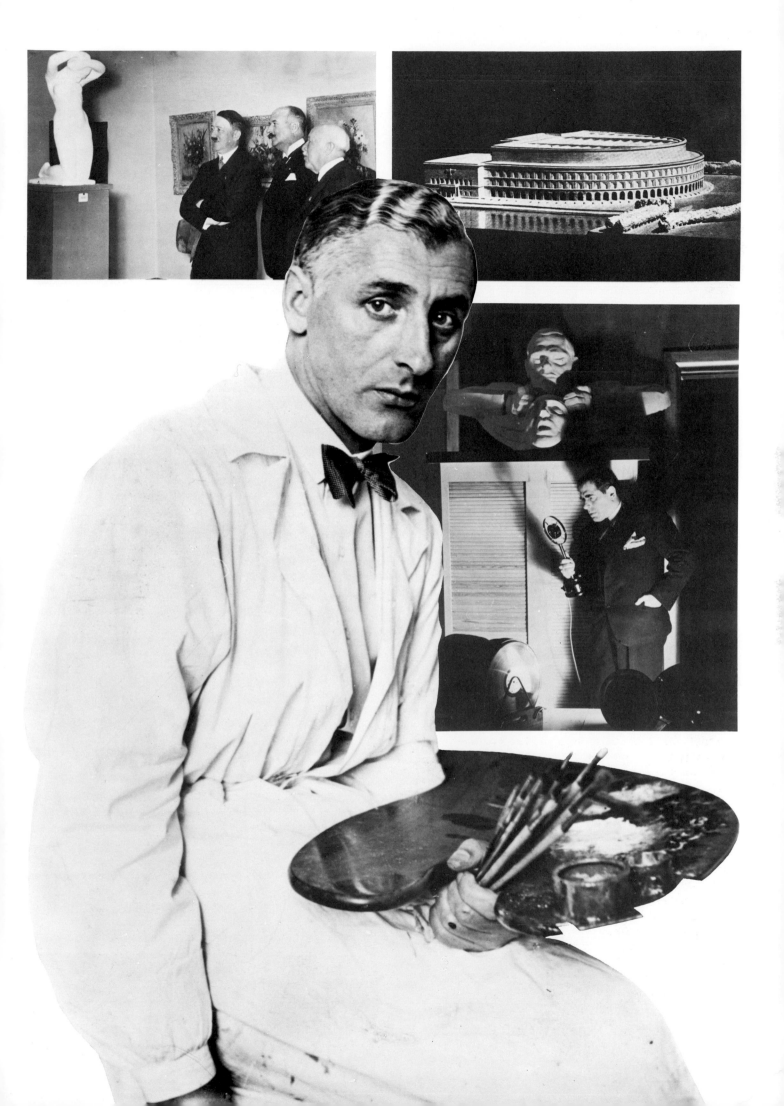

Above left: George Grosz (1893-1959) in his atelier in 1930. This great American artist and his work were banned by Goebbels after the Nazis took power. He was forced to flee from Nazi Germany in 1932 and went to the United States. He returned to Berlin in 1959 where he died.
Above: The 'Eternal Watch' at the Königsplatz in Munich, under the archetypal, fluted columns.
Left: An example of 'acceptable' art, which could only be of interest to fervent Nazis.

accomplishment, as if a kind of pre-Raphaelite perfection of minutiae could compensate for lack of inspiration elsewhere. To this end technical institutions were opened and with them, research establishments studying such questions as color permanence.

*   *   *

Though the concepts of the regime permeated all artistic activity there was none in which it was felt more strongly than in architecture. This followed naturally from Hitler's stated belief that to be judged 'worthwhile' by history, epochs had to erect their own monuments.

There was, however, a second reason. This was that political convictions apart, Hitler had a personal pre-occupation with architecture stemming back to his pre-party days. Having failed to get into the Viennese Academy of Arts, he next tried to enter the Academy of Architecture. Throughout his life he was never so animated as when talking about buildings and, in particular, his own plans for new ones. In this sphere he regarded himself as a pre-eminent expert.

Conscious of this, his minions knew that there was no more pleasing flattery of their master than to speak of him as 'Master-Builder of the Reich.' Gifts sent to him would often be dedicated in these terms. In a painting at an official art exhibition in 1939 he was portrayed as an architect, the new Reich rising behind him.

National Socialism, claiming to be a way of life more than a political creed, had of course developed its ideas about the forms of German architecture before it ever became a system of government. One article of this was an implacable opposition to all the ideas that the *Bauhaus* had stood for – fitness for purpose, the exploration of new styles, techniques and materials. Thus, when Otto March, who had been put in charge of the design of the stadia for the 1936 Olympics, produced a plan for a concrete structure with glass partition walls, Hitler vetoed it. The glass partitions with their *Bauhaus* overtones were ordered to be eliminated and instead a steel skeleton was clad in natural stone.

What was repellent to the Nazis was not just that some of the leading members of the *Bauhaus* were Jews. It was also that it preached a doctrine of environmental humanity, of buildings scaled and formed to human needs – influences still at work in the best modern architecture. In contrast, National Socialism called for the recording of its achievements in buildings which were overpoweringly grandiose. For them the sole purpose of an edifice was to gather together the greatest possible number of men and women so that they could listen to the party message fresh from the mouths of its prophets. Hence priority was given to sports arenas (also capable of being used for political rallies), gigantic assembly halls, cinemas and theaters. Hitler scoffed at the fact that one city with a population of 150,000 people had recently completed a theater capable of holding only 1200.

Mere buildings, however, were not enough. They had to be put in their proper setting so that even as he approched them from a distance, the individual felt the power of the state. Accordingly, site plans would frequently include broad processional avenues to be decorated with sculpture and trees.

In the styling of these structures, the Nazis always harked back to their beloved 'Nordic' Hellenism, oblivious to the fact that classical design had always been related to human proportions. A man might be dwarfed by the Acropolis, he was not overpowered by it.

The problem of the human relation to domestic architecture became even more important, of course, in the case of domestic architecture. For this the only acceptable source of inspiration was the Germany of the Middle Ages with its steeply pitched, high-gabled roofs. This was the very antithesis of the flat roofs then becoming popular and made possible now that new materials could render all surfaces impervious to the elements so that there was no need to pitch a roof to be sure rain and snow drained from it.

A meeting of a secret society, The White Rose, in a jubilant mood. Such societies were tolerated during the early days of the Reich.

To the Nazis, however, the flat roof was a reminder of the Middle East and hence the Jews. From that time on – and the practice continued throughout the Nazi period – even newly-built blocks of flats were given high-pitched roofs. The result was an incongruous and unpleasing combination of mock-Medieval townscape with modern needs, but it was also a reminder that the government was master here as everywhere else.

It was symptomatic of the same nostalgia for a past in which Germany seemed somehow more German, that the Nazis were led to think in terms of small cities: 150,000 was regarded as the maximum. To reduce some of the larger cities to this number considerable movement of population would have been necessary: notwithstanding the inconvenience and even hardship this would have caused, the Nazis were quite prepared to embark upon it, and in a few instances actually did.

Hitler admired certain architects – Troost and Thorak in particular and some years before his coming to power a young architect joined his entourage and was to remain there until neither Hitler nor entourage any longer existed. He was Albert Speer, himself a pupil of Troost, who while still a student had attended local party meetings and fallen under Hitler's spell.

His first professional activity on the party's behalf was less in the form of architectural than of theatrical design. After criticizing sketches for the planned settings for a mass rally on Berlin's Tempelhof Airfield he was challenged to do better. The result so pleased his party superiors that he was offered permanent employment as *metteur-en-scène* for the party's great gatherings.

The centenary of the Berlin Museum. Prof Waetzoldt, its director, makes his speech under the Altar of Pergamon.

Not long after the seizure of power, however, he was given openings for work of a less ephemeral nature when he was invited to plan and oversee the modernization of the Chancellor's official residence in Berlin, occupied by Hitler at the time. This brought the two into direct and often daily contact and the Führer obviously took a fancy to the twenty-eight year old architect. From now on his was to be the creative mind which was to realize or at least endeavor to realize his master's great plans. Speer was to sicken and revolt against what he had done to the extent that he alone of the defendants pleaded guilty before the Nuremberg Tribunal. Among the reasons he gave was his growing conviction that he had prostituted talent and training in producing work worthy only of a Cecil B de Mille film-set, and which when achieved in solid form came to appear to him as 'the very expression of tyranny.'

For all his later disillusionment, the advent of Nazi power found him involved like many of his fellow-architects in trying to give the Thousand-Year Reich three-dimensional form. For this, the Nazis had in mind what Lehmann-Haupt calls a 'total architecture.' Germany remade was to be the temple of Nazism's tutelary gods and, most especially, of its Messiah, while the air of dynamism which the sight of building construction everywhere gave to the new order was not overlooked either as a propaganda device. The entire country was to become a great mesh linked by the autobahns, the Roman roads of the Wehrmacht legions (and in due time those down which their enemies poured to overwhelm them) and its junctions were the towns and cities.

It was characteristic that titles were ascribed to these: Berlin was 'The Capital of the Reich,' for instance; Hamburg 'The City of Foreign Trade.' In this way the very

The Altar of Zeus at the Pergamon Museum in Berlin. Classical art and culture were revered by the Third Reich.

the monuments of previous great epochs, which had so impressed Hitler, survived largely as romantic and often beautiful ruins. But over the course of the succeeding millenia how would modern building materials like concrete and iron fare? They would become pitted, cracked, discolored and rust-marked, certainly no fit memorial to Hitlerism. So that even ruins should possess a proper dignity, all building work was ordered to be carried out in the most durable materials – stone and granite – irrespective of cost.

So totally pervaded were National Socialist ideas with religious symbolism that in the building of the rally site at Nuremberg, Speer admits that he was influenced by the great Altar at Pergamum, built in honor of the Greek god Zeus and his Nuremberg edifice with its great flights of steps and its colonnades inevitably remind one of a place of worship. Only the proportions differed from the classical models. Hitler's altar had a length of thirteen hundred feet – almost twice the length of the Bath of Caracalla, one of the great buildings of the ancient world.

Set against such a backdrop, the human figure was nothing but a pigmy. A Gothic cathedral might remind man of his insignificance. It was, all the same, an insignificance measured against the magnitude of a great and ultimately merciful God. Here, he was reminded only of his relation to the tyranny which ruled him.

Yet all this was no more than a beginning. In 1938 Hitler decided the time had come when his Chancellery must match his status. Speer was offered the commission, accepted although, typically, he was given no more than a year to do it, and was given as the site the entire length

place-names were made to carry their message and become a further means of surrounding the people by the environment of National Socialism.

Not everyone took these intentions seriously and they were openly made the subject of jokes. However, when the cabaret comic, Werner Fink, tried to involve his audience in the fun he was promptly sent to a concentration camp.

In fact, work began early, not only with the building of the road network but also with the building in many of the towns themselves. Munich ('Capital of the Party') got its Brown House as party headquarters. At Nuremberg ('City of the Rallies') work started on the construction of a constellation of arenas and stadia. Even here the overblown notions of Nazism influenced building. Speer realized that

H O Hoyer's 'In the Beginning was the Word,' a painting widely reproduced for domestic consumption during the era of the Third Reich.

Left: A meeting place of the underground society, Ever True, after its destruction by Nazi youths.

of one of Berlin's main streets, the Voss Strasse. The long, squat building which sprang into being there 48 hours in advance of the scheduled deadline brought Nazi neoclassicism to the nation's heart. There were the usual flights of steps and Doric columns – here square in section. Above the main portals, carved out of the gray stone blocks, an eagle grasped the laurel-wreathed swastika in its claws. At the foot of the columns, as hardly more than architectural decoration, SS men of the *Leibstandarte Adolf Hitler* stood guard, their black uniforms, helmets and boots set off by white belts. Within, visitors passed down a gallery 400 feet long or twice the length of the Hall of Mirrors at Versailles to reach the holy of holies, the Führer's office. And lest the propaganda value of this was overlooked, Hitler made it explicit: passing the building's endless facade, entering and then walking down that gallery, the visitor would be reminded of the might of the Third Reich.

Still greater plans were yet to come. In the greatest of the tasks entrusted to him, Speer was to refashion the whole of Central Berlin, its existing buildings to be replaced by the grimly unsmiling edifices of which the new Chancellery was a fair sample. The city's whole orientation was to be based on a central east-west axis which was to take the form of a vast, wide avenue, based on the Champs Elysées. An entirely new, even more massive and grandiloquent Chancellery would stand at one end, while down the several miles of the boulevard would be government offices, shops, plazas, two luxurious cinemas – one for the premières and the other – larger – for more everyday purposes. There were to be no fewer than three theaters, a new opera house, a new concert hall, a twenty-story hotel, variety theaters, restaurants and even an indoor swimming pool which was to be as large as the baths in Imperial Rome. Midway down there would be an 'Arch of Triumph' and this was to be nearly twice the size of Napoleon's in Paris.

At the very end of the avenue would be its greatest glory, a building with cupolas of such proportions that superlatives run out in describing it. The dome alone would be the biggest in the world. It would be surrounded by water, the Spree being diverted to this purpose, and there would be a lake on one side. On its other side there would be a great plaza, to be called the Adolf Hitler Platz, where the May Day rallies normally held at the Tempelhof Field would take place.

Militarism, always near to Hitler's and the Nazis' heart, was far from being forgotten in this grand design. There would be a wide arena, paved with great stones, not only for military displays, but also for exhibiting the trophies of war – great guns and tanks.

For Hitler's personal benefit a big scale model was made of it all to show how the refashioned city would appear. He so delighted in it that he would rush guests off to see it,

Far left: The Königsplatz in Munich after its reconstruction by the Nazis.
Left: The exterior of the House of German Art in Munich. This massive monument was used to exhibit the German art treasures which had been approved of by Nazi officialdom.

Hitler, Goering and other Nazi leaders attend a concert given by the Berlin Philharmonic under the baton of Wilhelm Fürtwängler.

sometimes squatting on his haunches to get his eye down to the level at which he could see how a pedestrian of the future standing in its midst would feel. He would not allow even the exigencies of war to interfere with the realization of these plans and refused to accept that enemy raids could destroy it if it was built before final victory had been won. Preparatory work such as arranging for the purchases of land, negotiating contracts for materials, many of which had to be obtained from abroad, began. When, in July 1941, Speer suggested that all work on projects not essential to the prosecution of the war should stop, it was decided to delay a few weeks before putting this radical proposal to Hitler and, in fact, it was never submitted.

When the early victories of the Wehrmacht in the USSR gave Germany access to the resources of granite available there so that it was no longer necessary to buy from Scandinavia, Hitler was jubilant.

Not a single stone was ever actually laid, though quite late in the war there was talk of beginning work on site clearance. The Germans were never called upon to undertake it. The Allied bombers did it for them.

In later life, looking at the photographs of his model, Speer was to realize what it would have looked like had it been built. It would have been, he said, an architectural bore. But 'bore' is too innocuous a word. Prisons, too, are boring buildings. Yet this is not the quality that most impresses the prisoner. For him, the looming masses of stone and iron are the restatement of his condition. So it would have been with the Nazis building plans.

The irony, whereby the enemy's undiscriminating high explosive brought those plans to nothing, has not escaped even German writers. Perhaps Lehmann-Haupt best sums it up: 'I find it impossible to free myself of the notion that Adolf Hitler and the men round him really did tempt the Almighty who took frightful vengeance and destroyed what they had built.'

Lilian Harvey and Willy Fritsch, two of the greatest stars of German cinema, make a broadcast. They starred together and individually in a number of films before the English actress returned to her native country at the outbreak of war.

FLICKERING IMAGES

After the takeover of power in January 1933, the National Socialist regime was determined above all to make the German people feel its presence quickly and nowhere did this determination seem better exemplified than in the cinema. On 2 February, three days after the takeover, a film called *Morgenrot* (Dawn) received its première in Berlin. It was a film about the U-Boat service in World War I, but in contrast with the pacifism of so many other war films, it discussed themes which lay close to the heart of National Socialism – comradeship, heroism, the sacrifice of the individual for the common good.

The opening was made something of a state occasion and the following day the Nazi papers were full of praise for it and for its director, Gustav Ucicky, who was to become a rising star in the Nazi film firmament.

But it was the sheer speed of the achievement which astonishes. How was it possible, given that the production of a film from scenario to final print can take anything from two months to a year? The key lies in the name of Alfred Hugenberg, former Krupp's managing director, Reichstag deputy for the Nationalists (to which the Nazis were for a time allied), press baron and owner of UFA, the country's biggest film production company. He had used his influence over UFA to insure that at least part of its output was of films intended to combat the pacifistic and 'degenerate' trends so deplored by nationalism. *Morgenrot* was one such attempt, and though it was chance that it was ready when it was, it was a chance the Nazis did not fail to utilize to the full.

For the assistance he rendered their cause since as early as 1931, Hugenberg was made head of the new government's Economic Department. The appointment was not a success and lasted a bare five months; nonetheless his UFA company together with a second one, Tobis, continued to be principal producers of films during the National Socialist period.

If, by his support for it, Hugenberg hoped to buy a degree of independence from government interference for the German film industry, he was disappointed, though oddly enough only a small proportion of the films produced was overtly propagandistic. Of the 1363 made during the twelve years of the Nazi regime, the Allies found it necessary to ban only 208 on account of ideological content.

There were two reasons for this. The first is that ideology of National Socialism, unlike that of say Communism or Christianity or, some would insist, of capitalism, cannot readily be woven into the fabric of life. It was not possible to take a basic story and by a little shifting of emphasis and interpretation make it convey a message. It needed specially created vehicles. The second, as a corollary to the first, arose from the shrewdness of the Propaganda Minister himself. He wanted to fill the cinemas so that when he had an important idea to express the audience was there and knew they would soon tire of an unvaried diet of propaganda.

Of course this did not mean that production companies did what they pleased. Nor that the industry throve creatively in the years from 1933. With some notable exceptions fully described by David Stewart Hull in his comprehensive *Film in the Third Reich*, the fare provided was largely pap and it required a real effort to remind oneself that this was the product of a cinema which with *The*

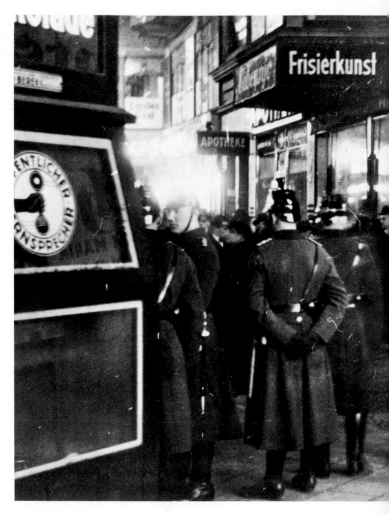

Cabinet of Dr Caligari, The Testament of Dr Mabuse, The Blue Angel or *Metropolis* had done so much to pioneer the film as an art form. In the films of the Hitler years one can praise actors' performances, photography – often superb, editing or special effects which could be stunning as in *The Adventures of Baron Münchhausen*. But there the praise usually has to end.

Certainly there was never any question of the government's overlooking the cinema. On the contrary, its fate was sealed long before the Nazi takeover, for as Hitler was preoccupied with architecture, Goebbels was preoccupied with film. He was longing to get his hands on the industry. This was not just because he saw in it an ideal medium of persuasion, though with its combination of sound married to moving naturalistic image, he knew it certainly was. He chafed when he saw it presenting 'negative' ideas before 1933 as in Erich Maria Remarque's *All Quiet on the Western Front*. To disrupt its première Goebbels and a group of his rowdies released white mice and snakes among the audience.

But his basic reason was that he was film struck in the way that others are stage struck. He liked the milieu, he was at his happiest with film people and many of his notorious love affairs, (he nearly had to break with Hitler over one), were with film stars.

These two factors guaranteed that the film industry was not to be spared Ministry attentions. In any case, even if he had left it alone there were others in the party who would have moved in on it. Among them was Rosenberg, who had already raised the question of Jewish influence

Left: The opening of Erich Maria Remarque's *All Quiet on the Western Front,* an anti-militarist masterpiece of the German Cinema, occasioned mob violence on the part of Nazis opposed to its pacifist theme. These 'Schupos' or *Schützpolizei* protected filmgoers.
Above: Henny Porten, great German actress of the 20s and 30s.
Below: A demonstration against the film of the Remarque novel on opening night, 8 December 1930. The film was banned after the Third Reich was established.

Hitler before and during a speech made on Reichs Party Day, 1935.

within it, claiming that because of it the *Volk* was being infected with lascivious images. Even much later he was to whisper into the Führer's ear the suggestion that the cinema was not doing enough to present political issues.

From Goebbels' point of view the ideal solution would have been to bring the industry directly under his own control by means of nationalization. This proved impossible because of the often complicated contractual arrangements companies had with foreign producers and distributors. The nearest the state came to ownership was in 1937 when Hugenberg agreed to sell out his large shareholding in UFA to Goebbels.

As an immediate, practical step the industry was, like all the other artistic media brought under the wing of the relevant Reich Chamber. The Film Chamber's ten departments were responsible for every aspect from matters of policy down to the employment of usherettes in individual cinemas. It also maintained a film archive and was responsible for the publicization of the German film as such. Through it even the distribution of raw materials was controlled, while as with other chambers, it was used to exclude Jews from employment.

Its organization went down to *Gau* level and it operated in collaboration with the Reich Film Credit Bank which made money available on favorable terms to reliable film directors so that they could work without feeling themselves under financial stress. The chairman of this was actually the President of the Film Chamber.

Corresponding with the Film Chamber was the relevant department of the ministry, Department V. Its terms of reference were 'to direct German film production in all its artistic, economic and technical aspects.' In practice this meant that it became involved before the first frame was shot, since all scripts had to be submitted for approval of its censor. Before sanctioning production, investigations were made as to the suitability, racially and politically, of the scenarist, the director, the stars and all involved in the production. Once approved, shooting could go ahead, but here producers might find themselves facing the personal interference of the minister himself. Such was his enthusiasm for the medium that he made himself an expert in all stages of production and filled with clear, dogmatic ideas on the theory of film, he would demand cuts, additions and sometimes changes in the cast or even the director. Often this had nothing to do with propaganda; it was plain meddling excused on the ground that he was concerned for the film's box-office success, since, after all, public money, often in considerable sums, was involved.

Even when shooting was finished, and despite all that had gone before, the film's troubles were not over. It was subject to a second process of censorship as a finished product and could still be banned, though there was machinery for appeal, if the decision went against the producers. It was felt, however, that appeals were little more than a formality and in the rare cases where the ruling of the censor was overthrown, the Ministry still had the last word since it could use or withhold its influence in promoting the film. In most cases, producers shrugged their shoulders if their finished work was banned, remembering perhaps that it had been made with government money! Often the reasons for the ban were extremely capricious and personal. In a film version of Kleist's *Broken Jug*, Emil Jannings portrayed a lame village magistrate. Rightly or wrongly, Goebbels, who was neurotically touchy on the subject of his foot, took it to be a caricature of himself and banned it. (Hitler was said to have revoked the decision and mischievously ordered it to be shown in the biggest cinema in Berlin, but according to Speer, his orders were ignored.)

As the first measures to control the film industry began to take effect and it was realized that government was to play both midwife and policeman, a deep and fundamental crisis in morale developed. No one took kindly to the picture of himself as a tool in the state's indoctrination plans.

There was, accordingly, some initial resistance to the various *diktats* forced on the industry to compel its acquiescence in its new role, but given the government's ruthlessness and the limited means at the resisters' disposal it was bound to be insignificant. In the end filmmakers had to make the best they could of the conditions or go out of business. In many cases, individual directors and performers, some of them Germany's best, chose to leave the country. One, Conrad Veidt, asked to fill in a form detailing *inter alia* his racial credentials, wrote Jew across it in large letters, though he was an Aryan, and went to Britain where he became a popular and much-loved star.

This drain of talent was obviously a matter of concern to Goebbels who went to considerable lengths to try to stop it. Shortly after coming to power, for example, he summoned one of the nation's finest directors, Fritz Lang, to his office. There he praised his work, apologizing for the fact it had been found necessary to ban *The Testament of Dr Mabuse* (it dealt with a schizophrenic with aspirations to world domination), and offered him a key position in the revamped industry. Lang protested that he had Jewish blood in his veins. Goebbels waved this aside, recalling Lang's distinguished war service. The director asked for time to consider and made use of the opportunity to arrange to leave the country to which he never returned during the Nazi regime.

Goebbels also made numerous attempts to induce Marlene Dietrich to return to Germany from America, since *The Blue Angel* was one of the films he most admired. It took him some time to accept that she was not to be persuaded.

These were exceptions, however. The majority worked out a *modus vivendi* with the new government and swallowing their bile, settled down to doing what they were told. Goebbels made it perfectly clear that he regarded them as state servants and during the war went so far as to compare them with soldiers whose only duty was to obey. Indeed, at that time, disobedience was punished by a speedy call up for the forces.

Its functions of supervision and surveillance apart, the Propaganda Ministry also saw itself, as with the other arts, playing a sponsoring and encouraging role in the cinema which meant assisting not what was best in the film, but what was most likely to help the regime. To begin with it tried its hand at film production. The results of this were films like *Blutende Deutschland*, *SA-Mann Brand* and *Hitlerjunge Quex*. The first was something approximating to a documentary. It showed the struggles of the NSDAP under the Weimar Government, and was heavily loaded with the main themes of Nazism – the crime of Versailles, the responsibility of British and French in bringing about World War I, and its consequences in the economic depression. The Jews and Communists were blamed for the continuation of this state of affairs and the SA were shown as heroes struggling against the malignant forces. It ended with jubilant scenes after Hitler became Chancellor.

SA-Mann Brand was also the story of Hitler's rise to power, but told in feature film form and as seen from the point of view of the Brand family. The father is a Communist: the son a member of the SA; the mother tries to pursue a path of conciliation between them. After various crises and family quarrels, the father, too, is won over to the Nazi cause. Among the aims of the film is that of discrediting trade unionism which is shown as corrupt and profiteering, while also wholly subservient to the Communists, who are represented as lawless thugs against whom the Nazis must struggle to reinstate basic human decencies. Looked at critically it is a shoddy production out of a small studio and one is forced to conclude that its sponsors became disenchanted with it while it was still

Elisabeth Bergner, one of Germany's greatest actresses, with Willy Forst in the film *The Dreaming Mouth* in 1931; she went on the forbidden list after 1933 because of her Jewish connections.

Max Schmeling, sometime world heavyweight boxing champion, in a film scene from *Love in the Ring*, a coarse cinematic melodrama.

on the studio floor. But even at the casting stage nobody seemed to think it merited a star and the players were all little known performers.

Hitlerjunge Quex, produced under the patronage of Baldur von Schirach, the leader of the Hitler Youth, was an altogether more ambitious production, extravagantly financed. The central character, Quex or Heini, was played by an anonymous member of the movement and his parents by two leading players, Heinrich George and Bertha Drews. Like Brand, the young Quex's loyalties are divided between movement and home (in his case both parents were Communists). The story is based on an actual case, that of Herbert Norkus, and like the proto-Quex, the fictional one is murdered in a drunken brawl by alleged Communists – the actual occasion had given Goebbels an opportunity for a stirring graveside oration. Thematically, the film was meant to show the contrast between the disciplined Hitler Youth and the disorderly frightfulness of its opponents. Although Holba and Blobner in *Jackboot Cinema* speak of it as having been regarded as 'the film' among the young, there is little evidence that in fact it was regarded as anything but a classic bore.

A fourth film in the same genre was *Hans Westmar*. This was actually an expurgated version of the story of Horst Wessel, the Nazi protomartyr. Horst Wessel, the twenty-one year old law student and son of a parson, had been one of the most active SA leaders in the Berlin Party, but his main claim to fame in his lifetime was his poem *Die Fahne Hoch* (Hold High the Banner!). The banner in question was, of course, that which bore the swastika and the place in which it was to be held high was the street. Its most significant lines were those which extolled the fallen Storm Troopers as 'comrades, shot dead by Red Front and reaction' and declared that they would go marching with the living, inspiring them in the battle.

It was first published in a special issue of Goebbels' *Der Angriff*, but shortly after its appearance Wessel seemed to lose all interest in the movement. The reason was that he had formed a liaison with a prostitute, Erna Jancke, whose procurer, a Communist called Höhler, happened to finish a jail sentence while their affair was still at its height.

In a fit of jealousy Höhler went round to challenge Wessel and a fight broke out in which Höhler drew a gun and shot the young SA man, who was rushed to hospital. There he lingered long enough for Goebbels to visit him and write touchingly of the dying Wessel in a way that overlooked his withdrawal from the movement. Then, obligingly, he died, so providing the movement with a name and a song whose aggressive, street-march rhythm still has the power to evoke National Socialism.

Above: Author and medical doctor Alfred Döblin during the film production of his novel *Berlin-Alexanderplatz*.
Left: Germany's most famous actor between the wars, Emil Jannings, who starred in the pre-Hitlerian *Blue Angel* as well as in *Bismarck* and other Goebbels-approved post-1933 epics.

It was, of course, understandable, that Wessel's story could not be made into a film as it stood, hence the expurgation. The dubious sexual relationship was omitted and with it the doorstep squabble leading to his death. In the film-version, the blue-eyed, square-chinned Hans Westmar, played by Emil Lohkamp, is portrayed as a young university student aware of and concerned about the gap which appears to exist between intellectuals and workers. He discovers in the NSDAP a means of bridging this gap. In all this, he was the cinematic realization of the Michael of Goebbels ill-fated novel, who had been exercised by this very problem and in the end resolved it by joining workers, to die, romantically, in a mine disaster. As a member of the SA, Hans Westmar 'holds high the banner' on his party's behalf, finally to succumb to the bullets of Communist hooligans. He dies muttering 'Germany' and is, like Horst Wessel, commemorated in a song which is the setting to music of his own poem.

As propaganda it is unrelenting. The Weimar republic is shown as depravity personified with corruption at every level. Under its lax rule even patriotism is perverted: Westmar goes into a bar only to hear a Negro jazz band playing its own irreverent arrangement of *Die Wacht am Rhein*. Communists in the film are never anything but low-browed Neanderthal brutes. Unlike the other three propaganda films it did, however, possess certain merits. Claire Trask, writing in *The New York Times* after its première, praised it as having a kind of eyewitness reality.

All the same, when taken as a whole these essays in film-making were singularly unsuccessful. Every attempt was made to lure the public to them with publicity and lavish first-nights. (At the opening of *Hans Westmar*, SA men lined the streets to the cinema.) In the main, they encountered only indifference and, to the annoyance of their sponsors, audiences showed plainly by their patronage that they preferred American offerings like *I Was a Fugitive from a Chain-Gang* which was playing at other theaters when *Hans Westmar* was on.

In any event, from this time the Ministry concentrated on problems other than film production, though in 1935 some 140 shorts, dealing with party and governmental topics, were made and shown through mobile cinemas which toured the country.

There was, nevertheless, one exception to the general policy of leaving well alone in matters of production. It manifested itself in the slim, trim vivacious figure of Leni Riefenstahl. There was in the German cinema a genre as peculiarly national as the Western is to America. This is the so-called 'mountain film' in which men challenge some capricious peak to rescue foolhardy tourists, to reach the survivors of a wrecked aircraft or simply to prove their machismo. Previously an actress, Leni Riefenstahl had produced one of the more distinguished of the brood, *Das Blaue Licht* (The Blue Light). It was on the basis of this that Hitler, over everyone else's head, appointed her to make films of the party rallies. Speer, who was one of the first to meet her after her appointment, speaks of the difficulties she had in dealing with the officials of a party by tradition antifeminist. Using every sort of wile she outmaneuvered them, and critics were silenced anyway once the first of her rally films was shown.

As a result of these it was decided to make a full-length film of the 1934 rally. In ordering that this should be done, Hitler, whose idea it was, had more than purely propaganda objectives in mind. That year the party had struggled through the Röhm affair. Ernst Röhm, commander of the SA, had shown himself dissatisfied with certain trends in the party. Hitler, who in his turn was fearful of the power possessed by the SA as an army within the party, had taken the initiative to purge it. In a lightning sweep, hundreds of SA men were arrested, tried by party kangaroo courts and in a large number of cases, executed. The victims included Röhm himself. The filming of the rally was intended, therefore, to show that the party had been left undivided after this trauma.

The resulting film, *Triumph des Willens (The Triumph of the Will)* has, of course, survived to be something of a cinema classic. Two hours long in its full version, it shows the great rally from every aspect: the arrival of the various contingents – the SA, the SS, the Hitler Youth; life in the camps; the arrival of Hitler and his welcome by the Mayor of Nuremberg and by party dignitaries; the various arena events and displays; the adulatory crowds round the Führer wherever he moves.

It was given its première in Berlin on 29 March 1935 and as befitted such an occasion guests included foreign diplomats, army officers, party leaders, while a band from the *Leibstandarte Adolf Hitler* played on the stage before the film began. It was hoped that it might be shown outside the country, but this was not to be and only a few nations friendly to Germany ever screened it, and even then in a drastically cut version.

Those who have sat through its full two hours agree that its main fault is what the French call *longueur*, tedious length. It suffers from something else, as well, the fearsome and detestable repetition of a single theme: that of the invincibility of naked, organized brute force. If this is to be reckoned as art, it is pure unadulterated Nazi art, the nearest approach to what Speer says was missing in Nazi Germany – 'a style of the Third Reich.' It has sometimes been suggested that Leni Riefenstahl was primarily an extremely gifted film editor, as if the deployment of a purely technical skill somehow made her involvement with Nazism pardonable. This is plain nonsense. The skill with which the message of *The Triumph of the Will* is hammered home depends almost entirely on the choice of camera angle. Typical of this are those sequences in which the frame is filled with men, depersonalized under their deep steel helmets, all turned towards the far distant podium or where athletes, seen from high above, cease to be people and become abstract geometrical shapes. This is strictly the province of the director, the creative mind behind the film.

One incident, recorded by Speer, indicates how much propaganda efforts owed to artifice and how little to spontaneity. When it was found that the footage of Leni Riefenstahl's film in which Hess introduced Hitler to the audience had been spoiled, Hitler ordered it to be reshot in the studio. A replica of the podium was built there and Hess was filmed, arm upraised in the *Hitlergrüss*, saying in an empty studio, precisely in the tone of voice he had used on the original occasion, 'My leader, I welcome you in the name of the Party Congress!'

The Triumph of the Will demonstrated its director's talent for handling large crowds and movement, and it was this which led to her choice as director of the film of the 1936 Olympics in Berlin. The ideological message, if here less openly aggressive, was in tune with the views of the Nazis just the same. They – and the film's director – shared an adoration of the human body, though only when healthy, young and unmarked by disease.

The film that was finally produced was divided into two parts and to make explicit the link with 'Nordic' Hellenism, it began by seeking to re-evoke the atmosphere of Attic Greece. Altogether it took two years to complete and much of this time was spent by Leni Riefenstahl working at the editing bench to produce the maximum drama and balance in the montages which are one of its main features. The result has to be admitted as a masterpiece which still has the power to leave behind it a sort of breathless excitement, so that one does indeed feel as though the character of the original Hellenic festivals has been recaptured.

These two films, though they did more for the National Socialist film than anything hitherto and most things subsequently, were produced in spite of rather than because of Dr Goebbels. He had a personal detestation for Leni Riefenstahl and, rarely able to separate personal and professional feelings, did his utmost to thwart and denigrate her. Against Hitler's unconcealed admiration, however, there was little he could do but snipe, while at the same time demonstrating that if his department might

Above : Adolf Wohlbrück in *The Bartered Bride*. He left the Third Reich voluntarily just before the war and subsequently starred in English films under the name Anton Walbrook.

have failed to distinguish itself in the field of the feature film, it could hold its own in the cinema of actuality, which was Leni Riefenstahl's province.

Because of his strongly journalistic bent, Goebbels had from the beginning seen the newsreel as the most important part of cinema entertainment. Once the audience was in the theater, it was possible to use its comparatively brief compass for indoctrination purposes. They would be prepared to sit through a newsreel before a film they really wanted to see, while they would not go to a full length propaganda film unless it was executed with the greatest skill.

To make sure that the public saw his newsreels, the showing of the so-called *Wochenschau* was made compulsory. Although, naturally, it was dependent on the hazards of the week's news for what was actually presented, the final result was governed by a strict policy of selection and emphasis. The head of the Ministry's film department was in charge of newsreel organization and decided on the treatment of stories, their planning and production. This

alone showed the importance attached to it. The aim was unambiguous: carefully chosen shots, skillful editing, to juxtapositions and the employment of mood music and sound-effect (usually added in the studio as news film was then, as largely now, shot mute). All tended to one end, made explicit by the strongly slanted commentary accompanying the images. The overall objective was to produce mass-intoxication and mass approval for everything the state did. Usually consisting, in the manner of newsreels of the time everywhere, of several topics, the *Wochenschau* would occasionally be devoted to a single one. This was the case with a newsreel intended to commemorate Hitler's fiftieth birthday, which occurred only a month after German troops had occupied Prague and four months before the outbreak of war. It was later to be used as a model of its kind. As a piece of propaganda, it was to be part of the Führer-cult. Although actually made by UFA, production was under the control of the Ministry. The twelve cameramen assigned to it were each given his particular area and altogether some 10,000 meters of film was shot, of which about 500 was finally used, a wastage level well above normal.

The film showed first the final preparations on the birthday eve: the completion of the tribune from which Hitler was to take the salute and other such details intended as suspense builders. Then it cut to the birthday proper with the band of *Leibstandarte Adolf Hitler* playing outside the Chancellery. Crowds begin to gather and break into spontaneous songs of jubilation; when Hitler appears on the balcony this turns into frenzied cheering.

Elsewhere on the parade troops arrive and begin lining the route. At the tribune party and government dignitaries assemble and are shown and identified: Himmler, Goering, Goebbels with his children in white, craning necks to see everything that is happening. Then a significant shot of an empty chair – the one Hitler will shortly occupy.

Back at the Chancellery, the powerful cars and motor-

Below: Leni Riefenstahl with Heinrich Himmler (left) during the filming of her propaganda masterpiece *The Triumph of the Will* in Nuremburg, on Party Day in 1934.

Poster for the film *Jew Süss*, a nasty bit of anti-Semitism based on the true story of Süss Oppenheimer, a financial adviser to an 18th century provincial aristocrat who enriched himself at his master's expense.

This was *Der Ewige Jude* (The Eternal Jew), a particularly foul piece of anti-Semitism, produced, under the aegis of one Dr Fritz Hippler, about the time that the Final Solution to the Jewish Problem was being implemented.

Every conceivable means was used to associate Jewishness with degradation. In one sequence shots of groups of Jewish people were montaged with shots of rats in sewers and the whole tone of the film was of this order. Meanness, mercenariness and other allegedly Jewish traits were exhibited, backed by borrowings, often out of context, from other films including foreign productions. The Jews shown were all picked for their repellent ugliness and, for the purposes of the film, a great deal of shooting was done in the Warsaw ghetto where Polish Jews had already been reduced to depths of abjectness through cold, hunger and, most of all, fear. As a consequence there was no difficulty in showing them as cringing, shuffling wretches without self-respect. The final obscenity is in the last scenes which show a Kosher ritual slaughterhouse. Blood spurts and drips, hens flutter in long death-throes, animals grunt and heave in their last anguish. The impression given is that frightful suffering is being imposed on innocent creatures, when, in fact, Jewish ritual slaughter has the precise object of inflicting a speedy, painless death in accordance with Talmudic Law.

cycle escorts start their engines, then drive past the crowds on the parade route. At the tribune Hitler steps from his car, climbs to occupy the seat previously shown empty. Now the parade of the detachments of the armed services, the most important part of the film, begins, unit after unit of marching men, others in vehicles, tanks, guns, pass before the Führer.

The cameraman's recapitulation of events might seem a poor substitute for presence at the event itself. This was just what the producers were out to disprove. The audience, seeing the film, was shown not only more aspects of the parade, but more intimate aspects of it than were available to any single spectator. Thus, even those who had seen the event would be tempted into the cinemas.

In wartime, the newsreel cameramen were to come into their own, not only in producing material for the *Wochenschau*, but also in the production of full length war documentaries such as *Feuertaufe* (Baptism of Fire), showing the eighteen-day Polish campaign, and *Sieg im Westen* (Victory in the West) about the campaign in France. From this time on Goebbels seldom failed to comment on the weekly newsreel and with his notes on the subject attached short summaries of the reports on the morale of the people which were sent to him by the Security Service.

Newsreel apart, however, there was still another film for which the government's direct agency was responsible.

At the very end, examples of Aryan German life are shown so that the contrast will not be missed. David Stewart Hull rightly describes *Der Ewige Jude* as 'perhaps the most hideous three-quarters of an hour in film history' and compares its horrifying effect with that of the concentration camp newsreels seen in the latter stages of the war. So horrifying is the slaughterhouse footage that the commentator goes so far as to suggest that those of delicate sensibilities close their eyes through it!

Goebbels, a convert to anti-Semitism, sought to make the film hard-hitting in the interests of rendering the Final Solution acceptable to the German people (as, in general, it never was). He certainly succeeded, but may be accused of over-stating his case so that its arguments rebound on the producers. The fact is that another hand may have been behind it. This was Rosenberg, who never missed a chance of striking at his party enemy and may well have suggested to Hitler that Goebbels was 'going soft' on anti-Semitism. It could well be that *Der Ewige Jude* was an attempt to refute this suggestion.

This piece of official poison was matched though certainly not surpassed by the private enterprise ones. Outstanding examples of these were *Die Rothschilds Aktien von Waterloo,* and *Jud Süss.* The former was directed by Waschenecke and united anti-Semitism with anti-Britishness, presenting a history of the Rothschild dynasty in which truth is stood on its head and ending with the well-known incident of the pigeons which flew up from the battlefield of Waterloo after Wellington's vistory. According to this version, for which there is not the remotest historical sanction, the family gave out that Napoleon had won. There was a panic on the stock exchanges and in the process the Rothschilds made fresh fortunes. It ends with a roller caption superimposed on a background of the Star of David and a map of Britain. The caption read: 'As this film is completed, the last members of the Rothschild family are leaving Europe as refugees and escaping to their allies in England, where the British plutocrats are carrying on.' Few took its message seriously, which is hadly surprising as the film lacked any artistic quality and was singularly unentertaining.

Jud Süss was something quite different. In 1925, the gifted Jewish novelist, Lion Feuchtwanger, published his eponymous novel based on an actual historical character, Josef Süss Oppenheimer. The real Oppenheimer had wormed himself into the graces of the Duke of Württemburg in the 18th Century to become a species of tax-collector. His extortions enriched both the duke and himself and Oppenheimer instigated and maintained a reign of terror. After the duke's death, however, he was brought to book for a whole series of offences, including the debasement of the currency for which he was duly hanged. None of these distasteful details did Feuchtwanger attempt to conceal, but his Süss is shown to have departed from the moral teachings of Judaism to which he returns while in the condemned cell. Such, in outline, is the story to which Feuchtwanger added an enormous *dramatis personae.*

After the Nazi takeover his works were among those consigned to the flames and it was only later that it occurred to anyone that here was a stick to strike at the Jews twice over – once from history and once from the mouth of a fellow Jew.

A script was prepared by Wolfgang Müller, regarded as gifted both as a writer and propagandist. So vicious was it, that when its members read it, a shudder of horror ran through the film industry. Actors and directors, many of them remembering their Jewish friends of pre-Nazi days, recoiled as from excrement. One director, Teich, refused outright to handle it and was fired by Goebbels. A second, Peter Paul Brauer, who was drafted, went the same way when he ran into casting difficulties. Goebbels accused him of showing insufficient authority. Next to be approached was Veit Harlan, a director who specialized in quick, low-cost productions and who had produced a number of them. He pleaded prior commitment and thought he had escaped the unpleasant task only to find that the Propaganda Ministry had discovered a clause in his contract which allowed for his secondment under its direct orders.

Similar problems occurred with casting. After going through a number of possibles, including Emil Jannings, Ferdinand Marian accepted, but only after a humiliating

Left: Adolf Wohlbrück being seduced by Dorothea Wieck in *The Student from Prague,* 1935.

bullying from Goebbels. Shortly after the war Marian died in a car crash, said to have been suicide resulting from the guilt feelings with which his appearance in the picture had left him.

While this interpretation of his death may be legend, there was reason enough for bad conscience. After seeing the film members of a Hitler Youth band in Vienna were so affected by it they kicked to death the first Jew they saw on the streets thereafter. And this is a single incident from many. With *Der Ewige Jude*, it was required viewing for the SS mass killing groups before they were sent east to carry out their massacres. Its numerous uplifting moments include a rape scene, one of torture and there is a long, gloating finale of the execution of Süss.

Although Harlan destroyed the negative of the film after the war, others were plainly made and some are known to be circulating even today in the Middle East. One is said to be in the personal possession of an Arab sheik, who has it projected at intervals for his personal delectation.

Besides such contributions to the canon of anti-Semitic art, the commercial film-makers were providing other sorts of propaganda vehicle. One of the earliest was *Flüchtlinge* (Refugees), directed by Ucicky, who had been responsible for *Morgenrot* and who was destined to become one of the select band of film-makers to the National Socialist state. The message of *Flüchtlinge* was primarily anti-Bolshevik and it described the sufferings and humiliations undergone by a group of German refugees at Soviet hands in 1928. As a kind of incidental target, it took a side-swipe at the League of Nations from which Germany had withdrawn after the Nazi seizure of power. It was shown as impotent and cynical. Unlike previous efforts this was an effective piece. Soviet treatment of the Germans in Russia was well-known and had been universally condemned, it therefore began with the advantage of being firmly grounded in fact. Leaving the cinema after seeing it, one can well understand that audiences must have felt that relief one knows when awakening from a nightmare, as they realized they now lived in a Germany growing steadily stronger so that foreigners could no longer feel able to kick their compatriots around with impunity.

Selpin directed *Die Reiter von Deutsch-Ostafrika* (The Riders of German East Africa). This was a slightly ambiguously anti-British piece. Although the British colonizers were shown primarily as drink-sodden brutes, particularly given to the ill-treatment of the settler-families of other nationalities, the main figures in the plot were a British and a German officer whose lifelong friendship suffers the interruption of World War I. In the end, though not before the British have committed a series of atrocities, friendship triumphs. This happy ending was to have embarrassing repercussions for all concerned with the film. In 1939, when Germany was once more at war with Britain, it had to be banned.

Ich für Dich, Du für Mich (Me for you, You for Me), directed by Carl Fröhlich, could well have been described as the feminine counterpart of *Hitlerjunge Quex*. The female equivalent of the Hitler Youth was the League of German Girls and this is the story of a group of its members, engaged in a year's voluntary service on a farm. The scenario was novelettish trash and dripped with ideology,

Wohlbrück, this time with the popular Renate Müller, in a picture produced by the singer and actor Willy Forst, *Allotria*. Goebbels believed light films contrasted well with the newsreels.

mainly contrasting the healthy, natural outdoor life of the girls with the fetid hothouse of urban intellectualism, and it occasionally added the little anti-Semitic prod to boot. Strangely enough a less heavy-handed and more documentary treatment might have made it more effective, for, as we now know, many of those who were girls in Hitler's time, and by no means all of them Nazis, thoroughly enjoyed these periods of farmwork and look back on them with a positive nostalgia.

Into a separate category of propaganda film comes *Der Herrscher* (The Governor), also directed by Veit Harlan, and his first major vehicle. This was heavy, dynastic drama with some roots in Thomas Mann's *Buddenbrooks*. The governor of the title is a German steelmaster whose domain is both his family and his factory. It is allegorical in that the father is intended to symbolize the Father of the Nation – the Führer. As is often the case, the analogy begins to break down and the message becomes more and more confused, especially as other ideas are dragged in. One of these was the recently introduced property and inheritance laws. Also an endemic fault of allegory, there was the tendency for the audience to be caught up in the story, *per se*, and thus miss the wider implications.

If *Der Herrscher* was used to make comprehensible and acceptable such state acts as changes in the property laws, *Ich Klage an* (I Accuse) was intended to create a public acceptance of the euthanasia measures which were being introduced. The centerpiece of the film is the trial of a doctor accused of the mercy-killing of his wife, a concert pianist who develops multiple sclerosis. Euthanasia, like sterilization, was very much part of the Nazi platform, but the measures actually introduced ran into entrenched hostility. This had led to Himmler's having to bring them to an end and to have the euthanasia institutes closed until such a time as their necessity was understood. It may have been, therefore, that his influence was behind the picture. It has to be said, however, that the director, Wolfgang Liebeneiner, treated it with considerable objectivity, presenting the arguments of both sides through the cases of prosecution and defense during the trial.

By the mid-'Thirties, the various contracts between German and foreign film companies were running out.

This, of course, meant that fewer foreign films were reaching the German cinemas which must have been a relief to the Propaganda Minister, though they were, naturally, subject to censorship and large numbers banned. It meant, nonetheless, that from now on the country's cinemas were more than ever dependent upon the home product and efforts were made to see that every film made contained some element of indoctrination. One source of this was history and in consequence a series of biographical films describing the lives of famous Germans of the past were made. Among them was *Robert Koch*, the story of the man who proposed the bacterial theory of disease. Others included *Friedrich Schiller* and *Wilhelm Tell*, the first one of the last German films to be shown abroad. Later productions were devoted to the lives of Rudolf Diesel, inventor of the Diesel engine, and Prince Otto Bismarck, the famous unifying Chancellor, whose activities gave ample scope for parallels with the life of Hitler. In the middle of the war, Goebbels conceived the idea of another film showing the correspondence between the Führer and a great man of the past in *Friedrich der Grosse*. At this time, the German people were oppressed by the growing numbers of their enemies. *Friedrich der Grosse* concentrated, therefore, on that period during the Seven Years' War when he had experienced a similar crisis. Goebbels did his personal best to boost the film. A great première was organized at which the audience consisted almost entirely of holders of the Knight's Cross, together with wounded soldiers and workers from the armaments factories. The Propaganda Minister chose the occasion to tell his audience that it had been selected as 'Film of the Nation' and that its star, Otto Gebühr, had been made 'Actor of the State.' He commented in his diary that the film was intended to make politics. 'It is a good expedient in the struggle for the soul of our people and in the process of a permanent hardening of the German power of resistance which we need in order to pass successfully through this war,' he reflected.

The war also brought other changes in film policy. There were, of course, more war films, such as *Über Alles in der Welt* describing the lives of soldiers and *Stukas*, devoted to the almost legendary dive-bombers and the men who flew them. There were, too, the spy films in which the villains, when unmasked, invariably turned out to be Jews. There were a few comedies, such as *Quax, der Bruchpilot* (Test pilot Quax) with the comedian Heinz Ruhmann in the lead.

Also a result of the war was a recrudescence of the anti-British film, while anti-British touches – often so outrageous even German audiences roared with laughter – were added to other films wherever possible. Of the specialities in this line there was Hans Steinhoff's *Ohm Krüger*. Ostensibly the story of the great Boer leader, it reminds the audience that concentration camps were a British invention. This inspired half-truth by which the piece of terminology which the British did invent (and were to use even during the war) is confused with the actual institution as it existed in Hitler's Germany, persists in the German mind even today. The high-point of the film is perhaps the one in which Krüger visits Buckingham Palace, where its incumbent, Queen Victoria, is discovered to be a whisky-soaked crone, lurching and slurred of speech. Yet another of the same ilk, *Mein Leben für Irland* (My Life for Ireland), offered itself as an account of British treatment of that unhappy island.

One of the cardinal mistakes of the Nazi propagandists was to forget that even in wartime there was still some sort of foreign audience for their productions. These were to be found both in the neutral and in the occupied countries. Had they stuck more closely to the fact films like *Mein Leben für Irland* might well have been more effective reminders to the rest of the world of matters Britain would rather have had forgotten. They were so outrageous and exaggerated that few took them seriously. The British Foreign Office could safely ignore them or, if it mentioned them, did so only with derision.

The story of the German cinema in Nazi times, like that of the theater and all other aspects of the arts and entertainment world, came to an end in the last months of the Third Reich when, in a last frenzied effort of total war, most of the production companies were closed down. Perhaps in many ways the story of the propaganda cinema is the nastiest of all. Paradoxically, the projected images of light and shadow made to move by the phenomenon of the persistence of vision have a strange kind of immediate conviction lacking in the other arts. It behooves all who are involved in producing them to remember their high responsibility and to hold honesty and integrity most worthy of virtues. When the cinema is perverted, as it was by the Nazis, what it distils is a peculiar kind of venom, as likely to destroy those who produce it as those who consume it.

Below left: Hitler at Bückeberg during a folk festival.
Below: Girls of Bückeberg in their folk costumes. These events were filmed and circulated widely to identify the Nazis with traditionalism in Germany which they had already undermined.

Trumpeter of the *Leibstandarte Adolf Hitler,* his personal bodyguard, opening a concert on behalf of the 'Winter Help,' one of the Nazis' approved 'charities' which contributed to economic relief in East Prussia.

POMP AND CIRCUMSTANCE

Throughout the consideration of National Socialist propaganda, one factor must be kept in sight: the end it served. Frequently this is presented as though it were no more than a cult of one man, Adolf Hitler. This, of course, is an over-simplification. No one would have followed him merely for himself. He attracted followers by what he stood for. He was the prophet of a system of ideas called National Socialism. In the end, however, prophet and message are always mutually interdependent and inseparable, and often the ideas take the prophet's name – Buddhism, Mohammedanism, Christianity are obvious examples. At the same time, some put the emphasis on the ideas, others on the person. Alfred Rosenberg, who liked to be seen as an intellectual of the movement, fell into the former category; Paul Josef Goebbels, into the latter.

For Rosenberg, National Socialism subsumed everything else, including the state itself. So he wrote in one of his *Völkischer Beobachter* editorials that what had taken place in 1933 was not the establishment of the 'state's totality,' but of the 'totality of the National Socialist movement . . . The state is the tool of the National Socialist philosophy of life.'

In characteristic language, Rosenberg explained why this was so: 'The state is not an end in itself, but only a means to the preservation of the people. The form of the state changes and its laws decay: the Volk remains . . . .'

While comparatively few in the party carried their ideas to Rosenberg's lengths, this was a view to which most of the leadership would have paid lip service in some degree. The mystical resonances attached to words like *Volk*, 'blood and soil' (as the twin matrices from which the *Volk* had been molded), 'community' and 'Fatherland,' were all part of the same ethos. So too was the appropriation of religious terminology to express political concepts.

Goebbels, however, was mainly preoccupied with the prophet. Indeed, he was so utterly mesmerized by the man from the moment he began to show an interest in the young journalist that he carried hero-worship to something near idolatry. His diary entries on this subject make nauseating reading. No doubt it was for this reason that Goebbels succeeded in his Führer's eyes, where Rosenberg failed. As megalomania and self-intoxication swamped Hitler's personality he became increasingly concerned only with that which kept him in the center and forefront. He even went so far as to cast doubt on the prophecy itself as laid down in *Mein Kampf*. He had made a mistake, he told friends, in allowing himself to be pinned down to specifics so early in his career.

This does not mean that Goebbels' terminology differed much from Rosenberg's. His propaganda outpourings are rich in words more usually associated with religion, like 'miracle' and 'mission.' On the evening of the Rhineland plebiscite, for instance, when Hitler addressed the nation by radio, he wrote in his diary that there was a feeling 'as though Germany had been transformed into one big church embracing all classes and creeds.' He did his utmost to convey the idea of a Germany united as a single

Top right: Memorial in Munich for those who fell in their attempt to overthrow the Weimar government during the Beer Hall Putsch of 9 November 1923.
Right: Hitler lays the foundation for another monument to the glory of the Third Reich.

126

Hitler flanked by Hess and Goering at a rally held at Tempelhof Airfield in Berlin.

Hitler Youth members beat their drums on the Party Day of Freedom in 1934.

community under its new leader in the same way that Christendom had once been united under the single authority of the Catholic Church. But perhaps because as a propagandist he saw more clearly the need for concrete imagery, he always placed the accent on the leader himself. He was perfectly conscious of the necessity in totalitarian regimes for a charismatic leader. He saw that such a leader might well attract as followers those who wanted nothing to do with the party or its program, and in this he was perfectly right. He was probably not exaggerating too greatly when he claimed in 1941 that 'millions of Germans drew a distinction between the Führer and the party, refusing to support the latter while believing in Hitler.' One cannot help suspecting that had his own relationship to Hitler been quite different from the adoring one it was, he would almost certainly have used similar terminology and similar techniques in projecting him.

With an unfailing intuition he saw just what sort of characteristics the leader should have. He must be father-figure and wise-elder of the community, a successor to to community elders of the past. He had to be a superman and a fellow-being, at once distant and near. On the one hand he had to be simple. The picture of Hitler as vegetarian, eating frugally; as non-smoker and non-drinker; as lover of nature, of simple flowers, of children, all this

was assiduously repeated in news stories, photographs, newsreels, magazine articles, even in reading primers at kindergartens. On the other hand, he must possess genius and cunning sufficient to get the better of those with whom he was called upon to negotiate on the nation's behalf, as well as to defeat enemies. In one speech, using typically *ersatz* religious language, he sums all this up: 'You started from below as every great leader does. But like all leaders you have grown to your task. You became greater with it.' And it was Goebbels who coined the term 'Führer' in 1931, insisting that it was employed throughout the party. Later, when after the death of Hindenburg, Hitler assumed the mantle of head of state, he also proposed that the title 'Führer' be substituted for the more formal 'President.'

To show that he was approachable to the masses, Hitler was frequently portrayed surrounded by a host of adulatory admirers. Speer claims that such occasions arose without any manipulation, but this does not alter the fact that the Ministry of Propaganda was perfectly capable of providing the crowds when necessary. It was, in fact, his boast that he could do just that. At short notice he could organize any kind of crowd from schoolchildren to workers, depending upon what was needed. They came to be called his 'cheering levies.'

Yet, even among the crowds of admirers there was something else Goebbels always laid stress upon: the

Hitler listens as a young girl recites a poem she made up in his honor during one of the four elections held in 1932. This was a deliberate attempt to give Hitler a 'family man' image.

of Germans. Hearing how, in Italy, the walls of even the smallest villages were bedecked with posters in praise of '*Il Duce*,' he commented that such expedients were totally unnecessary for him. His greatness was to be seen by all. *Si monumentum requiris, circumspice.* On another occasion, discussing the nationalist movements in other countries and their leaders, Degrelle in Belgium, for example, or Mosley in Britain, he declared that they were merely pale shadows of himself.

Parallel with the cult of the Führer were the myths and rituals of National Socialism, which both Goebbels and Rosenberg exploited in their own ways. Rosenberg was preoccupied with the warrior past of the Germanic tribes and based many of his ideas round the notion of the 'unknown soldier,' using it as a symbol of the 'twelve million men of white race' killed in World War I. In this way the entire struggle is made to appear as if it had been some kind of racial conflict or crusade of the white races. This was such manifest nonsense that he was forced to modify it and to focus his devotion on the two million German war dead instead. These became the 'blessed warriors' whose strivings are rewarded by a place in the Valhalla of the race-soul, wherever that might be. National Socialists were heirs and trustees of the heritage they had won. The re-forming of the German Army after the Nazi takeover of power was a demonstration of the potency of the warrior-myth. 'Today's rebirth,' he wrote, 'is the sign that countless men and women begin to understand what it is that two million heroes represent: martyrs of a new myth of life, indeed of a new faith . . . .'

Rosenberg did not in the least mind adopting the symbolism of Christianity when it could serve his purpose. As he pointed out, Christianity had purloined these from the pagan anyway. On the other hand, he believed many Christian symbols must be rejected. Among these was the cross. In its place would stand the war dead. 'The men of the coming age,' he declared, 'will transform the heroes' memorials and glades of remembrance into places of pilgrimage of a new religion; there the hearts of the Germans will be constantly shaped afresh in pursuit of a new myth.' Since they were the inheritors of the warrior-heroes, the National Socialists' own 'fallen' were entitled to be remembered equally. So Horst Wessel, the child Herbert Norkus, Leo Schlageter or those killed in the Kapp Putsch were also martyrs.

Goebbels, too, made full use of the hagiology and martyrology of Nazism. Writing of Horst Wessel after his death he used his most repellent tones of blasphemous idolatry. The dead man was 'a Christ and a Socialist!' He was 'one who calls through his deeds: come to me: I will redeem you.' Even as the unsavory details of Wessel's life were brought out at the trial of his killer, there was no modification in the tone: Goebbels continued to proclaim him a national hero.

He also organized the huge funeral. Its high point was a roll call in which when the name 'Horst Wessel' was

loneliness of high office, of decision-making and bearing the responsibility for those decisions.

Finally, so that his subjects might be overwhelmed with gratitude, their Führer was offered as a man to whom power was nothing but a distasteful duty which he had assumed out of his deep love of the German people. By inclination an artist, he was longing to return to this calling and set the trappings of power aside.

But of all the attributes which were ascribed to him there was none which Goebbels thought more important than luck. At all costs, the masses must be persuaded that their leader was fortunate. His endeavors had, therefore, to be crowned by invariable success. This not only inspired greater confidence in him on their part and increased their willingness to follow where he led; it also made it appear that he was under the protection of Providence. The unconscious attitude he was seeking to foster was one in which ordinary Germans would say to themselves that it was useless to oppose the Führer, because he would always turn out to be right in the long run. He was the man touched by the hand of destiny. This, of course, was perfectly consonant with Hitler's own description of himself as the sleep walker blindly executing a higher mission.

Indeed, one might say that he was taken in by propaganda about himself no less thoroughly than the majority

A massive rally in 1933 waits for the arrival of Hitler.

called out, Hitler Youth boys shouted back 'Present.' This was in the same style as the words of Rosenberg in *Völkischer Beobachter* in which he proclaimed that the Nazi martyr was 'not dead.' 'Unseen and yet perceptible,' he wrote, 'the souls of the "dead" struggle together with us for a new life.' From this time on the dead of the movement were said to have been 'summoned to Horst Wessel's standard.'

There were the others, however. Leo Schlageter had been shot by the French occupying forces in the Ruhr. After the abortive Kapp Putsch in Munich a swastika flag had been recovered stained, it was alleged, with the blood of the sixteen who died in it. Given the name of the 'blood flag' it was used thereafter to dedicate other flags of the movement starting at the rally of 1929. Later, the bodies of the sixteen were taken from the graves and, with-

out the permission of their relatives being sought, given a new resting place in a party mausoleum in the König-platz in Munich. The ceremony was attended by Hitler and, as at Wessel's funeral, when he called out the names on the coffins, members of the Hitler Youth answered 'present.'

Matters of ritual did not, however, end with funerals or the commemoration of the dead and Goebbels claimed that he himself was the originator and the guiding light behind all party and state ritual. For this purpose there was a special department of his ministry. It was he who instituted a Calendar of National Socialism, having in mind the church's calendar of feasts, so that almost every month the public was reminded of the society in which it lived. On 30 January the seizure of power was recalled; on 24 February the Foundation Day of the NSDAP was celebrated; on 16 March it was the Day of Remembrance of Heroes; 20 April brought the Führer's birthday; ten days

Hitler inspecting young members of the *Hitlerjugend* and BDM at Youth Day in Potsdam in 1932.

A crowd scene taken on the same day, three months before the Nazi takeover of power.

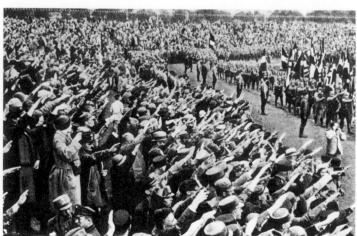

later on 1 May, there was the People's Day of Unity; 21 June was Midsummer's Day. This often included mass meetings at which important policy statements were made. At one of these held at the Olympic Stadium in Berlin in 1939, for example, Goebbels gave the first hints of what his government's attitude was going to be towards Czechoslovakia

In September, there was the party rally. October began with a Festival of the Harvest, which had little to do with the Harvest Thanksgiving services held in Christian churches. Again it was an occasion for mass meetings, some involving a million people, and for electrifying pro-Nazi speeches.

On 9 November there was a day of remembrance for the Kapp Putsch. It included solemn dedication, the worship of heroes, and a Ceremony of the Resurrection restating the national faith in immortality through the *Volk*. Between these events were lesser ones, times one might say of practical sacrifice or contemplation, such as the annual collections for the Nazi *Winterhilfe* (Winter Relief) in which Goebbels always played a prominent part himself.

In his calendar only one festival was left untouched. This was Christmas. But if he was unwilling to interfere with it, there were others who were. Rosenberg, Himmler and Martin Bormann formed part of an avowedly anti-Christian wing of the party. Of the three Bormann was undoubtedly the more fanatical and railed against the delaying of an all-out *Kirchenkampf* (Struggle with the Churches), using his influence with Hitler to this end. Himmler on the other hand was constantly trying to substitute ideas consonant with National Socialism for those of Christianity. Included in this were attempts to reshape Christmas, which was celebrated on 21 December – Midwinter Day – in some SS circles. Every effort was made to convert it into a Germanic 'Festival of the Light' with paganistic overtones, in the place of the celebration of

Below: The German Workers' Front on 'German Corner' in Berlin in 1933.

The Hitler Youth dedicate themselves to the service of the German nation, 1 May 1933.

Above: Hitler and Röhm, leader of the SA, at Party Day in Nuremburg September 1933 view the march past of SA troops. It was only nine months later that Hitler decided to liquidate Röhm to eliminate the SA threat to his regime.
Right: Cyclists of the SA in another march past in Dortmund, 1933.

the birth of the Christian Saviour. A Nazi children's Christmas book which Lehmann-Haupt came across totally omitted any reference to the Nativity, to Santa Claus, to shepherds, angels, or anything else redolent of the traditional aspects of the feast. The place of Saint Nicholas was taken by 'Frau Holle' and the angels by 'emissaries of Nature' and of some undefined sun-cult. Indeed, the whole book is permeated with notions more in keeping with sun-worship than anything else. For example, the festival was intended to mark the point at which the darkening day gave place to the miracle of the growing light.

The catalog of ceremony and ritual is indeed almost endless. There were initiation rites for everything from the League of Schoolchildren to the SS. In the Hitler Youth there were religious ceremonies which completely aped those of the church, but included such transpositions as readings from *Mein Kampf* instead of the Gospels and the recitation of a so-called Hitler Creed. Almost inevitably one's mind turns to the Black Mass where the main change is that the name of Satan is substituted for the name of God.

Still other Hitler Youth ceremonies took place when the young members received their daggers. Then they would be reminded of their duty to defend the Fatherland to their last breath. In others they would be warned of the

need to harden their young and malleable hearts for whatever harsh but necessary tasks National Socialism might require them to perform. Before this, personal scruples of morality or pity were as nothing.

The dark eminence behind all these was Dr Goebbels operating through his system of propaganda wardens which reached down into every *Gau.* Always the aim was to demonstrate how a particular group could serve Führer and party, and to gain from it a greater degree of commitment. In one ceremony held at the Nuremberg rally, for example, the Labor Service was involved. The assembled battalions, mustered as an army on parade, stood at attention before Hitler, polished spades at the 'Present.' They were addressed by a voice over the loudspeakers: 'Once a year, the spade shall rest. Once a year there comes for the time to stand before our Führer for whom we work day by day. In this hour, new faith is kindled.' The youths called back: 'We are ready.' Then, in the manner of a Litany, the voice went on: 'No one is too good . . .' and the answer: '. . . to work for Germany,' and so on.

After reaffirming their love of 'Germany, our Father-

Right: 'Germany Awake' on every banner as Wehrmacht troops parade on Party Day in Nuremberg, 1933.

132

land' and their willingness to follow the Führer 'wherever he leads,' it ended: 'We lift up our hearts and think of our brothers who suffered in the trenches, and of the others who fought murder and hatred in the streets. They died for Germany.' The final response was: 'But today we can live for Germany.'

In other rites, such as those involving the SS, the elements of neopaganism and Himmler's 'blood and soil' were more intimately incorporated. Himmler, who had added ancestor worship to other SS cults, squandered great fortunes on archaeological inquiries intended to show the persistence of German pagan ideals through history and culture. At one time graduates of archaeology could invariably find well-paid jobs in the ranks of the SS assisting these sterile investigations.

But Goebbels, while claiming to scorn such ideas and to deride the solemnity surrounding the SS oath-taking ceremonies, was not past using such expedients himself. In his early days as *Gauleiter* of Berlin, he took his SA units out in the countryside. Against an enormous pyre of burning wood, reminiscent of the burning cross of the Ku Klux Klan, an oath of allegiance to Hitler was sworn.

Left: A fireworks display on Labor Day, 1 May 1933.
Below: Part of the crowd of 151,000 who listened to Hitler's speech on Party Day in Nuremberg in 1933.
Right: Saarlanders salute the Führer on a visit he made to the territory then under League of Nations suzerainty. The populace voted to join the Reich in 1935.

However, as the party took over the government, the more important rituals became those involving the greatest numbers. The crowd was mutually supportive and it helped to create the feeling of a pan-German community. This was, of course, the essence of the integration of all Germans into a single, comprehensive ideology. But there was still another reason why Goebbels, at least, regarded these mass occasions as important. Participation in them was the regime's substitute for actual participation in policy-making. It was, indeed, regarded as superior to the part played by the ordinary citizen in democracies. It showed the National Socialist leaders feeling the pulse of the people, where in other societies leadership operated through a complex machinery which shielded them from people's inner feelings.

Goebbels would often suggest that the measures his government was implementing were simply the expression of public demands which had been detected in some way by speakers as they addressed them on mass occasions. In an ingenious piece of casuistry the *Frankfurter Zeitung*, in an editorial in 1937, took up this thesis and tried to prove how even the most demagogic, rabble-rousing oratory was equivalent to a test of public opinion. 'The address as an instrument of politics, this is the egg of Columbus discovered by National Socialism,' it wrote. 'In a manner so far unknown, the masses have felt they have been participating in the political process by way of speech and address.'

Of all the great public occasions of National Socialism there was one which represented a climax, combining as it did pageantry, ritual and the participation of huge numbers. This consummating act was the annual party rally at Nuremberg. The idea behind it was not, of course, new. The church had always had its great festivals and processions. Even the anti-clericals of the French Revolution had seen the need for some kind of substitute for these and adopted as the solution something akin to the National Socialist rally. Then, too, art and music were joined to pageantry, symbolism, oratory and political slogan as in the great gatherings in the Champs de Mars or that notorious occasion in the Cathedral of Nôtre Dame when a naked actress sat on the altar to symbolize the spirit of the new age while the Phrygian-capped revolutionaries cavorted frenziedly round her.

The Nazis were perhaps a little too respectably *petit bourgeois* for open displays of nudity, but the rest was there. Art in the special 'official' shows which often ran concurrently with the congress or, if one admired that sort of thing, in the architecture of the stadia, enlarged or 'improved' almost every year; music in marching bands of party groups or services, in the special gala performances of *Die Meistersinger* or the movement from a

Hitler is mobbed by an enthusiastic throng in Nuremberg on his way to a party rally.

Bruckner symphony which always preceded Hitler's great cultural speeches.

And pageantry, pageantry, pageantry: there were marches through the bunting and swastika-hung streets of the Medieval city; gymnastic displays by the Hitler Youth or the League of German Girls; parades of the SA, the SS, the Labor Service, the women's organizations, the functionaries of the party.

Lasting anything up to eight days, the rallies were the culmination of the year's activity, not only of the party but after the takeover, of the government as well. From 1934, for example, army parades and displays were included. They were made by Hitler occasions for policy-making and, particularly, intimidation. In 1938, the rally took place just after he had wrung the consent of France and Britain to the splitting of Czechoslovakia. Secure in the knowledge of their acquiescence he played the part of the angry leader of his people and, constantly interrupted by the cheers, spoke openly of going to war if need be. We know from history, or from personal memory, of the chill those moments evoked through Europe.

The true focal center of the rally activity was the party congress proper which took place in Nuremberg Town Hall, but it was on public displays that the eyes of the world were focused. For these a succession of arenas were built starting with the Zeppelinwiese (Zeppelin Meadow)

Right: Hitler and Hess (right) on the podium before the speech given on Party Day in Nuremberg in 1933.
Below: Ernst Röhm, the SA leader.

just outside the city, so named because Count Zeppelin had once landed one of his dirigibles there. To this a further three were added over the years: the Luitpoldheim, the Märzfeld and the German Stadium. A broad straight east-west avenue sixteen miles long and 240 ft wide was laid down from the Luitpoldheim to the Märzfeld, which was intended for military displays (Märzfeld is a German rendering of 'Field of Mars'). Giving off the avenue, itself designed for parades, were the Zeppelinwiese on the right and the stadium on the left.

In this way, Nuremberg had been made into one huge temple of Nazism, and it was appropriate, therefore, that the climax of the great annual sacrifice which took place there should be a sermon from the high priest.

Projection of the Führer was of course, one of the main aims of the occasion. At Nuremberg he appeared, in Ernest Bramsted's graphic words, as 'both Caesar and comrade.' As comrade he moved among the party-members, the 'Old Fighters'; or the hundreds of thousands of spectators, smiling, waving, accepting posies from shy, clean, photogenic children. It was as Caesar he made his appearance at the arena, stalking down the 'Road of the Führer' which divided it in two, with his henchmen about him. His progress would be paced to the rhythms of solemn marches, for his first act was to join the assembled multitudes in a tribute to the dead. Then, with that stiff, folded-hands on belly, hunch-shouldered gait of his, he

Left: The SA troop their colors.
Below: The parade of the SA colors on Party Day, 1933.
Right: Reichs Youth Day in Potsdam, 1932.
Below right: Hitler Youth leader Baldur von Schirach salutes his followers in Nuremberg, 1933. Note the contented expression on Julius Streicher's face in the foreground. This bald Nazi was perhaps the most virulent of all the anti-Semites in the Nazi Party.

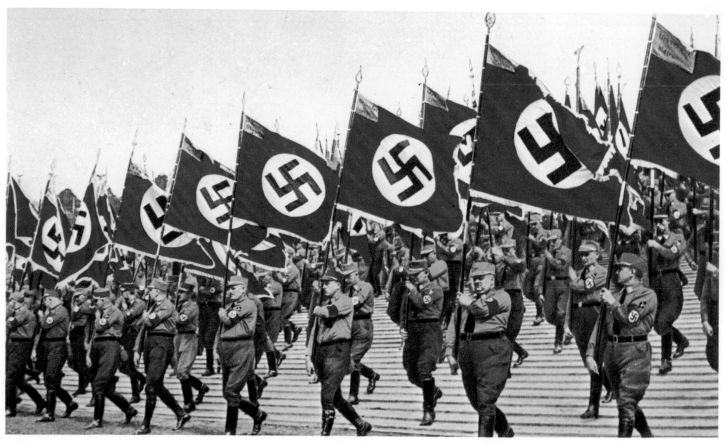

Above: The banners are lowered in honor of the martyred dead of the Beer Hall Putsch on Party Day in Nuremberg.

would lead the way up the steps to the podium with its banked microphones. There he would be greeted by wave after wave of 'Heils.' He in his turn would greet his assembled janizaries of SA and SS as 'My men.' And they would shout back: 'My Führer.' *Ave, Caesar, morituri te salutamus. Ave, ave, ave . . .*

In the course of their evolution, the rallies had been shaped by the ideas of many men. Though Goebbels always claimed to have worked out the style and technique of the party's great occasions, it had actually been Rudolf Hess who had suggested the notion of a great victory rally in 1933 and it was the success of this which had led to its becoming an annual event.

The man who had done most to provide settings, the essential splendid backdrop without which they would never have achieved the fame they did, was Albert Speer, however. His efforts began as early as the 1933 rally for which he designed an eagle with a wingspan of over a hundred feet to stand behind the tribune for Hitler and party leadership. From then on work on the rally sites was virtually continuous through the year. Between 1933 and 1934 teams of workers, numbering hundreds in all, installed concrete review stands. These were flanked by two eagles, which though smaller than the original were more permanent. During the following year one entire arena was paved with granite. Towers for huge flags, colonnades illuminated by spotlights, metal bowls in which open fires could be kept burning through the sessions were among

details added year by year. As the site extended and more and more buildings were completed 40,000 oak trees were planted to give greenery, the oak being chosen because of its associations with ancient Germany. In another case the enormous buildings round the arena were clad in natural Jurassic limestone, giving them a blinding fluorescent whiteness.

At the same time, Speer was also responsible for the presentational effects, acting as a sort of massive pageant producer. Of all the various effects he employed he regarded his most beautiful as the one he used at the 1934 rally and repeated subsequently. Hitler's speech on this occasion was so timed that its close corresponded with nightfall. As the sky darkened, the beams of 130 spotlights placed at intervals of forty feet began throwing their beams straight upwards. 'The feeling,' he says, 'was of a vast room with the beams serving as mighty pillars of infinitely high outer walls . . .'

Sir Nevile Henderson, the British ambassador to Berlin, an unswerving hater of the Nazi regime, was even more enthusiastic. 'I had spent six years in St Petersburg before the war in the best days of the Russian ballet,' he wrote in his memoirs, 'but for grandiose beauty I have never seen anything to compare with it.'

In the totality of the rallies this was one more element in the vast agglomeration of rhythms which assailed the senses – flags, banners, flaming torches, all forming regular but moving patterns in the hands which held them; the tramp of thousands upon thousands of feet, the goosestep rattling on the hard granite of the arena, the clatter of hooves, or the clank and squeals of tanks as they

Above: Hitler receives the salute of youth and workers on Labor Day in Berlin's Lustgarten in 1934.
Below: Spotlights shine on the podium and banners during a rally held on Labor Day in Nuremberg.
Right: Hitler salutes Wehrmacht troops at Goslar in 1934. The Reichswehr was the 100,000 strong army allowed Germany by the Treaty of Versailles. In 1934 it became the Wehrmacht.

Left: Over 100,000 massed troops of the SA and SS at an early Nuremberg rally. These September rallies were the climax of the Nazi Party celebrations and usually lasted for three days.
Above: Saxon youth hail their Führer in Erfurt in 1933.

maneuvered; parades, drills, gymnastic displays. All, in some way, acting upon the minds of the spectators like voodoo drums, rousing them to frenzies until they were in a trance.

The production of this effect year after year was, of course, an organizational *tour de force.* Overall control was in the hands of Goebbels as head of party propaganda, through the *Hauptstelle Grossveranstaltungen,* but actual organizational work devolved upon a council headed by Robert Ley. This was housed in offices in the Feldmarschall Hindenburg Platz in Berlin and each member of it headed a group with a specific area of responsibility. Their work went on all through the year.

Central to it all was, of course, the program itself. This could comprise some thirty or so major events, plus an even larger number of smaller ones. Apart from the great arena displays involving thousands and sometimes hundreds of thousands, there was the party congress proper; receptions for the press, national and foreign; for diplomats and important foreign guests; public parades through the streets; torchlight processions; fire-works displays which grew more spectacular year by year; the laying of foundations for new buildings on the rally site.

Outside of the program, however, was the overall organization which arranged for the movement of people to the city, for their accommodation and feeding and so on. For example, parking spaces had to be decided and allocated; areas kept traffic free with only those of the highest rank being allowed to use their cars. During the rallies themselves nearly 500 special trains had to be run to carry participants, while a further 200 were set aside for the special use of the leadership and for the guests they might be bringing. To take all this extra traffic new railway stations were built near the rally site and were built in record-breaking time.

Accommodation included rooms in hotels for the more important guests, in private homes for lesser ones, as well as dormitories in schools, public halls and even

Left: The tribune in front of the Frauenkirche in Nuremburg in September 1933.

factories or warehouses. For this purpose metal bed-frames were used and these were kept in a store between rallies. Accommodation for a further 240,000 people was provided on campsites.

Food came from canteens and field kitchens and there were, in addition, special contracts with breweries and some retail chains. Provisions were bought in bulk by a special committee, and during the rallies restaurants stayed open round the clock, though no alcohol was served after midnight. Each province of the country had its own dining hall offering local specialities at low prices.

Yet another department was responsible for looking after the press, film and radio and for liaison with the Propaganda Ministry. Plans never realized included the building of a special press hotel in the city with accommodation for 285 guests and incorporating its own post and telegraph office and telephone exchange with world-wide connections.

The construction program between rallies also occupied the entire year and required special planning, since it was always expected that work begun one year would be at least at one stage of completion by the following so that rallies did not take place amid scenes of building construction. Because of the grandiose scale and the limited time enormous work-teams were needed. On one occasion when a new arena was being built, a central tower was set up for the supervision of workers who were directed by loudspeaker.

Other details of organization included the collection and delivery of mail, first aid facilities and health care. By the time of the 1938 rally there were 1000 doctors, 1200 nurses, 4000 medical assistants, as well as 200 temporary hospitals on the site. Licenses were issued to street vendors and for those selling anything edible, all of whom had to keep strict hygiene rules while the police watched prices. Souvenir stands were the monopoly of the party and articles offered included postcards, bookmarkers, pennants and swastikas for cars. In addition, stores were open from five in the morning until eleven at night.

Quite separate were such problems as sound amplification and the lighting of the arena for events at night. For the first a system of loudspeakers was developed, the range of which was such that the microphones could pick up the ticking of a watch and boost it until it sounded like the pounding of hammers in a steel-foundry. To avoid echoes, special huge, mushroom-shaped speaker housings were developed. As to lighting, a single example gives an illustration of its scale: on the Luitpold Arena alone there were 150 huge spotlights which consumed 40,000 KW of electricity each evening. The Greek pillars of the enormous grandstand were lit up by 1200 spotlights, while a further fifty were used to pick up the speakers' stands, spectator areas, flagpoles. So brilliant was the illumination that the light reflected in the sky could be seen in Frankfurt over 100 miles away!

For the participants, drilling and the planning of parades filled the entire year. Each of the party organizations taking part was instructed to look out for those among its members who showed a special aptitude – the best marchers, singers, athletes. Once selected they were expected to give up four nights a week to training for the great event and this was stepped up to five, finally with

Massed bands of the SA parade through Berlin's Brandenburg Gate in the torchlight parade staged the night Hitler took power in January 1933.

weekends added, as it approached. Just before the rally each individual was given printed instructions, telling him the number of the truck on which he would travel, its starting place and time of departure and his own seat number, as well as details of his accommodation and where it was in Nuremberg. He was expected to pay for his participation and the single flat fee of 25RM covered travel, tent, bed and meals. Anything else was extra and was the individual's own responsibility.

On the Saturday before the rally's commencement, the special trains would also begin arriving with 800 men in each. They would assemble on the platform and march the four kilometers to the campsite. Everyone was given a city directory to help find his way round and another to guide him round the camp itself which was usually enormous and was divided into streets named after party members killed in the early 'struggles.' Within the camps there were strict rules including lights out at 2230 hours by which time, too, all fires had to be extinguished. The camps were guarded and passes were necessary for entering or leaving them.

This precise and detailed planning was carried right up to the moment the formations entered the arena. Cues were set to the second so that bands, for example, would begin to play at a pre-set distance from Hitler. Columns marched twelve-men deep with thirty inches between one marcher and the next. For those outside the armed services, who of course were carrying their weapons, there was even an exact ordering for the placing of the hands. The right was swung in step, the left was placed on the belt buckle, thumb inside it and behind, while the fingers which were outside were slightly bent, touching the right edge of the buckle.

Participants and spectators easily outnumbered Nurem-

Left: The Congress Hall within the Luitpold Hall in Nuremburg on Party Day 1933.

berg's population of 420,000, indeed by as early as 1934 the Zeppelinwiese was capable of taking 400,000 spectators. For the citizens, the rallies were not merely an annual excitement, but also a source of considerable profit.

In their choice of the city, the Nazi propagandists had acted with their usual complete calculation. It was, in almost every respect, the very model of a German Medieval city. It had first come into prominence in 1050, when the Emperor Henry III had allowed it to establish mint and market. In 1219 it was designated an 'imperial town' and this allowed its citizens to ply their trades without the risk of interferences from local princes.

As they grew in wealth the merchants of Nuremberg sought to express their status in buildings. Ignorant of the architectural forms being developed in Italy and France and copied elsewhere, they established a totally German style, thereby further endearing their city to their National Socialist descendants. At this peak of prosperity, with its high-gabled, richly ornamented buildings, it became a cultural center. Albrecht Dürer, the great German artist lived there; local poets developed forms based on the Medieval *Minnesang* and this led to the *Meistersinger* in the 16th Century.

Although it later went into decline, it is easy to understand why it was chosen as the embodiment in town planning of the Nazi ideals of Germanness. It had not, however, been the original home of the rallies. The first took place in Munich in early 1923 and involved some 5000 Storm Troopers. Parading *en masse* with the swastika and the red, white and black flag, both of which were making

Below: Hitler advances to the podium at another rally in Bückeberg in 1934.

Hitler addresses new recruits to the HJ (Hitler Youth) and BDM (League of German Girls) in front of the Feldherrnhalle in Munich.

their first public appearance, the whole object was to demonstrate that Hitler and the party was to be taken seriously. Besides speeches by Hitler, in which he attacked the Jews and the 'November traitors' who had stabbed Germany in the back by putting their names and hence the nation's to the Treaty of Versailles, there were, during the three days of the rally parades, consecration of flags and hymn-singing.

Völkischer Beobachter spoke of it as a triumph and predicted that the swastika would become the symbol of all Germany in due time. It spoke also of harassment of party members and threatened dire retribution in the future for their persecutors.

A further rally was held in September of the same year, this time the site was actually Nuremberg. Guests on this occasion reflected the growing prestige of the party, for they numbered among them General Erich Ludendorff, who with Marshal von Hindenburg had commanded the German forces in World War I, as well as Admiral Scheer, one of the country's most distinguished sailors. Events, besides marches, parades and the dedication of flags, included a religious service conducted by a sympathizing pastor who, in his sermon, launched an attack on the Jews. In other speeches, Hitler and other leaders reiterated the themes of party policy: Germany was financially enslaved by foreigners, the victim of the unjust Versailles Treaty.

Behind these could be detected the great enemies of Marxism, the Jews, pacificism, Weimar, majority rule and international capitalism.

The years 1926 and 1927 saw the rallies in Weimar itself and again in Nuremberg. An American reporter describing the second, declared it had been poorly attended with the Nurembergers taking little interest in it. This time the SA formations were swelled to 30,000 but, said the American newsman, not even the arrival of formations from Berlin, where they were banned, did much to excite the crowds. He concluded: 'The gathering was so dismal ... that it was resolved not to hold a congress in the following year . . . .'

However, the Nazi stage-managers seemed to have learnt their lesson, for by 1929 the rally was vastly reorganized with, among other events, torchlight processions with brass bands added and it had for its climax the greatest firework display Nuremberg had ever seen. The finale was a setpiece of a swastika, surrounded by green leaves and crowned by a huge eagle.

All these were dwarfed by the sequence of rallies held in the years after the seizure of power. It was then that construction began on permanent sites, vast stadia with stands for hundreds of thousands of spectators. The trend-setting rally was the one held to mark the National Socialist victory in 1933. Every available area which could be used to provide sleeping accommodation was reserved, including unused halls, restaurants, and schools. The SA, the Hitler Youth and similar organizations were to sleep in encampments of which the largest was one near the Zeppelinwiese with tents capable of taking 400 men or 600 boys in each.

To bring the 400,000 party members attending, 250 special trains were organized and highways throughout the city closed. From 1 September no private car was allowed into it and planes were prohibited from overflying. There was a huge press contingent, including 200 foreign reporters, while other guests included diplomatic representatives conveyed to the city by special sleeping cars in which they lived throughout the rally to save hotel space. Among the visitors was a party from the Austrian SA.

Below: Hitler meets some German workers in the company of Dr Robert Ley (just behind him).
Right: Hitler inspects the standards presented by the SA on Reichs Party Day.

149

Hitler restages the march to the city center of Munich in a re-enactment of the Beer Hall Putsch with Hermann Goering at his side. In this scene in 1934 Hitler did not fall to earth and Goering did not bolt as they did in 1923.

The events, witnessed by some 100,000 spectators, were all highly spectacular and included a parade of 160,000 party leaders. While they stood in columns, waves of flag-bearers ascending over the top of an embankment at the far end of the field, marched between them. These displays of flags were repeated in a Hitler Youth display later.

The 1934 rally was still bigger both in numbers of participants and spectators, as well as in the length of the program. This was the first rally to last a full week and it was attended by some 500,000 people. Parades included one by the Labor Service, formed in the previous year, in which the bare-chested youngsters marched into the arena with the sun glinting off their polished spades. There were also massed choirs provided by the Strength Through Joy organization, as well as gymnastic displays and tableaux telling the story of Germany, past, present and future.

Hitler arrived from Berchtesgaden, his mountain retreat, in a Junkers 52 and in his speech declared that there would 'not be another revolution in Germany for a thousand years,' while also warning churchmen not to oppose the government's measures. He threatened annihilation to all who stood in the way of it or the party.

The last day of the rally included Army displays for the first time. Cavalry units charged onto the arena, machine guns and flame-thrower demonstrations were given; there was target shooting by the artillery; demonstrations by motorcycle groups and mass evolutions in which the entire formations took part. At this first open manifestation of German armed might, the crowd showed 'frenzied excitement,' in the words of one observer. On the evening of the last day eight bands in the square in front of Hitler's hotel serenaded him, while the torchlight procession, already a tradition of the rallies, brought it to a triumphant end.

Their growth continued throughout the succeeding years. The Army displays especially were expanded from year to year, symbolizing Germany's might and offering their menace to any who might stray across her path. In 1936, Air Force displays were incorporated with nearly 400 aircraft maneuvering over the crowds. The completion, in 1937, of the Märzfeld, devoted to military displays meant that half a million spectators could now be accommodated. Foundations were also laid for the stadium for sports events with accommodation for 200,000 spectators.

There were other innovations too. By 1938, the choice of entertainment outside the arena events had become bewildering in its variety. Besides the gala presentation of Wagner's *Die Meistersinger*, there were vaudevilles, folk dancing displays, even puppet shows and shooting galleries. Tribunes, allowing 100,000 people to watch the events on the Zeppelinwiese, were completed that year and for the first time, leading German writers and composers were invited to attend. Foreign guests included

Above right: Motorized SA pass before their Führer on Reichs Party Day in 1935.
Right: An enthusiastic welcome for the Führer in Bückeberg in 1935.

some 100 delegates from the Arab countries, a group of nations in whom the Nazis always took the keenest interest and established close relations. The 1938 rally was also the first one in which full radio coverage was provided with 'Echoes of Nuremberg' presenting a nightly review of highlights. It was also at the 1938 rally that the 'Nuremberg Laws' were proclaimed, giving Germany's Jewish population, which had included so many of its most loyal and distinguished men and women, the role of uninvited guests in the Reich.

This was, in fact, the last rally, for the 1939 one, to surpass all that had gone before, was canceled as the threat of war loomed closer. Throughout the war only local party meetings were held, though there was a wave of large scale mass meetings in the fall of 1943 aimed at stiffening German will to resist at the time when events were beginning to run against them. During these years Hitler continued to dream of future rallies and had plans to increase accommodation in Nuremberg many times; the dream stadium with a seating capacity of 400,000 which he envisaged would have been without parallel on earth. In fact, during the war work continued on one project. This was a new Congress Hall for which the cornerstone had been laid in 1935. It was to be 670 feet wide, 870 feet long and 150 feet high, making it bigger than the Colosseum in Rome. There would have been seating for 40,000 people plus standing room for a further 8000, and the whole was to be surrounded by an artificial lake. It was never finished and what had been built was ultimately destroyed, a fate perhaps symbolically appropriate.

Yet the ghost of the rallies, more than anything else connected with the Third Reich, lingers on. As Bullock says, even to see films of them is to be recaptured by their hypnotism. Bands, flags, the background buildings against

Above left: Military attachés from many countries accredited to Germany take the salute on Party Day in Nuremberg.
Above: Peasant women gather for a Labor Day festival in 1933.

the cloud-hung skyline, the ordered rectangles of men, their uniformity broken only by the slowly fluttering banners above their heads – all combined to convey a feeling of might, unity and confidence. Equally, it is impossible to dwell on them without feeling something of what both spectators and participants must have felt. For the former, there was the sense of being in a city *en fête*; the kaleidoscope of events in the streets, dazzling to eye and ear; the tension of excitement within the stadia.

For the latter, there was the atmosphere of the occasion, life in the camps; the ever-present smell of grass crushed underfoot; the *al fresco* meals and the odor of woodsmoke in the nostrils; most of all the heady, almost unbearable excitement of being an actual part of this swaggering immensity, marching side by side with a thousand, ten thousand, a hundred thousand like oneself.

Almost everything about the Hitler regime had about it the power to shock and revolt – posters, speeches, newspapers with their crude and brutalizing terminology. The rallies are no exception. Yet they alone had the power to affect the stranger, for no knowledge of the language, for instance, was necessary to understand them. And in understanding he found his reaction to them, inevitably, a love-hate one. In this he was, for a moment, at one with the Germans as they were affected by Nazi propaganda.

Left: Motorized heavy artillery parade before the tribune in Nuremberg on Wehrmacht Day, 1935.
Below: Hitler and General Staff members on the reviewing stand.

BARKING OF THE DOGS OF WAR

The purely ideological propaganda of National Socialism and the projection of the Führer addressed at the German people, did not, of course, cease with the war. In some directions it was actually redoubled to make up for the fact that its favorite medium, the mass meeting, was no longer available. The period also saw a drastic reduction in public appearances and addresses by Hitler, which in the latter half of the war virtually ceased with Goebbels largely stepping into his shoes.

In point of fact, the war could be said to have solved at a single blow one of the Propaganda Ministry's greatest problems. Much prewar effort has been directed, as we have seen, towards creating a sense of community among Germans who, after all, had been welded into a nation for considerably less than a century. Once faced with the challenge of an external enemy, unity was brought about virtually automatically and this was in some ways encouraged by aspects of the Allied war policy.

How far Goebbels had planned for the contingency of a European conflict we have no way of telling. Certainly, if he did not accept its inevitability, he accepted the possibility and there was little evidence of *ad hoc* improvisation about the way his ministry set about adjusting itself to the new situation. Each one of the departments and agencies under his control made a smooth transition from peace to war: journalists, broadcasters, artists, musicians, actors, movie-directors dropped into their allotted place in the new scheme like soldiers forming up for a parade – which in one way was what they were and how the government regarded them. As a matter of fact, a long list of artists who were exempt from military service was drawn up at the beginning of the war. In doing this, Goebbels was actuated partly by his somewhat capricious but very real

regard for the arts (he had always had a personal inclination to put artists in a special category, even when their work did not accord with National Socialist principles). His policy was also motivated by the belief they could serve the nation better at home than at the front.

Of primary importance in wartime were, naturally, the news media, and here Goebbels' decisive and efficient methods stand in sharp contrast with those of the Allied side. For the German propaganda minister was first and foremost a journalist and understood and sympathized with the problems of his kind. On the British and French side liaison with the press was in the hands of those who, as professional soldiers, regarded it as potentially hostile, remembering among other things the public drubbing commanders had received from writers like *The Times'* correspondent, Colonel Charles Repington and from Basil Liddell Hart during and after World War I.

For the soldiers, the ideal situation would have been one in which journalists could have been kept away from the armies altogether. Failing this they would have to be held at bay, which in practice meant harassing them and placing such restrictions on their work as to make it virtually impossible. The thought that the public needed to be informed was one which appears never to have crossed their minds.

Philip Knightley in his *The First Casualty* tells a story of bumbling chicanery at British and French High Commands while they sought to put off the fateful day when

Below: Goering salutes the gun carriage passing with the body of Reinhard Heydrich, assassinated in Czechoslovakia. Formal ceremonies of this type replaced the monster rallies of prewar years.
Right: Wartime poster shows a Nazi 'St George' slaying the Communist dragon on behalf of 'Europe's Freedom.'

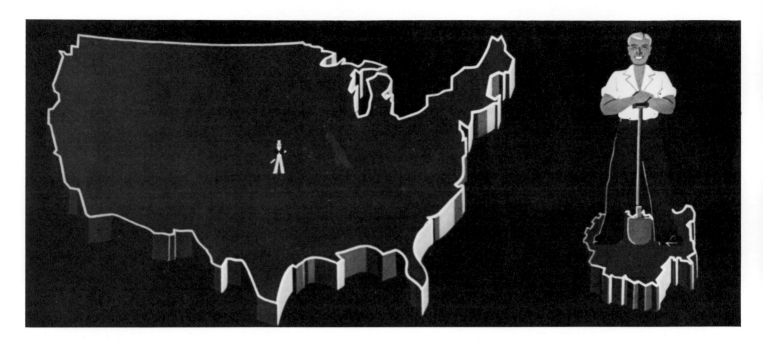

they would actually have reporters somewhere near the armies. Accreditation was delayed, then there were difficulties with transportation. As a sop, while editors chewed their fingernails to the bone, the British General Staff offered them its so called 'Eye-Witnesses.' Regrettably, since he was also, perforce, a journalist, he was not trusted either and hence was successfully prevented from witnessing anything. When the newspaper correspond-ents at last reached France things were no better and when it came to trying to cover the French Army a good deal worse. Four copies of every story had to be lodged with the various censors and when they had done their worst with it, it was passed over to a representative of the British Ministry of Information for dispatch to London as communications were under government control. All in all, a reporter was lucky if his story reached the papers

Left: Still from a propaganda film stressing Germany's requirements for *Lebensraum*. The caption states that Germany's population density was 135 people per square kilometer while the United States had only 16.
Right: A typical SS medal of the period. Designers of military insignia and medallions had a field day during the Third Reich developing new styles and modifying old ones for the new orders and units designated by the Nazis. Goering helped design his own uniforms, including the cream-colored greatcoat shown below.

correspondents to visit it. They would go back to Berlin to write of 'magnificent defense works.' Ironically enough, the line was actually only half-finished in 1939. An attacker could quite simply have walked through it. Needless to say, the visiting journalists were kept away from these sections.

American correspondents in London or Paris, accustomed to a situation in which access to news was a constitutional right, fell into angry despair which was reflected in the disdain with which they treated Allied accounts of the war.

By an enormous, scarcely credible paradox American editors began applying to their Berlin correspondents for the true facts. Here a totally different situation prevailed. Goebbels had realized that Germany would get a better press internationally if it greeted the reporters from neutral countries generously. There may not have been freedom of information as others understood it, but there was a complete freedom for correspondents to write what they liked – even if it was detrimental to Germany or to the performance of her armed forces. What was more they could reach their home offices in a matter of minutes; from London it took eight hours.

Every possible facility was offered by the Foreign Press Department of the Propaganda Ministry and there was even competition 'to be nice to the press' from Ribbentrop's Foreign Office which had had its propaganda domain extended at the beginning of the war on the personal orders of Hitler. In consequence reporters were given all manner of special privileges: extra rations, gasoline allowances and an advantageous exchange rate for their currency. In some cases, there were secret arrangements by which the specially favored had all their bills paid by one ministry or the other. They were also invited to stay at a country retreat outside Berlin which had been specially set aside for the purpose.

There were, of course, snags. If a correspondent consistently sent stories displeasing to the regime he might suffer a certain amount of harassment and there were cases of telephones being disconnected. Besides this there was the risk of arrest for espionage, though this sanction was only once used and the arrested man was quickly freed. In any event, within a month of the outbreak of war the press corps in Berlin had swollen by about 100 because it was felt to be an altogether easier place for gaining information.

It might be thought, however, that the foreign press was in a special category and, indeed, this was to some extent the case. Nonetheless, Goebbels took the responsibility for keeping the home public in touch with the battlefront very seriously indeed. It was, he argued, only by giving it a real insight into the war as those at the front experienced it that the civilian population would make its maximum effort and accept the sacrifices demanded of it. This, among other reasons, was why he decided in advance that there were to be no war correspondents with the German forces. War correspondents might well become a privileged category of men and, as such, kept from the action which

in two days. The official releases of news frequently contained exaggerations of a type which would make the most sensationalist reporter blush. Sometimes they were manifestly untrue. Anyone alive at the time can remember the interspersion of 'limited patrol activity in No Man's Land' (in which the enemy was always worsted) with alleged breaches of the German Siegfried Line. The latter were easily refuted by the Germans who simply took neutral

Left: Goering leads the funeral parade of SS men on the occasion of Heydrich's death, which had been prompted by British intelligence working with Czech émigrés and the Czech underground.

The launching of the pocket battleship *Admiral Graf Spee* before the war occasioned an outburst of patriotic propaganda which convinced both Germans and potential foes of Germany's growing sea power.

was precisely what he wanted German audiences to see. Besides, correspondents were interested in the wider issues: in whether a battle was a victory or a defeat; in explaining to readers its tactical or strategic importance; how much territory had been gained by it; what casualties had been inflicted – and sustained. All these were questions the Propaganda Minister believed must be left to his own personal arbitration. Instead, he wanted concentration on the texture of war – trees so that wood might be overlooked.

For this purpose he decided to form Propaganda Companies (in German: *Propaganda Kompanien*, or PK, for short) which consisted of men who were actually serving in the forces. He recruited them from those who in civilian life had been journalists, photographers, film cameramen, broadcasters, illustrators, even poets, publishers and printers, the whole being under the command of Major General Hasso von Wedel.

Inducted into the services in the normal way, they underwent basic training and then took their places in Army, Navy or Air Force. They fought with their units and suffered casualties in roughly the same proportions as the German forces as a whole. But all the time they were reporting back on the war as they saw it, first hand. The results of this policy can be seen by comparing the quality of reportage, at least in the early phases of the war, in

Germany and in British and French newspapers. This is especially noticeable in photographs: paratroops are shown as they are about to leap or actually in mid-air; advancing infantry crouch tensely behind tanks; landing forces don life-jackets before wading ashore under enemy fire: prisoners are shown at the moment of capture – dirty, depressed, demoralized. Early in September before a single correspondent reached French or British fronts, men of the Propaganda Kompanien were with the triumphant German Armies pushing across Poland.

The material they gathered was made freely available to neutral reporters with the consequence that American newspapers were filled with German accounts (often corroborated by the papers' own correspondents when they were allowed to follow the armies as they often were in times of victory). Picture papers printed in New York carried the same photographs as those in Berlin. German newsreels were shown at the cinemas, while all Britain and France could provide were dull and uninteresting pictures of events behind the front or of men trying to while away the hours in the bunkers of the Maginot Line.

The men of the PK did not serve merely as reporters, however. Briefed to 'influence the course of the war by the psychological control of mood, at home, abroad, at the front and in enemy territory,' they also set up propaganda

Right: 'Victory at any Price' is the slogan of this wartime propaganda poster. Ironically the price was higher than even the Propaganda Ministry bargained for.

SIEG
UM JEDEN PREIS

Reichspropagandaleitung, Plakat Nr. 28

Druck: Waldheim-Eberle, Wien

Heinrich Himmler, SS chief, flanked by Generals von Rundstedt and Sperrle, in Berlin.

operations to reach the enemy through leaflet raids, over loudspeakers capable of carrying across the lines, or by 'black propaganda' radio stations. There was nothing freebooting about this. They acted under the direction of Berlin where the policy lines were laid down and the wider issues kept very much in mind. In broadcasts to France during the 'Phoney War' period, for example, every effort was made to show that that country was not regarded as

Co-operation between the munitions workers and the fighting soldiers at the front lines is stressed by this wartime poster for purely internal German consumption.

the primary enemy. Banners visible across the lines declared that there would be no firing from the German side so long as they were not themselves attacked (a similar technique had been successfully employed on the Russian front in 1917 and contributed to the breakdown of the Imperial Armies). There was even (again, as in Russia in 1917) some secret fraternization in which, on the German side, PK men played a persuasive role.

The true foe, it was constantly stated, was plutocratic, Jew-dominated Britain, prepared now as in 1914 to 'fight to the last drop of French blood.' Right-minded Frenchmen, therefore, would see Britain as the common enemy.

The theme was taken up in announcements between items in concerts beamed to the French soldiers. From Stuttgart, there was 'Radio L'Humanité (L'Humanité was the name of a French Communist newspaper). It was run by a former German Communist deputy in the Reichstag, Ernst Torgler, and employed the French traitor, Ferdonnet. In its Diary of a Prisoner of War it taunted the poilus with the idea that while they were manning the Maginot Line, their British comrades were seducing their girl friends.

Leaflets the color and shape of autumn leaves dropped on the French lines reminded the troops that they, too, could fall like 'les feuilles d'automne' and invited them to consider whether the cause was worth the sacrifice.

Adding effectively to this seductive bombardment was the actual performance of the Allies when it came to the battle. And this in its turn, combined with their reluctance

Schafft Waffen für die Front

to provide adequate information, operated to their detriment in the world's press. In Norway, for instance, PK men filed 200 dispatches, sent in 250 photographs and shot 54,000 feet of film. All achieved world-wide distribution. Britain offered only its official communiqués believed by few. Since the campaign ended in a total German victory and an ignominious British evacuation, the supposition gained ground, and was publicly stated in the neutral press, that the Allied reticence was a cover to prevent the harsh truths from being known. The German *blitzkrieg* of May 1940 merely seemed to confirm this view.

Through this campaign, such purely military matters as the issuing of announcements of victories, Hitler retained under his own control, but Goebbels was responsible for presentation. This included fanfares, hymn-singing by choirs and a three minute silence after which Hitler's favorite *Badenweiler March* was played. At one point such was the speed of the German advance that programs were being broken into for these special announcements at intervals of approximately three hours.

The Battle of France left Germany the unchallenged master of much of Western Europe, but throughout the struggle correspondents with the French and British Armies had been treated by the commanders with undisguised suspicion. What little information they were offered was often so manifestly untrue that it was greeted with laughter. It was common for officers briefing newsmen to have less idea about the true situation than the reporters themselves.

Those in the higher ranks of command, who might have been expected to know, simply ignored the press. German generals, by contrast, realizing the PK men were servants of two masters were glad to provide interviews or allow themselves to be photographed since this might help to bring them to the attention of Berlin.

The work of the PK men did not end with occupation. Once the German Armies were installed they established themselves in newspaper offices and radio stations, not only censoring but taking an active part in their work. The day after the surrender of the Dutch Army, for example, PK radiomen began arriving at Hilversum, bringing with them complete sets of transmitting equipment to replace any that might have been damaged and enough recorded material in Dutch to last for two weeks. At the same time, the normal broadcasters were allowed to carry on so that listeners hearing their familiar voices might be reassured about the occupation. One Dutch announcer chanced to see the trucks of a radio unit which had not been unloaded: it contained some two months of program and was marked for dispatch to Britain.

Men of the PK were responsible for the production of *Signal*, the very high quality picture magazine published in Paris in German, French and English. It was, in fact,

'Total War Makes a Shorter War' was the slogan above this rostrum in 1943 where Goebbels made his dramatic appeal to the German nation to wage total war. He thought this slogan would make the defeat at Stalingrad more acceptable to the German people.

In command of the PzKw 1, the tank developed by Germany in Russia during the 1920s, which made its appearance on maneuvers in the mid-1930s and in Poland and France in 1939 and 1940.

knew, they said, that the war could not be won, though there was no hint of when victory would come. By August, with Britain still undefeated, the question raised in *Das Reich* which had just begun publication was: 'Why is Britain losing?' By September, it was being asked what form the collapse – still inevitable – would take. But the note of caution became still more marked. Goebbels had no wish to build up hopes in Germany which would only be dashed. From the end of September there were no further references to the enemy's 'desperate situation' nor to 'hammer blows' in the offing. Nonetheless, to keep the enemy on edge the hints were still maintained. While the preparations for 'Operation Sealion,' the invasion of Britain, were being dismantled along the Channel coast since the defeat of the Luftwaffe had made the endeavor untenable, Hitler went on offering his threats. He told a mass meeting in the Berlin *Sportpalast* on 23 September: 'When the people in England are curious and ask: Why does he not come? The answer is: Take it easy. He will come.'

But Britain's refusal to surrender was having repercussions elsewhere. Even in occupied Europe hope began the rekindle, the resistance groups began to form. Europe might be occupied but it was not yet vanquished.

Among the neutrals, harboring their secret hopes that the detestable National Socialist system might not after all prevail, there was a growing tendency to take Britain seriously as a contender. One can see how exercised the Propaganda Ministry was by all this, using every means to counter the worrying trends, though in the main unsuccessfully. Such reverses as Britain was experiencing, as for example its heavy shipping losses on the Atlantic trade routes, were exploited to the maximum. But plainly they were not going to prove decisive and even the most optimistic of Goebbels' writers could not pretend that attrition alone could influence the war in anything less than years.

There was also a change of emphasis. German propaganda had become more markedly anti-British in tone since the Czech crisis. Britain was the plutocrat of plutocracies, ruled by its effete aristocracy – a notion which became so imbedded in the German mind it must have been due to something more than Goebbels' efforts. Hess, flying to Britain to try to persuade its government to make peace speedily, mistakenly supposed he had only to make for the nearest peer to ensure that his views reached the Cabinet. At the same time Britain was presented as a worn-out imperial power in a state of racial ferment which was liable to boil over at any moment. In international affairs the prime British attribute was hypocrisy.

Through this farrago, however, an attempt had at first been made to distinguish leadership and people. The latter were said to be full of sympathy for German aspiration, even to envy them their leader as a man like themselves, knowing their problems. By the end of 1940 and the beginning of 1941, British working class attitudes to Hitler and

through the outpourings of the PK men in local newspaper offices and the pages of *Signal* that many people in the occupied countries made their first contact with the National Socialist ideology.

The process was extended in every way. Libraries were emptied of books considered to be undesirable and in 1942, on Goebbels' direct orders, plans were laid down for new dictionaries to be used in the occupied countries. These were to stress the National Socialist conception of the state and its ideology.

The year 1940 could well be described as the year in which German propaganda reached its high-water mark but the Allies failed to respond. From that time on there was a gradual reversion. In the first place Churchill began to feel secure in his position as Premier, a position which he had assumed in the darkest days before Dunkirk. A former journalist himself, he was anxious that the public should be told what was happening. In the second place, the Battle of Britain was by no means having the anticipated result for the attackers. By degrees, confidence in a quick victory as expressed through Nazi propaganda began to falter. In June 1940 they were declaring, unconditionally, that Britain's fate was sealed. By July there was some slight modification: the Briton-in-the-street

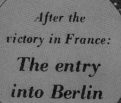

Signal

Belgium Fr. 2.— / Bohemia-Moravia Kr. 2.50 / Bulgaria Leva 10.— / Denmark 50 Öre / Estonia 40 Sent / Finland Mk. 4.50 / Greece Drs. 11.— / Italy Lire 2.— / Yugoslavia Din. 5.— / Latvia 50 Sant. / Lithuania 60 Centu / Luxemburg Fr. 2.— / Netherlands 20 Cents / Norway 45 Öre / Portugal Esc. 2.50 / Rumania Lei 16.— / Slovakia Ks. 2.50 / Spain Pts. 1.25 / Turkey Kuruş 15.— / Sweden 50 Öre / Switzerland 45 Cts. / Hungary 36 Fillér / U.S.A. 10 Cents

No. 9

*After the
victory in France:*

**The entry
into Berlin**

SS Wir alle.

Wir alle tragen das gleiche Kleid in Feldgrau mit silbernen
Schnüren. Wir alle stehen zum Kampf bereit, wenn
Runen und Totenkopf führen. Sollen wir klagen, wenn
dunkelste Nacht wieder den Glauben an dich hat gebracht,
Deutschland, mein Deutschland, Deutschland, mein Deutschland?

Worte: SS-Obersturmführer Max Hanig   Weise: SS-Rottenführer Becker

Wir alle haben die gleiche Pflicht.
Wer wollte sein Los je bereuen;
Soldaten gehören sich selber nicht
im Willen, ein Reich zu betreuen.
  Sollen wir klagen, wenn Morsches zerfällt?
  Großdeutsche Taten erobern die Welt!
  Deutschland, mein Deutschland,
  Deutschland, mein Deutschland.

Wir alle schworen den gleichen Eid
dem Führer in heiligen Stunden;
das Herzblut haben wir ihm geweiht,
mit ihm sind wir schicksalverbunden.
  Sollen wir klagen? In Not und Gefahr
  steht deine schwarze, verschworene Schar;
  Deutschland, mein Deutschland,
  Deutschland, mein Deutschland.

Wir alle sterben den gleichen Tod
und fürchten nicht Teufel noch Hölle.
Im Scheiden stirbt auch das Abendrot,
und doch strahlt der Morgen in Helle.
  Sollen wir klagen, wenn Leben erwacht?
  Jubel umbraust deine ewige Pracht,
  Deutschland, mein Deutschland,
  Deutschland, mein Deutschland.

Words and music for 'We are all SS,' one of the rousing songs which accompanied the Waffen-SS into battle. The propaganda effect of thousands of men singing in perfect cadence as they marched had a devastating effect upon the opposition, especially the civilians.

their conduct in the war made this obvious nonsense. It was plain that people and leaders in Britain were very much at one. Perhaps frustrated to find his calculations proved so faulty, Goebbels stopped making the distinctions. Instructions given to editors to omit the people in their attacks on the British government fell into abeyance. There was now nothing to redeem either: all classes were alike in their blind incomprehension and enmity for Germany.

The start of the war with the USSR inspired hopes of an entirely new turn in German fortunes, the *Drang nach Osten* by which all problems would be solved. This seemed to be coming towards realization in the initial, successful stages of the conflict. Once more, Hitler produced his *Sondermeldungen* (Special Announcements) interrupting normal programs with their fanfares to announce new victories. And, although it was Goebbels' personal view that they were over-used, the special announcements losing precisely that quality, they were still produced.

Once more the men of the PK were in the van of the advance, and once more the product of their labor was seen in Germany, in the neutral countries and now also in the occupied territory. It is hard to forget the strident, crowing tones of triumph which marked the propaganda of the time. This was the showdown between ideologies (so long predestined) and in the event there seemed no reasonable doubt which was the superior. Russian living standards after twenty-five years of Bolshevism were even lower than had ever been supposed. Villages and entire areas of many towns proved to be no more than collections of log buildings topped with turf or

thatched roofs reaching down almost to the earth. Roads were broad stony tracks, dusty in summer, thick mud in winter.

There were stories of Orthodox churches used as factories, even as public lavatories by the godless Bolsheviks. There were, besides, accounts of atrocities committed by the retreating Red Army, usually accompanied by gruesome photographs of the dead, and these were given wide exhibition not only in newspapers and newsreels, but in displays in shop windows.

As to the men who made up the enemy's forces they were never anything but 'subhuman Slavs' or 'Mongols,' a nomenclature which might have helped to make it seem permissible to treat them with such hideous inhumanity. Those who saw Soviet prisoners whose only crime was to defend their own country against an invader, herded as beasts, debased by hunger, reduced to bootless bundles of rags, found it hard to forget the sight. It was not difficult to decide who most deserved the title of 'subhuman,' captives or captors.

It was a strange quirk of Nazi propaganda that it expected the people of occupied Paris, Copenhagen or Amsterdam to regard the activities of the German forces with the same enthusiasm that the forces might have encountered in Berlin. Little adjustment in emphasis was made in presenting propaganda to the occupied countries. The military communiqués were simply translated and then presented as though the readers were waiting agog to hear of fresh German victories. For example, for the benefit of the English-speaking population of the Channel Islands, newsreel commentaries in English were provided. The strident-voiced German lady employed for the purpose

Left: Cover of the propaganda magazine *Signal,* published every two weeks throughout most of the war. This issue shows the triumphal parade of the Wehrmacht through Berlin's Brandenburg Gate after the conquest of France in 1940.
Overleaf: An anti-American article published by *Signal* in 1941.

The Pg.

The Party member, the man one meets everywhere in Germany and recognizes by the badge in the left revers has become a familiar figure in Germany today. He can be the labourer paving the street; he can be the chauffeur driving the car along that street; or he can be the merchant or manufacturer sitting in that car. Social position is of no importance where membership of the Party is concerned. The form of address used by a Party member is "comrade", and "Mr" or

The party membership book

In the bottom left-hand corner is the Leader's signature. The number of the book is 36,555. The member is, therefore, a veteran and holder of the gold Party Badge which was awarded to all Party members below 100,000

any other title is omitted. The salutation is "Heil Hitler", and at the same time the hand is raised according to the ancient German custom. Whoever becomes a member of the Party is not merely joining an organization; he has become a fighter in the German movement of liberation, and that implies much more than paying a subscription and attending meetings. The Party member binds himself to put aside all selfish interests and to devote all his energies to the welfare of the people. In the National Socialist German Workers' Party only the best National Socialists are to be accepted as members in accordance with the decision of the Leader. It is his will that the Party should be a sworn community of political fighters. Every German national of German blood can be admitted. In order to avoid admitting unsuitable members, each application is sent to the block supervisor of the block where the applicant lives. The block supervisor must form a clear and accurate judgement of the applicant before accepting his application. The financial situation and the profession are immaterial, but a good reputation and a firm character are decisive factors. Young members are given the preference on principle.

At the local group headquarters of the Party:

Solemn reception of a new member

The right arm is raised in the German greeting, and the oath of loyalty is pronounced: "I solemnly promise to be loyal to my Leader, Adolf Hitler. I promise to respect and obey him and the leaders he has appointed at all times." Then the local group leader hands him his membership book with the words: "In the name of the Leader, remain loyal to the Party"

Number of members up to the assumption of power

1919	6	1929	176,000
1925	27,000	1930	389,000
1926	49,000	1931	806,000
1927	72,000	1932	1,200,000
1928	108,000		

. . . and a page of pictures showing the various activities of the men and women in the National Socialist German Workers' Party

The German vocabulary has become larger since 1933. Words have been created to designate ideas previously non-existent. Words already existing have likewise changed their meanings. A "Pimpf", for example, is a lad from 10 to 12 years old in shorts and a brown shirt, with freckles on his face and with an enormous appetite after his spell of duty. The "Pimpf" is a familiar sight everywhere. "Strength through Joy" connotes a holiday trip to the mountains, a production of "Faust" at the municipal theatre or the crowded bus taking you out into the country on a Sunday morning. All these illustrations consequently have their own particular significance, each one vividly represents a side of contemporary life — these pictures are symbols

The People's Car

Everybody knows it and after the war there will be hundred thousands of them on the roads. It was designed at the instructions of the Leader by the German Labour Front for employees and workmen, it costs RM 975.— and can be bought on an easy purchase system with weekly payments of RM 5.—. The car has a marvellous performance. It can keep up an average of 62 m. p. h. along the German arterial motor roads. Petrol consumption is approximately 33 ¹⁄₂ m. p. g.

The "Wilhelm Gustloff" is one of the ships in the "Strength through Joy" fleet. It was launched in May 1937 and since then has taken innumerable comrades of every class on journeys to foreign lands. It is fitted with every comfort and all the luxuries of the modern passenger steamer—theatre, bathing pool, and sports deck. The accommodation, consisting of outer cabins only, is sufficient for 1500 passengers. A trip on this vessel costs only from five to seven marks per day

The House of German Art in Munich

The "German Art Congress" is held in this building every July. The Führer and his staff are the first visitors. Photographs of the opening ceremony and of the procession of the six thousand can then be seen in every newspaper. For weeks on end people stream through the exhibition rooms and by the last day every picture has been sold

ROOSEVELT—
Emperor of the World?

In this number "Signal" is beginning a series of articles on Roosevelt's policy. The first article that we are publishing today shows how the tentacles of dollar imperialism are reaching out over the whole world. A second article will show how Roosevelt's plans to stir up the American people's enthusiasm for war succeeded. The third article will answer the question: "Are the U.S.A. capable of ruling the world?"

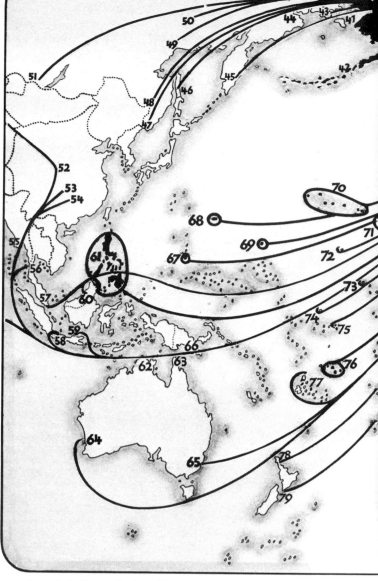

Recently "Current History," perhaps the best political periodical published in the U.S.A., contained an article on "America's Destiny" by Basil C. Walker. "Current History" belongs to the publishers of the "New York Times" and has at its disposal all the home and foreign news services of this widely distributed newspaper whose close connections with leading political and economic circles in America are well known.

"Our day has come"

In his article Walker writes that it is the task of the Americans to master the present situation with bold decision and to force events into a path which leads to a world such as they wish. The only kind of peace in which they are interested is a "pax americana" similar to the one-time "pax romana" and "pax britannica." By helping Britain, he goes on, they are wearing out the arch-enemy. America's history has prepared her for the rôle she has to play. Present day developments in the world point to America as the only nation fitted for the position of leader —not to save Europe or the European system, but to make America the leader of all free people in the whole world in the American epoch that is dawning. The longer they hesitate, the harder and bloodier will be the task. A quick decision is the cleverest. Their day has come, he says. They must advance without delay.

At last, in these few sentences, the leading political monthly of the U.S.A. has made Roosevelt's real aim as clear to us as we could wish: it is not the defence of the democracies or of the western hemisphere, not even defence against the "aggressors," but purely and simply world domination, the economic and political conquest of the world. For "pax americana" means nothing other than the conquest of the world by Washington, just as "pax britannica" is nothing other than the pseudonym of that system which has subjected to the interests of London vast expanses of the earth which were not allowed to develop their own.

What Basil C. Walker reveals in his article is the programme for a campaign of aggression not only against Germany but against the whole of Europe and the great complementary territory of Africa, not only against Japan but against the whole of Asia and the South Sea countries. The fact that the South American States are treated as mere political vassals by their big brother in the north interests Germany particularly because many of them are united to her by ancient ties of friendship. As for the rest, Europe, England excepted, has always respected the Monroe Doctrine. We have always left the states in the two Americas to settle their own affairs among themselves. We do not interfere.

All the more urgently, in consequence, do Europe and Eastern Asia demand respect for their own "Monroe Doctrine." It is up to Amernica to do as much as she will for the defence of the western hemisphere, but even a child cannot be persuaded that this hemisphere must be protected in Central Africa, in Batavia, or in the Urals. Roosevelt wants to make himself the Emperor of the World. He would like to play the rôle of a modern Louis XIV for whom the whole world offers just enough scope for the realization of his imperialistic ambitions.

Two world powers fade into nothingness

Roosevelt has already to his credit two big successes in which nobody would have believed two or even one year ago. The two greatest powers of modern times, the British Empire and the Soviet Union, have resigned their leading positions in favour of the U.S.A. and from day to day are becoming more and more dependent on Washington. Today these two powers are begging America for help and are ready to surrender in return their most valuable possessions, even their independence, if one were to believe what many Britons say. They know that without this help they cannot stand out alone against Europe which is defending herself with supreme energy. For this small Europe is fighting stubbornly, tenaciously—and victoriously against the hideous danger of Bolshevism. And at the far end of the Euro-Asiatic continent is Japan watching, silent and patient, and prepared to reply to each move with a counter-move. But both are occupied. One is busy with the war against the Soviets, the other with the war against Chungking. They are, therefore, not in a position to defend themselves as efficiently as if they

were free. And Roosevelt is taking advantage of this situation to encircle Europe and Japan, to place around their necks the rope with which he intends to strangle them. He is even prepared to make an alliance with Moscow if it will facilitate a landing in the Asiatic continent from where he can launch an attack on Japan.

America is trying to establish herself in every corner of the world which offers a starting point for attacks on Europe and Eastern Asia. She is prepared to use any means to further her aims: economic pressure, military power, political intrigues, cultural propaganda. A tour around the world will be sufficient to prove it.

Stepping-stones across the Atlantic

As the "New York Times" reports, the U.S.A. wants to induce Brazil to take over the protectorate of the Azores. Portugal's firm attitude in the face of the only too clearly manifested "interest" of the U.S.A. in the islands off the west coast of North Africa has made Washington cautious.

Perhaps—they are saying in the U.S.A.—the Portuguese will be less hostile to the occupation of the Azores if it is done by Brazil and not by the U.S.A., for Portuguese is spoken in Brazil too. Perhaps this proposal will succeed in sowing discord and mistrust between Portugal, the little mother country in Europe and Brazil, the big daughter in South America. Every attempt to upset the relations between

Europe and South America is welcome. Portugal has, however, consistently reinforced the garrisons of the Azores, of the Cape Verde Islands, and of the Madeira group. Washington does not yet dare to use force, for using force against the tiny country of Portugal would serve to reveal its clear intentions only too clearly, and therefore Brazil is pushed forward.

The occupation of these islands to which the Spanish Canaries also belong, would do more than protect South America from the "aggression" of the totalitarian states. More important is the fact that if she controlled these, America could control the sea routes between Europe and Africa south of the Sahara. Washington knows well enough that South America is threatened neither by Germany nor Italy—it wants to gain control of the stepping-stones across the Atlantic from where it would be able not only to attack South-Western Europe but also to extend its influence far into Africa. This is what the Americans have in mind. They want to build themselves a bridge-head in West Africa against Europe.

Why Wavell had to go

As the "Washington Times" reported in the middle of July, the difference between Churchill and Wavell which led to the recall of the latter from the post of Commander-in-Chief of the Eastern Mediterranean were due to the fact that Wavell, like the Americans, was of the opinion that Britain's posi-

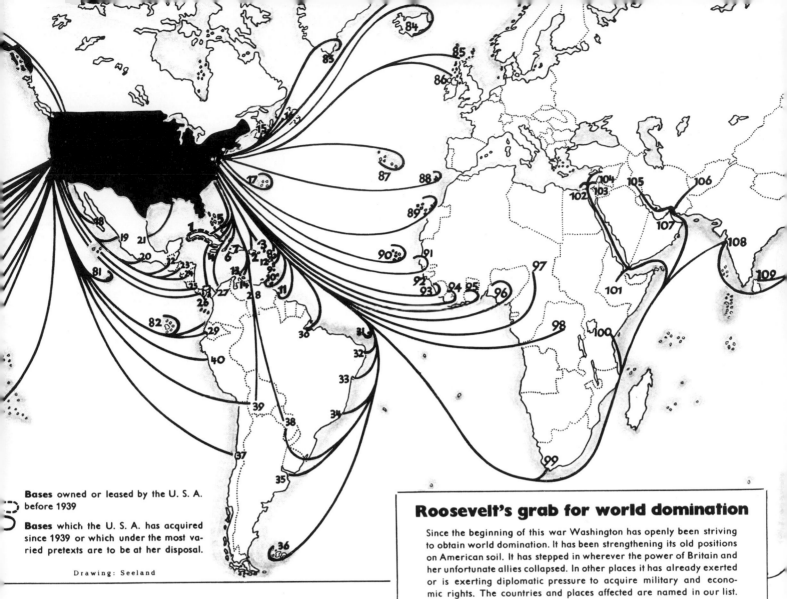

tion in the Eastern Mediterranean was untenable in the long run. The front should be moved back to a line running south of the Sahara across Africa. This would mean that the hard pressed British Mediterranean Fleet would be free for action in the Atlantic. The Americans and the British could then concentrate their energy on West Africa. Wavell had a good press in the U.S.A., but he was not able to put his plans into action. Instead he was transferred to India. The attack on Dakar has not been repeated up to now.

The encirclement of Europe

To accomplish this, comparatively unimportant harbours on the African coast were garrisoned with American consuls, regular air lines were opened up and the steamship companies put on more steamers. In 1940 as compared with 1939 the U.S.A.'s foreign trade with Africa increased approximately 40 %. Since 1939 America has been exporting to Africa important armaments and articles for the equipment of troops. This fact is explained if one recalls that the southernmost part of the French Empire in Africa, French Equatorial Africa, has split away from the Vichy Government and is under the control of people who have joined forces with de Gaulle. From French Equatorial Africa across Belgian Congo which is likewise hostile to Europe, to Anglo-Egyptian Sudan and across Kenya to the eastern projection of Africa an American cordon which is to be prolonged across Egypt northwards

to Palestine, Transjordania and the territories of Syria and Iraq that have been forcibly suppressed.

In the Persian Gulf the tentacles radiating eastwards from America over the whole of Europe meet those reaching out across the Pacific and the Indian Ocean to strangle East Asia. For in the petroleum fields in the Behrein Islands American capital supplies oil to the British troops and ships in the Indian Ocean and the Red Sea. From the Persian Gulf the encirclement of Europe is extended to include India. Here the intermediate links, Turkey and Iran, are missing. Although these states desire nothing more passionately than to preserve their neutrality, from day to day it becomes more and more apparent that the Anglo-Americans will display just as little respect for the sovereignty of Iran as they previously did for that of Iraq and Syria. As usual the "intrigues of German citizens in Iran against Britain" must furnish the pretext although the Iran Government officially announced that the behaviour of the 650 Germans in Iran is correct in all respects and a threat is out of the question. Under the most varied pretexts the Americans and the British are trying to induce Afghanistan to join the front against Europe.

Europe, an American economic colony?

If one bears in mind also that the Union of South Africa, with its gold

Roosevelt — Emperor of the world?

production as the deciding factor, is almost entirely dependent on the U.S.A.'s willingness to purchase—for the agricultural products of the Union are practically unmarketable today—and that that part of Africa which lies south of the Sahara urgently needs the U.S.A. who are the only customers on whom it can reckon, one can clearly recognize the U.S.A.'s intention of making the whole of Africa dependent on her good will and finally of bringing the continent not only under her economic but also under her military and political control.

When one hears that American engineers, technicians, and trained workmen are building aerodromes, landinggrounds and living quarters on African soil (British Gambia south of Dakar), that intervention in Liberia has already been announced, that the occupation of Greenland and Iceland are already accomplished facts, and that American experts are developing air bases in Northern Ireland, one realises beyond a shadow of a doubt that America desires to subdue not only Germany and Italy but also the whole of Europe, England included. She hopes to be able to prove that Europe depends on America's good will for her food supplies and that at the same time the U.S.A. can even mete out military chastisement. Europe, including England, is to be transformed into an economic colony that owes obedience to America, and the difference between the indivi-dual European states is to disappear.

Finally, when one observes the unconditional support given by the U.S.A. to the Soviets whose designs on Europe have been established facts for some time—if they had succeeded Europe as a cultural conception would have been destroyed—the whole body of the European states reveal themselves as a community facing a common fate and with common rights to live which must be defended against the threats of a common enemy.

The tentacles reaching out for Asia

With the same consistent ruthlessness as in the case of the Atlantic the U.S.A. are reaching out to seize Asia. Here it is Japan and powers allied or friendly to her, Manchukuo. Nanking-China, French Indo-China, and Thailand, that are exposed to the ever increasing pressure exerted by America. Here, too, Roosevelt is trying to tighten his grasp. Using all the strength and means at her disposal, whether military, political, or economic, America is proceeding with the encirclement of Japan, the leading power in Eastern Asia.

Since Bolshevism, hard pressed by the fighting forces of Europe, is taking refuge in a vassal relationship to the U.S.A. as has already been done by the British Empire, it has been possible for Roosevelt to approach Japan from the north, a move which had had up to now only very imperfect success. Alaska, the western point of which is only a few miles distant from the extreme eastern point of North-East Siberia, and which combined with the long chain of Aleutian Islands provides a kind of bridge to the north-east of Asia, was already a long time ago developed into an important American air and naval base. The naval port Dutch Harbour on Unalaska, one of the large islands of the Aleutian group, was built up into a northern counterpart of Pearl Harbour on Oahu, the most important of the Hawaiian Islands. Hawaii was the heavily fortified key position of the American naval forces concentrated in the Pacific.

In the north no real progress was made because frequent storms and dense fog lessen the strategic value of the Aleutian Islands and the south coast of Alaska. Now the Americans, who do not grant help to the Soviets for nothing. want the Bolshevists to make over to them bases in North-Eastern Siberia. As they have already promised support to the Soviets in a formal agreement, one can safely assume that they have already landed or are about to land soon in Kamchatka, on the coast of the Ochotski Sea, at the mouth of the Amur, perhaps even in Vladivostok. They could send formations of the Air Force there by this route across the Asiatic continent without even touching Japanese spheres of influence. By so doing they would be within easy reach of the heart of Japan. It must be mentioned here that the northern part of the long island Sachalin that lies at the mouth of the Amur belongs to the Soviet and the south to Japan.

In the central Pacific, America striving for supremacy has been becoming more and more apparent. The bridge from Hawaii to the Philippine to whom the U.S.A. have promised mock-freedom dating from 1946, an which today extends on to Thailand Singapore, the Dutch East Indies an British India, was systematically im proved. The bases on Johnston an Palmyra— south-west and south of Hawaii—were completed on the 15th of August. Farther to the south-west wor is in progress on the islands of How land and Enderbury in the Phoeni group. The American naval and ai base Tutuila in the Samoa Islands i already old, having been completed some time ago; with the British Fiji Islands it completes the bridge to New Zealand and Australia. Farther to the north, in the direction of the Philippines Midway, Wake, Marcus, and Guar are being developed.

The U.S.A. is working at high pres sure on the further development of Corregidor and Cavite in Manila Ba in the Philippines. American bomber flew to Java, for the Dutch East Indie have long since degenerated into mere tool of American politics. In Bor neo aerodromes are being built which will serve to protect Singapore from the flank in the southern Chines Ocean. Singapore itself, in a case o emergency, could perhaps be defende only with the help of American nava and air forces.

The existence of a military alliance between the U.S.A., England, Britis India and the Dutch East India, Chung-

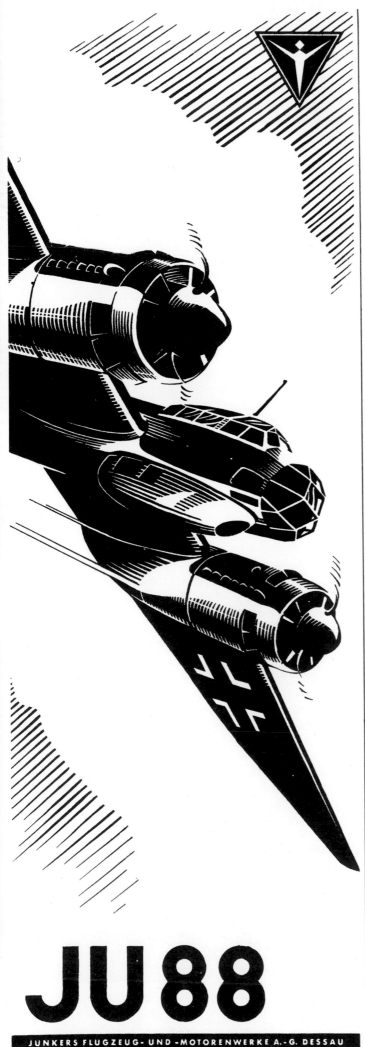

JU 88

king China, Australia, and New Zealand is an open secret in the Far East. In connexion with this co-operation which is under the guidance of the U.S.A., America has set aside 40 million dollars for aerodromes in the south-west of China. The U.S.A. and England wish to prepare 600 machines for service in Kweiyang and in other places in South-Western China, and to detail 200 pilots there. In addition Hopkins, Roosevelt's Extraordinary Ambassador in Moscow, has prepared the conclusion of a military alliance between the Soviet Union and Chungking. Further, Moscow is to undertake to complete with Anglo-American help the branch of the railway running eastwards from Turksib to Central Asia as far as Lantschau in Kansu straight across Hsingkiang.

Along the Thailand, Indo-China, and China frontiers of Burma, petrol dumps, hangars, and living quarters are being erected by American engineers with the help of American money. The reinforcement of the British garrisons in Singapore, the Malay States, and in Burma point at the unmistakable fact that an Anglo-American action is being prepared against Thailand which would be offering similar violence to a small state as was offered to Iraq and as British policy has been offering to India and Egypt for many years. By making a timely agreement with the Japanese and by calling upon them to protect both of their interests the French Government has saved Indo-China from Anglo-American intervention. Thailand too, as her last actions prove, is inclining to the Japanese side.

It is a matter of course that there is something behind the granting of transport planes and the recent additional loans (10 million pounds sterling and 50 million dollars) to Chang Kai Chek, the tenacious defender of the rest of China He is the Anglo-American's continental dagger which is threatening the Japanese position in South-Eastern Asia and which under no circumstances must be withdrawn. For the Americans the important thing is to open up the gigantic possibilities of the Chinese market for exploitation by their economic imperialism. If the American plans succeed, Chang could retire after doing his duty. Just as Britain by her clever policy of the balance of power kept Europe powerless by always supporting the weaker side against a stronger adversary, so the U.S.A. today are acting in the gamble for Asia. They are supporting the weakened Soviet Union and Chang Kai Chek who has been driven back to the remotest provinces in the south-west in order to overcome Japan who has earned the leadership in the Far East by her achievements and her strength.

And why? Escape from her own problems!

Just as in Europe, the U.S.A. wish to prevent by all the means in their power that the states of the Far East should arrive at a suitable solution of their justifiable demands. If this were to happen America's attention would be directed to her own problems. In Roosevelt's own country all the questions and tasks which cannot be solved in the old-fashioned way are waiting for solution; it is easier to interfere everywhere and to make the world into the battlefield of American imperialism of the Roosevelt stamp.

Even though the countries belonging to the British Empire voluntarily content themselves with the position of vassals of Washington, it is no reason why the old homes of culture, Europe and Eastern Asia, should bow before that class of Americans whose standard of values is the dollar and for whom the films of Hollywood are cultural achievements of the highest grade.

appeared to have learned her English in the New York Bronx. She would present film of a British city being bombed with a savage delight as though expecting audiences to share her pleasure. The rasping and unfeminine relish with which she would describe the destruction of a Spitfire or a Hurricane in aerial combat, always ending with the phrase 'Shat Down!' soon made it a catchphrase.

Notable, and noticed by 'the Occupied,' was the fact that neither German aircraft nor German soldiers were ever seen to fall in battle. The true reason for this was actually a deliberate policy decision taken by the PK units, largely, in fact, from humane considerations. They felt it would be an unbearable sight for a German family to see son, husband or father die. To those as entrenchedly cynical as the people of the occupied countries rapidly became, however, its effect was to cast doubt on the entire authenticity of the newsreel. It was freely suggested that they had actually been made during maneuvers rather than on the battlefield.

As had happened in their struggle with Britain, the onset of the winter of 1941 proved that victory in the USSR, was to be elusive. There were, of course, a few triumphs left for the Wehrmacht, such as Rommel's victory in the Western Desert, bringing him within striking distance of Cairo. But here, as well, there was to be no final victory and success was to give place to relentless retreat.

In the place of the glowing colors he had used in the first phases Goebbels was painting the war in increasingly somber hues by the beginning of the third year. This, in fact, had been his personal inclination for some time. While glad enough in victory to suck the last drop of advantage at home and abroad, he cautioned and struggled against an over optimism which took every success for granted. In October 1941, the Chief of the Reich Press Department, Otto Dietrich, who was now more or less permanently attached to Hitler, announced that the war in the USSR was as good as over with nothing but mopping up operations left. With only the small nut of Britain remaining uncracked, the German people let themselves go in jubilation with even blackout restrictions lifted in many areas. For his part, Goebbels deplored this counting of unhatched chickens and was to regard Dietrich's statement – which had originated from Hitler – as the worst propaganda blunder of the war.

For his part, while he did not allow any doubt about the final victorious outcome of the war to gain expression, he instructed his minions to do their best to see there was no encouragement to false optimism and that people were made aware of hardships which might yet await them. He was aware of a weariness and irritability, a readiness to blame the government for events among the German people and was prepared to tolerate this as the result of

Die Wehrmacht

HERAUSGEGEBEN VOM OBERKOMMANDO DER WEHRMACHT

4. JAHRGANG · NUMMER 13 · BERLIN, DEN 19. JUNI 1940 · EINZELPREIS 25 RPF. UND BESTELLGELD · ERSCHEINT VIERZEHNTÄGLICH

Another arm of the propaganda machine was the cartoon which was meant to keep morale high within the Reich and the occupied territories. Here the British get the boot.

the anxiety and frustrations of inconvenience or hardship undergone apparently in vain. But actual pessimism he sought to answer. He did so by presenting Germany's situation in perspective. She still dominated Europe, holding territorial and strategic advantages which, to all intents and purposes, made her invincible. As against Dietrich's *faux pas* and its results, a Swedish journalist regarded this response by Goebbels to growing war-weariness as his supreme masterstroke of psychological calculation and regarded it as having fundamental effects on the nation's will to fight on.

What concerned him most were the reports of mounting anti-war feeling, reaching him through the confidential memoranda of the Security Service to which he was given access. He gave his unconditional support to measures to punish defeatists, but his purely propagandist efforts were actually assisted rather than hindered by two acts of the Allies. The first was the announcement, after the Casablanca Conference, that they would be satisfied with nothing less than Germany's 'unconditional surrender.' He was quick to see the effect of this: it meant that there could be no question of the Allies indicating any willingness to negotiate if the existing government was overthrown. Should there be groups in Germany hoping that this might provide a way out, they must abandon hope. At the same time, the indignity of unconditional surrender, especially after the sacrifices of war, was more than many patriotic Germans could accept even if they were anti-Nazi. The government could continue the fight, aware that it now had the people united behind it as never before.

A second act helped to cement their union. This was the Allies' Strategic Bombing Offensive. Materially and morally, the cost of the raids was appalling and the prob-

lem of morale was not assisted by the fact that the Luftwaffe was manifestly unable to defend Germany, let alone to make repayment in kind. On the other hand the raids, which Goebbels promptly dubbed *Terror Angriffe* as part of his consistent policy to give names to events, could be cited as proof that the Allies were striking not at the German war effort or even its government, but at the ordinary people. Forgetting Coventry, Exeter and London, he invited the question: what had the German people to hope for from enemies who employed such barbaric methods?

In public he promised revenge. By their acts, the British had incurred a 'guilt of blood' for which it would have 'to foot the bill.' When the time came terror would be broken by counterterror.

On a personal plane he visited the cities which had been attacked, having been appointed by Hitler as Reich Plenipotentiary for the Bomb-Damaged Areas. He walked and talked among the homeless and bereaved, seeking to demonstrate that government and party was at one with them in their plight. In Berlin, of which he was still *Gauleiter*, he even took charge of firefighting. At the same time much of the relief given to raid victims came through the party, while he himself instituted a body for Aid to Air-Warfare Victims. Thanks to these efforts, neither he nor his party had ever been so popular with the people.

But this was a small consolation when set against the growing magnitude and number of his problems. Among these was the increasingly successful Allied propaganda offensive. In particular, he was led to give frank acknowledgment to British achievements. On every hand, Germany and its rulers were being shown as the villains of the war. Stories coming out of occupied Europe only tended to confirm British declarations that the New Order was nothing more than a hideous tyranny.

A particular thorn in his flesh and one to which his diaries refer on several occasions was the British *Soldatensender Calais*. Purporting to be a Wehrmacht station in Calais it was actually operating from southern England. A great deal of its success lay in the skill and care with which its staff informed themselves about the ideas, grievances and fears current among ordinary German soldiers. Its air of authenticity was increased by its lauding of German victories when they occurred, at times even magnifying them. At the same time retreats were presented as 'planned withdrawals to previously prepared positions,' a formula increasingly being used in German broadcasts. Its insidiousness from Goebbels' point of view lay in its references to the extremely heavy casualties a particular action had involved and the implication that more troops were to be sent east or that those who had already served their time there might soon be sent back. Many of those hearing the station's transmissions were veterans of the Eastern Front, now transferred to safer and more comfortable duties. The thought of a further period in Russia was bound to sow discontent among them.

Through its home and international services, known to be much listened to in occupied Europe despite the risk of death or the concentration camp, the BBC reminded the world of German boasts in the early part of the war and what they had been brought to, and spoke of timetables of victory gone amok. It pointed out how rarely

A 'lights out' warning for civilians during Allied air raids, which increased in intensity in 1943.

Propaganda poster in Norwegian urging Quislings to join the Waffen-SS.

Hitler appeared in public and left open the door to speculation as to what had become of him.

In vain Goebbels rushed to the *Wolfsschanze* in east Prussia on several occasions to try to drag his leader away from the nervous poring over war maps for a few hours so that he could address the nation, to somehow revive the old mesmerism. He was left to do the best he could with articles in his newspapers and radio talks describing the Führer, lonelier than ever in his eyrie, a little more stooped and grayer of hair but as vital, as inspired as ever, still the infallible genius at the head of the German nation. He knew, with mounting desperation, that this was a poor substitute for the man himself.

Early in 1943 the heaviest blow so far fell. The Sixth Army under Paulus surrendered at Stalingrad. It struck a German people little ready to accept it. It was true that the seeds of a possible defeat had been sown. As the German *blitzkrieg* in the east began to stall, the PK correspondents had begun to pay frank tribute to the fighting qualities of the Russian soldier, seeing in him a tenacity only the British units in France in 1940 or in the Western Desert had so far shown. The Russians were something different from the Poles or the troops of a demoralized France (an unwarranted slur on the *poilus*, incidentally, who had fought and were still fighting with accustomed valor). Later there were continual references to the harshness of the struggle for Stalingrad. The fighting was

remorseless, casualties high. 'Death,' said one candid reporter, 'has ceased to appall the German soldier on the Russian front; he now regards it as his inescapable fate.'

Despite these warnings, however, there was still the fact that Hitler had promised the fall of the city, the target of special hatred as it bore Stalin's name, in the previous September. Whatever the cost few expected actual defeat and mass surrender.

In the treatment of the news of Stalingrad no attempt was made to mitigate its gravity or scope. First, German listeners were alerted to stay tuned and by their radios for a special announcement, which ominously enough was preceded by slow marches and rolls from muffled drums. In those moments an expectation of something yet more terrible must have been built up in the minds of the listening public. The announcement when it came, dwelt on the heroism of the troops, the crucial importance of their mission, and treated the whole disaster as a noble but necessary sacrifice, with the implication that through it the course of the war had been changed. After the playing of German, Rumanian and Croatian national anthems, all three countries having been involved in the battle, it was announced that all places of entertainment would stay closed for three days.

Overleaf: Cover and interior from the *Luftwaffe* propaganda magazine, *Der Adler*, published simultaneously in English and German.

Max Schmeling
in REIH und GLIED

Ein großer Sportsmann wird Fallschirmjäger

A Famous Pugilist

Turns Parachutist

The great German pugilist, Max Schmeling, "our Max", as he is known to youthful admirers, volunteered for active service with the parachute troops. After a thorough course of training, he is now waiting orders for the front. Stringently disciplined in body and mind, courage and tenacity, paired with an unyielding determination, have marked his career as a pugilist from the start and the "good sport" has proved himself to be a good soldier too. Max is enthusiastic about his new rôle and all who known him are loud in their praises of an exemplary comrade who is always ready to help. Without losing a word, he places himself with all his energy and decision at disposal for a new commission that calls for the qualities of a real man. He is a fighter by nature and it was a matter of course for him to take his stand in the very front line in Greater Germany's struggle for existence. When questioned about his training as parachutist Max replied that the only thing to it was to avoid getting "cold feet" at the first time of baling out. "Once that stage has been got over, parachute jumping is a fine sport that only needs a little courage and good nerves. I enjoy it quite as much as boxing", he said. Max Schmeling has proved as a pugilist that he knows how to hit hard and he will be ready when the gong goes

...schirmjäger angetreten! Max Schmeling in Reih und Glied; er überragt seine ...meraden noch um Haupteslänge. — Unten: Fertigmachen zum Start! Max Schmeling hilft einem Kameraden beim Anlegen des Fallschirms

...achutists fall in. Max Schmeling in the ranks; he is a good head taller than his ...nrades. Below: Making ready for the start. Max helps a comrade to adjust his parachute

Frühmorgens marschieren die Fallschirmjäger zur Übung. Das Transportflugzeug steht startbereit

Parachute troops march off to practice in the early morning. The transport plane is ready to take off

Wolken, Wellen, Weiten —
das Reich der Seeflieger

Clouds, waves, and far-flung wide open spaces —
there the seaplane pilots hold away

Aufnahme Dr. Wolf Strache

Der Jäger und seine Waffe

The Fighter Pilot and His Weapon

[I]mmer wieder melden die Berichte des Oberkommandos der Wehrmacht große Erfolge der deutschen Jäger. Unter ihnen setzen Männer wie Major Mölders und Major [Ga]lland die Reihe der berühmten Weltkriegsflieger fort. Das deutsche Jagdflugzeug hat [si]ch als eine Waffe erwiesen, die dem Gegner bereits schwerste Verluste zugefügt hat. [W]o deutsche Jäger auftauchen, da muß der Engländer auf der Hut sein; mit pfeilschneller [Ge]walt stürzen sie sich auf ihn und lassen nicht ab, bis der Feind zur Strecke gebracht ist

[Th]e bulletins of the German High Command again and again report the successful doings [of] the fighter pilots. Men among them like Squadron Leader Mölders and Squadron Leader [Gal]land perpetuate the line of famous aces of the Great War. The German pursuit plane [ha]s proved to be a formidable weapon that has already inflicted very severe losses on the [en]emy. British pilots must be very wideawake whenever German fighter planes suddenly [sw]oop upon them like an arrow from the bow, never to let go until the enemy plane has been shot down

[S]tart folgt auf Start, Einsatz auf Einsatz. Der Jäger ist stets bereit, sich auf den Gegner zu stürzen, wo er ihn auch treffen mag

[T]ake-off follows take-off, raid upon raid. The fighter pilot is ever ready to hurl himself upon the foe whenever encountered

[A]ufmerksam verfolgt der Jagdflieger (Bild rechts) auf dem Frontflugplatz die Rückkehr seiner [K]ameraden, die eben dem Tommy einen ihrer zahlreichen Besuche auf der Insel abgestattet haben

[R]ight: The fighter pilot at the front airdrome is attentively following the return of his comrades who have just paid one of their numerous visits to Tommy Atkins in his island home

Above and above right: Two covers of *Die Wehrmacht*. The soldiers are saluting the seizure (recapture, as they put it) of Posen (Poznan) in Poland.

This defeat marked a watershed in German propaganda. It was at a mass meeting at the *Sportpalast*, one of the few held during the war years, that Goebbels, beneath a banner proclaiming *Totaler Krieg* (Total War), asked his audience whether they wanted Germany to give in under the blows it had received or to go on relentlessly. The answer he received was unequivocal and its echoes carried across the country. It was not an unexpected response, since he had been careful to pack the audience with party stalwarts.

To divert the public mind from direct problems to the larger ones of the conduct of the war, he followed up his meeting by inviting anyone who wanted to, to send in suggestions about its prosecution. Most of those he received were impractical, a few crackpot; the usable ones, however, were adopted. What he was gratified to discover was that the public in general regarded measures so far taken as utterly inadequate. That revelation must have been poor recompense for the derision Allied propaganda poured on his scheme. They had several ideas of their own to tender.

Another by-product of the Stalingrad fiasco was a change in the underlying psychology behind the propaganda message. Now Germany was shown as sacrificing itself to save European civilization from the 'subhuman hordes of Bolshevism.' At the same time, every means was used to increase internal fears as to what might be in store

if these hordes reached the Fatherland. On a slightly more positive note he promised new secret weapons, now almost perfected, which would shortly exact retribution from the enemy for his barbarous destruction of German cities. Goebbels was less than totally convincing in persuading the people that this new hope lay in prospect as he had never taken these weapons seriously.

In this reshaping of policy, the PK men were given fresh assignments. From now on they had to play down defeats, casualties, retreat. They did so with such success that each successive withdrawal would sometimes be presented as though it were a victory. It was only by close study of the map that one could see that the most recent one had taken place considerably closer to Germany than had the previous. From this there arose the frequently heard comment, among Berliners especially, that 'a few more victories like this and we've lost the war.' The PK was also expected to play its part in stiffening resistance for the final struggle which by this time everyone knew must be inevitable.

During this period, Goebbels carried out a market research project to try to discover which of the PK's 'Special Correspondents' had the greatest following. The results were both personally alarming to him and indicative of the ultimate failure of his propaganda. Those taken most seriously were all the veteran professional journalists of pre-1933 days. Fearful that these men might have few scruples about informing people of the facts, he decided that reporting from the Russian front should be entrusted only to those who placed loyalty to the party

Recruiting poster for the Waffen-SS urges youths to join after they became 17.

'Front and Homeland: The Guaranty of Victory' urges support of the war effort by the civilian population.

before the demands of professional integrity. From now on older journalists were relegated to less sensitive areas.

In the fall of 1943 came a wave of mass meetings held despite the increasing air raids. In fact, the continuance of the raids was part of their motivation – they were used to whip up hatred against the western as much as the eastern enemies. They were also intended to provide the faithful with arguments to refute the case of the growing number who believed Germany could only be defeated. As in his political fighting days, Goebbels considered that argument must be defeated on the streets. Always ready to congratulate himself, he wrote in his diary describing how these mini-rallies had transformed public morale.

But the fourth year of war brought only its fresh crop of horrors: intensification of the air attacks, reverses in Russia – and no sign, as had once been hoped, that the Russians might be ready to make peace once they reached their own borders. Not even the Japanese, whom the Germans had to thank for bringing the USA into the war against them, were any longer providing the consolation of a few Axis victories.

And in June came the Anglo-American investment of Fortress Europe, only weeks earlier declared invulnerable. Hope renewed as the Allied armored-spearheads became bogged down in the Normandy *bocage*, only to fade as they broke out. The last waverers still questioning the likelihood of an Allied final victory were now con-

vinced. For the first time, even the PK men installed in the offices of newspapers in the occupied countries began hinting at the possibility of German defeat. But what, they asked bitterly, would come of it? The British Empire, the last great bastion of western civilization, would be broken up. Britain herself would become the lackey of either American dollar-culture or Russian Bolshevism.

Goebbels found solace in a philosophy of 'while there's life, there's hope'; in other words as long as Germany kept up the struggle there was the possibility of a reversal in Allied fortunes. In *Das Reich* he enunciated his theme: through the course of the war three nations had undergone radical crises. Two had survived them, Britain and Russia. Now it was the turn of Germany. If it, too, remained steadfast and survived, the chances of its presiding over an historical shift of forces were considerable. For example, the obviously tenuous and uneasy alliance between capitalism as represented by Britain and America and Communist Russia must be unstable and liable to break up at any moment. The war was like a marathon in which it could be that at the end, though faint and staggering, Germany would be left the sole competitor in the field. Through the remnants of his 'black propaganda' network he was, indeed, trying to drive a wedge between Western and Eastern Allies, though not with any notable success.

Side by side with his exhortations to hold out, ran the increased warnings of the terrors waiting a defeated Ger-

Above: Naval artillery protects 'Fortress Europe' on the Channel coast.
Below: Hitler and Goering salute their troops on Heroes' Remembrance Day in Berlin in 1943.

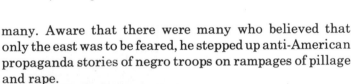

Hitler and Goering visit the reconstructed Richthofen Squadron of the Luftwaffe, Goering headed its namesake at the end of World War I.

'He bears the Guilt of the War' is the slogan on this rather heavy-handed, anti-Semitic poster.

many. Aware that there were many who believed that only the east was to be feared, he stepped up anti-American propaganda stories of negro troops on rampages of pillage and rape.

There was another brief dawning of hope as the pilotless 'V' weapons began their bombardment of southern England, but it was no more than a moment. There was yet another when Hitler survived the bomb-plot against him. In August, with Goebbels playing a role outside that of pure propaganda, Germany summoned up her last reserves. To release the last dregs of her manhood places of entertainment, drama schools, conservatoires, orchestras, publishing houses, magazines and some newspapers were closed down. The list of exemptions for artists drawn up at the beginning of the war was reduced savagely. Actors, producers, jugglers, violinists, ageing authors and journalists were given rapid courses in handling the Schmeissers and Panzerfausts with which they were to stave off the Red Army and marched off. With their reluctant departure for a front moving relentlessly closer to the Thousand-Year Reich, it was obvious that something else was going too: Goebbels was parting with the very means by which he disseminated his propaganda.

By the fall, the resigned calm of the sacrificial victim had settled upon Paul Josef Goebbels and was not to desert him. Germany had done her duty by western civilization,

more was beyond her powers. For all the world as though he believed his country had been assailed by the USSR instead of itself having been the assailant, he went on repeating the message that Germany had held back the storm – for a time. If they took advantage of the breathing space afforded them, the European nations and the whole west might yet regroup their forces, at last recognizing who the true enemy was. If they failed, the triumphant hosts of Bolshevism would deploy across the Plain of Europe to engulf it in a new Dark Age. Forgotten in this welter of sanctimonious self-pity was the fact that to the French, the Dutch, the Belgians, the Luxemburgians, the Greeks, the Norwegians, the Danes and to the people of what the Germans delightedly and persistently called 'the British Channel Islands'; to the Resistance fighter, to the family of the innocent hostage torn from them to be shot; to the inmate of the concentration camp; to all of these, National Socialism had brought its own Dark Age before which the original paled.

Prophetically in February 1945, he spoke of 'an Iron Curtain' descending upon the Russian occupied areas of Eastern Europe.

Then – once more – the brief instant of hope in April 1945, when he could deceive himself that perhaps if Germany dragged out resistance there might be a change in her fortunes. Franklin Delano Roosevelt, the American

Roosevelt sagt selbst:
„¹/₃ der gesamten Bevölkerung sind unterernährt und schlecht gekleidet."

president, died. Articles published in Germany rejoiced in the passing of one of the leading 'warmongers of the Judeo-capitalist camp.' Along the battlefronts however the advance hesitated not for a moment and Harry Truman was no less implacable an enemy of Nazi Germany.

That same month Goebbels meticulously burned all his personal papers, to prevent their falling into enemy hands. In a leader for *Das Reich,* headed 'Resistance at All Cost,' he demanded still greater efforts by the German people: life and death struggles before every last village; scorched earth as the enemy advanced. The paper never reached its readers; Goebbels was talking only to himself.

Then came his final exhortation to the people of Berlin to do what those of other towns had failed to do, even when failure meant summary execution: they must hold back the torrent. With a gift of self-delusion almost equal to Hitler's he spoke of reinforcements on their way. Within a week the Russians began pouring into the Reich capital. Their advance had been materially assisted by the autobahns built for the Wehrmacht by Fritz Todt.

Among the ruins of Hitler's splendid 1938 Chancellery they found the bodies of the lame little doctor Goebbels and his wife. They found, too, the corpses of the six children who had once elicited drawn breaths of fond admiration from German mothers when they had featured in the *Wochenschau* made to mark the Führer's birthday. They, at least, surely deserved a better fate. But then so did those others, naked and gangling like plucked chickens, laid out in rows as they were taken from the gas chambers. Both were, after all, victims of National Socialist propaganda.

Above: 'Roosevelt says it himself: one-third of the population is ill-dressed and ill-fed' says this still of an anti-American newsreel.
Below: A German stamp, typical of the period, with the slogan 'One People: One Reich: One Führer.'
Right: Wehrmacht, SA and Hitler Youth fight for the same cause in this wartime poster.

AFTERWORD

Like all propaganda, that of the Third Reich was a drug of the mind as fully insidious as any that pharmacy has devised for the body. It was one upon which large sections of the German people, a people as realistic, as pragmatic, as replete of goodwill as any in Europe, became wholly dependent for twelve years. It provided them not only nationally but individually with a sense of personal worth – the same sense an alcoholic acquires from the bottle. Like the alcoholic, they failed to notice that it was a mere distorted image of the reality. Like him, too, they were quite ready to accept the cost – impaired judgment and the perversion of reason.

It is tempting to see May 1945 as signaling the moment when the German people suddenly recovered from their dependency, feeling only amazement and disgust that they could ever have allowed themselves to surrender their minds and human dignity to it. In fact, as the new Germany proves, in very large measure this is what did happen. This is not a complete picture. All too often one hears today's young Germans expressing views which can be traced straight back to Dr Goebbels' outpourings, a sort of negative nationalism which is quite blind to the virtues of other nations, utterly unaware of their achievements.

It is equally tempting, as a non-German European, to believe that the gullibility which accepted propaganda of the kind the Nazis purveyed was a wholly German phenomenon. This is not true either.

No manifestation of the human consciousness is ever wholly evil, as none is wholly good. Both are simply general characteristics. A blanket attack on capitalism ignores how potent an agency for progress it has been (a fact which Marx quite openly acknowledged); a similar attack on imperialism fails to see what the colonizing powers did to raise the standards of living of their subject peoples (a fact Marx also acknowledged). If, on the other hand, one subjects Communism to the same treatment, one ignores the burning plea for social justice, humanity and decency which, though often distorted in practice, still lies at its heart.

The propagandist has succeeded just as fully when he has created total enemies for the views he has propounded as when he has created total supporters for them. In both cases he can mock beguiled humanity. The enemy often does his work more effectively than his supporters.

A case in point is the famous 'Battle of the Streets' in pre-Nazi Germany. By allowing his Communist rivals to persuade themselves that National Socialism was not only evil unredeemed but was on the brink of power, Goebbels provoked them to overreaction. Out of this came the excesses he had quite accurately ascribed to them. And the ordinary people's reaction to this was to join the Nazis, who were seen as the guardians of order in a society beginning to revolt against chaos and violence. The Communists had danced to Goebbels' tune as unthinkingly as his own Storm Troopers. It was he who said that the battle had to be won on the streets. They had simply accepted the challenge and by so doing had allowed themselves to fight on a battleground of the enemy's choosing.

In this way Nazi propaganda still succeeds. When one unthinkingly dubs this person or that group as 'fascist' or 'racist,' one is giving the real fascists and racists an opportunity to claim allies, adding to their respectability. Of course, one must attack opportunist politicians who see incitement of racial tensions as an instrument to power. Of course, one must warn of those psychologically disturbed individuals, who collectively inflict their fantasies on other races. But danger threatens when one attaches the same labels to those who, simply in the interests of improving relations between the races, point to possible differences.

In fact the overreaction to Hitler's racial ideas has made racism such a sensitive issue that few politicians dare to speak out. Until recently criticism of the conduct of the Israeli government was considered tantamount to Hitlerian anti-Semitism. Nonetheless it is the inalienable right of every individual to like or dislike other individuals, without consideration of race. As Sartre has pointed out in his very telling book on anti-Semitism, one is playing the racist game as much by treating every Jew as if he were sanctity personified as when one regards him as the Satanic polluter of the nations. The fact that both attitudes which run so counter to human experience and reality exist, indicates something fundamentally wrong, and is a tribute to the success of the propagandist. The effects of Hitler's propaganda have not entirely worn off, demonstrating the horrifying vitality of the twelve years during which Germany and Europe were under the spell of Hitler's Propaganda Machine.

Right: The three armed services fight on for the Third Reich.

BIBLIOGRAPHY

Goebbels and Propaganda in General

Bramsted, Ernest K, *Goebbels and National Socialist Propaganda, 1925–1945*, Michigan State University Press, 1965

Doob, Leonard, *Goebbels' Principles of Propaganda*, article in *Public Opinion*, Princeton University Press, NJ, 1950

Lochner, Louis P, edit., *The Goebbels' Diaries*, Hamish Hamilton, London, 1949

Manvell, Roger and Fraenkel, Heinrich, *Dr Goebbels: His Life and Death*, William Heinemann, London, 1960

Reimann, Viktor, *The Man Who Created Hitler: Joseph Goebbels*, tr. Stephen Wendt, William Kimber, London, 1977

Hitler and Other National Socialist Leaders

Bullock, Alan, *Hitler: A Study in Tyranny*, Odhams Press, London, 1952

Cecil, Robert, *The Myth of the Master Race: Alfred Rosenberg and the Nazi Ideology*, Batsford, London, 1972; Dodd, New York, 1972

Hitler, A, *Mein Kampf*, tr. J Murphy, Hurst and Blackett, London, 1939

Manvell, Roger and Fraenkel, Heinrich, *Hermann Göring*, Mentor, London, 1968; Simon and Schuster, New York, 1962

Speer, Albert, *Inside the Third Reich*, Weidenfeld and Nicholson, London, 1970; Macmillan, New York, 1970

The Arts

Lehmann-Haupt, H, *Art Under a Dictatorship*, New York, 1954

The Film

Hull, David Stewart, *Film in the Third Reich*, Simon and Schuster, New York, 1973

The Rallies

Burden, Hamilton, *The Nuremberg Rallies, 1923–39*, Pall Mall, London, 1969

The War

Knightley, Phillip, *The First Casualty: the War Correspondent as Hero, Propagandist and Myth Maker*, Deutsch, London, 1975

Rhodes, Anthony, *Propaganda: The Art of Persuasion in World War II*, Chelsea House, New York, 1976

The author would particularly like to thank the Wiener Library, London, whose helpful librarians enabled him to see many original examples of propaganda during the Third Reich.

INDEX

A

Adolf Hitler Platz, Berlin, 109
Adolf Hitler Schools, 13
Adventures of Baron Münchenhausen, 112
Aid to Air-Warfare Victims, 176
All Quiet on the Western Front, 112
Allied Strategic Bombing Offensive, 176
Amann, Max, 70, 75
Angriff, Der 35, 64, 70, 102, 116
Anti-Semitism, 20, 22, 27, 41–42, 50–53, 67–8, 70, 75, 86, 120, 188
Archipenko, Alexander, 99
Architecture, 104–109; Academy, 104; Domestic, 105
Arenas, 107, 139–40, 142, 145, 150
Art galleries, Purge of, 99
Art schools, Control of, 98
Art shows, Control of, 98
Artists, 94, 96–100
Association of German Newspaper Publishers, 75
Association of the German Press, 75
Austrian SA, 148
Austrian Social Democrats, 8
Autobahns, 106–107, 186

B

Badenweiler March, 163
Battle of Britain, 164
'Battle of the Streets,' 188
Bauhaus, 94, 105
Bäumler, Alfred, 100
BBC, see British Broadcasting Corporation
Berchtesgaden, 150
Berg, Alban, *Lulu,* 101
Bergner, Elisabeth, 94
Berlin: Adolf Hitler Platz, 109; Brandenburg Stadium, 60; Chancellery, 106–107, 109, 119, 186; Feldmarschall Hindenburg Platz, 145; Franz-Josef Platz, 100; Sportpalast, 18, 50, 55, 164, 182; Tempelhof Airfield, 106; University, 56, 100; Wilhelmplatz, 23
Bismarck, Prince Otto, 123
Blau Licht, Das (The Blue Light), 118
Blitzkrieg, 1940, 163
Blue Angel, The, 112
Blutende Deutschland, 115
Bolshevism, 24, 54, 70, 167, 182, 183, 185
Books, Burning of, 100
Bormann, Martin, 131
Bramsted, Ernest, 46, 140
Brandenburg Stadium, Berlin, 60
Braque, Georges, 99

Brauer, Peter Paul, 121
Brecht, Bertholt, 94
Breker, Arno, 102
Brennessel, Der, 64, 67
British Broadcasting Corporation, 176
British General Staff, 158
British High Command, 156
British Ministry of Information, 158
British propaganda offensive, World War I, 8
British *Soldatsender Calais,* 176
Broken Jug, 115
Brückner, Anton, 96, 139
Buddenbrooks, Thomas Mann, 100, 122
Bullock, Alan, 67, 152

C

Cabinet of Dr Caligari, The, 112
Capitalism, 188
Carmina Burana, Carl Orff, 102
Casablanca Conference, 176
Catholic Church, 20
Chagall, Marc, 99
Chancellery, Berlin 106–107, 109, 119, 186
Christianity, 17
Churchill, Sir Winston, 164
'Combat Art,' 102
Communism, 17, 22, 188
Concentration camps, 100
Crystal Night, 53
Cubism, 96

D

Dadaism, 96
Daily Express, 82
Dance, E H, *History the Betrayer,* 27
Das Reich, 64, 67, 81, 164, 183, 186
Degrelle, Léon, 128
Derain, André, 99
Deutscher Kleinempfänger (German Small Receiver), 82
Diary of a Prisoner of War, 162
Diesel, Rudolf, 123
Dietrich, Marlene, 94, 115
Dietrich, Otto, 25, 78, 174, 176
Displays: Air Force, 150; Army, 150; Brass bands, 148, 150; Fireworks, 148; Flags, 150; Gymnastics, 150; Tableaux, 150; Torchlight processions, 150
Drang nach Osten, 167
Drews, Bertha, 116
Dunkirk, 164
Dürer, Albrecht, 36, 39, 147

E

'Echoes of Nuremberg,' 152
Economics, Ministry of, 84
Edda Saga, 13
Emil and the Detectives, 100
Enabling Act, 22
Epp, Major General Ritter von, 64, 67
Epstein, Jacob, 99
Euthanasia, 20, 122
Ewige Jude, Der (The Eternal Jew), 42, 120–22
Expressionism, 96

F

Fahne Hoch, Die (Hold High the Banner), 116
Feldmarschall Hindenburg Platz, Berlin, 145
'Ferdonnet,' 162
Feuchtwanger, Lion, 121
Feuertaufe (Baptism of Fire), 120
Film, 26, 112–23, 145, 152–53; censorship, 114–15
Final Solution to the Jewish Problem, 20, 22, 53, 120–21
Fine Arts Criticism, Ban on, 101
Fink, Werner, 106
First Casualty, The, Philip Knightley, 156, 158
Flag displays, 150
Fluchtlinge (Refugees), 122
Folk-culture, German, 101–102
Foreign Office press club, 26
France, Battle of, 163
Franco-USSR Treaty, 1936, 86
Frankfurt University, 100
Frankfurter Zeitung, 78, 101, 138
Franz Eher Nachfolger GmbH, 70
Franz-Josef Platz, Berlin, 100
Freemasonry, 22
Freikorps, 67
French Air Force, 53
French Army, 158
French High Commission, 156
Freud, Sigmund, 100
Friedrich der Grosse, 123
Fröhlich, Carl, 122
Futurism, 96

G

Gauguin, Paul, 99
Gebuhr, Otto, 123
George, Heinrich, 116
German folk-culture, 101–102
German Foreign Office, 159
German Stadium, 140
German tribalism, 13
Gestapo, 12
Goebbels, Magda, 20
Goebbels, Paul Josef, *passim*
Goering, Hermann, 20, 51, 53, 90, 99, 102, 119
Gropius, Walter, 94
Grosz, Georg, 94, 99
Günther, Hans, 96

H

Handwriting: Copperplate, Gothic script, Italic, 102
Hans Westmar, 116
Harlan, Veit, 121–22
Hauptstelle Grossveranstaltungen, 145
Hauptstelle Rednerwesen (Head Office for Speakers' Affairs), 46–7
Heidelburg, University, 18, 20
Heine, Heinrich, 18
Henderson, Sir Nevile, 142
Herrscher, Der (The Governor), 122
Hess, Rudolf, 26, 118, 142, 164
Heuss, Theodor, 81
Heydrich, Reinhard, 96
Hildebrand Lied, 13
Hilversum Radio, 163

Himmler, Heinrich, 12, 17, 26, 119, 131, 134
Hindemith, Paul, 94, 98
Hindenburg, Marshal Paul von 41, 127, 148
Hippler, Dr Fritz, 120
History the Betrayer, E H Dance, 27
Hitler Creed, 132
Hitler Youth, 30, 36, 42, 47, 64, 116, 118, 122, 130, 132, 139, 148, 150
Hitlerjunge Quex, 115,–16, 122
Hofbräuhaus, Munich, 18, 32, 98, 107
Hohlwein, Ludwig, 36
Horst Wessel, 116
Hugenberg, Alfred, 112, 114
Hull, David Stewart, *Film in the Third Reich,* 112, 121
'Humanité,' *Diary of a Prisoner of War,* 162

I

Ich für Dich, Du für Mich (Me for You, You for Me), 122
Ich Klage An (I Accuse), 122
Illustrierter Beobachter, 64, 68
Information, 75, 78; *Vertrauliche Information* (Confidential Information), 78
Institute for the Investigation of the Jewish Question, 68
Iron Curtain, 185

J

Jackboot Cinema, Holba, Blobner, 116
Jannings, Emil, 94, 115, 121
Jancke, Erna 116
Jew of Malta, Christopher Marlowe, 100
Joyce, William ('Lord Haw-Haw') 82
Jud Süss, 42, 121
Justice, Ministry of, 84

K

Kaiser, Henry, 30
Kaiser Wilhelm II, 27
Kandinsky, Vassily, 94
Kapp Putsch, 128, 130, 131
Kastner, Erich, *Emil and the Detectives,* 100
Kirchenkampf (Struggle with the Churches), 131
Klee, Paul, 94
Kleist, Heinrich von, *Broken Jug,* 115
Koch, Robert, 123
Kraft durch Freude, 47, 97, 150
Kreisredner (District Speaker), 46
Krieck, Ernst, 100
Krupp Company, 112
Kun, Bela, 54
Kunst in Dritte Reich (Art in the Third Reich), 98

L

Labor Front (*Deutsche Arbeitsfront, DAF*), 47, 97; *Kraft durch Freude* (Strength through Joy) Movement, 97, 150; *Schönheit der Arbeit*

(Beauty of Work) Division, 97
Labor Service, 30, 132, 139, 150
Lang, Fritz, 94, 115
League of German Girls, 30, 36, 42, 47, 64, 122, 139
League of Nations, 122
League of Schoolchildren, 132
Lehmann-Haupt, Helmuth, 94, 106, 109, 132
Lenin, V I, 32
Lewis, Sinclair, 78
Ley, Robert, 97, 145
L'Humanité, Diary of a Prisoner of War, 162
Liddell Hart, Basil, 156
Liebeneiner, Wolfgang, 122
Life, 81
Life philosophies (Weltanschauungen), 12, 27
Lohkamp, Emil, 117
Lübeck museum, 99–100
Ludendorf, General Erich, 148
Luft, Friedrich, 81
Luftwaffe, 53, 164
Luitpoldheim arena, 140, 145
Lulu, Alban Berg, 101

M

Magic Mountain, The, Thomas Mann, 100
Maginot Line, 160, 162
Mahler, Gustav, 100
Mann, Heinrich, 100
Mann, Thomas, *The Magic Mountain,* 100
March, Otto, 105
Marian, Ferdinand, 121–22
Marlowe, Christopher, *Jew of Malta,* 100
Marschall und der Gefreite, Der, 41
Marx, Karl, 18, 100, 188
Marxism, 12
Märzfeld Arena, 140, 150
Mathis der Maler (Mathis the Painter), 98
Matisse, Henri, 99
Mayer, S L, 81
Mein Kampf, Adolf Hitler, 8, 13, 17, 46, 57, 126, 132,
Mein Leben für Irland (My Life for Ireland), 123
Meistersinger, Die, Wagner, 138, 146, 150
Mendelssohn, Felix, 100
Metropolis, 112
Michael: A German Fate, Goebbels, 18
'Mjölnir,' (Hans Schweitzer), 35, 70
Modigliani, Amadeo, 99
Morgenrot (Dawn), 112, 122
Morris, William, 94
Mosley, Oswald, 128
Müller, Wolfgang, 121
Munch, Edvard, 99
Münchener Beobachter, 64
Munich: Hitler in, 18; Hofbräuhaus, 18, 32, 98, 107; Königplatz Mausoleum, 130
Munich rally, 1923, 147–48
Music Chamber, 100
Musicians, Persecution of, 100
Mussolini, Benito, 56, 128

Mythus des Zwanzigsten Jahrhunderts (The Myth of the Twentieth Century), Alfred Rosenberg, 67

N

National Prizes, 100
National Socialism, 12, 17, 18, 24–5, 27, 30, 35–6, 42, 48, 55, 64, 70, 75, 78, 81–2, 90, 94, 96, 100–102, 104, 107, 112, 116–17, 128, 130, 132, 138, 164, 185, 186, 188; Calendar of Festivals and Ceremonies, 130–32; and Christianity, 17, 126–31; Posters, 30, 35
National Socialist German Workers' Party (NSDAP), 17, 18, 22, 30, 46, 50, 54, 115, 156
National Socialist Newsletter, The, 64, 67–8
National Socialist press, 64
National Socialist propaganda, 27, 30, 126
Nazis, see National Socialism
Neo-classicism, 96, 102, 109
Newsreel: Commentaries, 167, 174; *Wochenschau* (Weekly Newsreel), 119–20, 186
New York Times, 117
Nobel Prize, 100; for Literature, 1936, 100
Nolde, Ernst, 94
'Nordic' Hellenism, 102, 105, 118
Norkus, Herbert, 13, 116, 128
Northcliffe, Lord, 8
Nuremberg Congress Hall, 152
'Nuremberg Laws,' 1935, 22, 152
Nuremberg Rallies, 96, 107, 132, 138–40; 1923, 148; 1927, 148; 1933, 142; 1938, 139–40, 150, 152
Nuremberg Town Hall, 139
Nuremberg War Crimes Tribunal, 8, 106
Nuremberg, Zeppelinwiese, 18, 147

O

Observer, The, 81
Ohm Kruger, 123
Olympic Games, Berlin 1936; 78, 86, 90, 105, 118
Oppenheimer, Josef Süss, 121–22
Ordensburgen (Order Castles), 13
Orff, Carl, *Carmina Burana,* 102
Orthodox churches, 167
Orwell, George, *1984,* 42
Ossietzky, Carl von, 100

P

Party Meetings, 152
Paul, Bruno, 94
Paulus, Field Marshal, 177
Pharus-Saal, 30
'Phoney War,' 162
Photographs, 70
Picture Post, 81
Pictures, Burning of, 100
PK, see *Propaganda Kompanien*
Plank, Josef ('Seppla'), 41
Posters, 30–42, 49 153
Potsdam Army School, 102
Press: 26, 64–81, 90, 145, 156–64; Clubs, 26; Foreign, 78, 81, 90,

159; Religious, 75; War Correspondents, 156–64
Print, Bauhaus, Gothic 'Fraktur,' Roman, sans-serif, 102
Propaganda Kompanien (Propaganda Companies), 160, 162, 163, 167, 174, 177, 182–83
Propaganda Ministry, 23–4, 75, 78, 97, 101, 115, 119, 127, 145, 156, 164; Department V (Film),114; VI (Theater), 97; VIII (Literature), 97; IX (Fine Arts), 97; X (Music), 97; Foreign Press Department, 159; Press club, 26
'Protection Squads,' see *Schutz Staffeln*
'Protocols of the Elders of Zion,' 22, 67

Q
Quax, Der Bruch-pilot (Test-pilot Quax), 123

R
Radio: 81–2, 84, 86, 90, 145, 152, 162, 163, 167; British *Soldatsender Calais,* 1976; External broadcasting services, 82; Hilversum, 163; *L'Humanité,* 162; Reich Radio Chamber, 81–2, 84; *Reichs Rundfunk Gesellschaft* (RRG), 81–2, 84
Rallies, 142, 145–50; Adolf Hitler Platz, 109; May Day, 109; Tempelhof Airfield, 106, 109; 1938 rally, 145
Rassenkunde (Race Knowledge), 96
Red Army, 167, 185
Reich Association of German Publishers and Periodicals, 75
Reich Chambers, 96–7, 100, 114; Film, 114; Fine Arts, 36, 97; Fine Arts Committee, 1937, 97; Literature, 97; Music, 97, 100; Press, 75, 78; Theater, 97
Reich Film Credit Bank, 114
Reich Press Department, 174
Reichsparteileiter (Reich Party Leader), 24–5, 46–7
Reich Speakers' School, 46–7; Party Speakers' Certificate, 46
Reichspropagandaleiter, 47
Reichsredner (Reichs Speakers), 47
Reichstag, 20, 22, 30; National Socialist delegates, 20
Reich, Thousand-Year, 106
Reinhardt, Max, 94
Reiter von Deutsch-Ostafrika, Die, (The Riders of German East Africa), 122
Remarque, Erich Maria, 112
Repington, Colonel Charles, 156
Rhineland plebiscite, 126
Ribbentrop, Joachim von, 16, 159
'Richthofen Flying Circus,' 53
Riefenstahl, Leni, 118–19
Röhm, Ernst, 64, 118
Rommel, Field Marshall Erwin, 174
Roosevelt, Franklin Delano, 185

Rosenberg, Alfred, 12, 13, 17, 26, 67–8, 94, 97–8, 112, 121, 126,130, 131
Rothschild family, 121
Rothschilds Aktien von Waterloo, Die, 121
Royal Air Force, 53
Ruhmann, Heinz, 123

S
SA-Man Brandt, 115-16
Sartre, Jean-Paul, 188
Schacht, Hjalmar, 680
Scheer, Admiral, 148
Schiller, Friedrich, 123
Schirach, Baldur von, 116
Schlageter, Leo, 128, 130
Schönberg, Arnold, 94, 100
Schönheit der Arbeit (Beauty of Work), 97
Schutz Staffeln, 12, 26, 42, 64, 109, 118, 122, 131–32, 134, 139, 142
Schwarze Korps, Der (The Black Corps), 26
Schweitzer, Hans ('Mjolnir'), 35, 70
SD, see *Sicherheitsdienst*
Sealion, Operation (Invasion of Britain), 164
Security Service, see *Sicherheitsdienst*
'Seppla' (Josef Plank), 41
Shakespeare, William, *Merchant of Venice,* 100
Shaw, George Bernard, *Candida,* 100
Shock Troop Speakers, 47; Cadets, 47
Sicherheitsdienst, 12, 26, 97, 120
Sieg im Western (Victory in the West), 120
Siegfried Line, 159
Signal, 81, 163–64
Sixth Army, 177
Soldatsender Calais, 176
Sondermeldungen (Special Announcements), 167
Speakers' Information Section, 47
Speeches, 46–60, 148, 153, 167
Speer, Albert, 8, 22, 48–50, 55–6, 59–60, 68, 98, 106–107, 109, 115, 118, 127, 142
Sportpalast, Berlin, 18, 50, 55, 164, 182
SS, see *Schutz Staffeln*
SS-*Leibstandarte Adolf Hitler,* 118
Stadia, 60, 105, 107, 140, 148, 152–53.
Stalin, Josef, 177
Stalingrad, Battle for, 177
Steinhoff, Hans, 123
Sterilization, 122
Storm Troopers, see *Sturm Abteilung*
Strasser, Gregor, 18, 20
Strasser, Otto, 20
Strauss, 94, 100
Streicher, Julius, 68, 86
Strength Through Joy, 47, 97, 150
Stukas, 123
Sturm Abteilung, 12, 32, 41–2, 49, 64, 70, 75, 116, 117, 134, 139, 142, 147, 188
Stürmer, Der, 64, 68, 70, 86, 102

Swastika, 31–2, 36, 109, 130, 147

T
Teich, 121
Tempelhof Airfield, Berlin, 106
Terror Angriffe, 176
Testament to Dr Mabuse, The, 112, 115
Theater, Persecution of, 100
'Thing-plays,' 102
'Thing-Theater,' 102
Third Reich, 8, 26, 81, 100, 109, 118, 123, 152, 188
Thompson, Dorothy, 78
Thousand-Year Reich, 106, 185
Times, The, 156
Todt, Fritz, 186
Torgler, Ernst, 162
Toulouse-Lautrec, Henri de, 30
Trask, Claire, 117
Triumph des Willens (Triumph of the Will, 118
Truman, Harry S, 186
Tsar Nicholas II. 22

U
Uber Alles in der Welt, 123
Ucicky, Gustav, 112, 122
UFA (Film Production Company), 112, 114, 119
University of Berlin, 56, 100
University of Heidelburg, 18, 20

V
'V' weapons, 185
Van der Rohe, Mies, 94
Van Gogh, Vincent, 99
Vaterlandliebe, 60
Veidt, Conrad, 115
Versailles, Treaty of, 22, 86, 115, 148
Vertrauliche Information (Confidential Information), 78
Viennese Academy of Arts, 104
Völkischer Beobachter, 26, 64, 67–9, 70, 75, 126, 130, 148
Volksdeutsch, 24
Volksempfänger (People's Receiver), 42, 82

W
Waffen-SS, 42
War Correspondents, 156–64
War Crimes Tribunal, Nuremberg, 8, 106
Warsaw ghetto, 120
Wedel, Major General Hasso von, 160
Wehrmacht, 30, 102, 106, 109, 128, 174, 176, 186
Weill, Kurt, 94
Weimar Government, 20, 22, 27, 86, 102, 115
Weimar Rally, 1926, 148,
Wells, H G, 8
Weltanschauungen, 12, 27
Wessel, Horst, 13, 116–17, 118, 130
Western Desert, 174
Westmar, Hans, SA, 117–18
Wilhelmplatz, Berlin, 23
Wilhelm Tell, 123
Winterhilfe, 42, 131
Wochenschau (Weekly Newsreel), 119–20, 186

Wolfsschanze, 177
Woodcarving, 102
World War I, 27, 115, 122, 148, 156
World War I, British propaganda offensive, 8
World War II, 81
Writers, Persecution of, 100

Z
Zeppelinweise (Zeppelin Meadow), Nuremberg, 18, 139–40, 148, 150
Zionism, 22
Zweig, Stephan, 100

ACKNOWLEDGMENTS
The author would like to thank David Eldred, who designed *Hitler's Propaganda Machine,* S L Mayer, who assisted him with the captions and picture research, Fred Curl, who supplied some valuable photographic reference, and Rolf Steinberg, who found some of the rare and unusual material presented in this book through his picture research in Germany. He would also like to thank the Bison Picture Library for supplying all the illustrations for this book except the following:

Robert Hunt Library: 12–13, 13 (right), 16–17, 88–89.
Orbis Picture Library: 33, 34, 157.
Ullstein: 92–93, 94, 103 (three), 104 (top two), 108 (top), 112–113, 113 (bottom), 115, 118 (top), 120–121, 122.
Landesbildstelle Berlin: 96 (bottom), 97 (both), 98, 110–111, 113 (top), 117 (both).
Fred Curl Collection: 57 (top), 58 (top), 158 (top).
Rolf Steinberg Collection: 9 (top two), 11 (all), 12, 14–15 (four), 16 (two), 19 (two), 20, 21 (top right), 22, 23, (top two), 25 (both), 26, 27, 40, 41 (two), 65, 66, 67, (both), 68 (both), 69, 74, 75, 79, 80, 85, 86 (all four), 87 (all five), 90 (both), 91, 159, 167, 175, 182 (both), 183 (right), 185 (right).
Bundesarchiv: 1, 4, 5, 6, 8, 8–9, 9 (center), 16 (center), 17 (both), 21 (two), 23 (bottom two), 24, 28–29, 31 (both), 32 (both), 35 (left), 36 (right), 37, 38, 39 (both), 41 (top left), 42 (left), 50 (top), 52 (top left), 64, 82, 83, 84 (top), 96 (top), 105, 106, 107 (both), 116, 118 (bottom), 124–125, 146–147, 161, 162 (bottom), 162–163, 177 (both), 187, 189.